GLOBALISATION AND BUSINESS ETHICS

T0298749

Law, Ethics and Economics

Series Editors:
Christoph Luetge, University of Munich, Germany
Itaru Shimazu, Chiba University, Japan

Law, Ethics and Economics brings together interdisciplinary books which deal with at least two of the three constituents. Among other subjects, this series covers issues in ethics and economics, law and economics, as well as constitutional issues in law, economics, philosophy and social theory. The focus is on theoretical analysis that goes beyond purely normative considerations, thus aiming at a synthesis of the desirable and the feasible.

Also in the series:

Deliberation and Decision:
Economics, Constitutional Theory and Deliberative Democracy
Edited by Anne van Aaken, Christian List and Christoph Luetge
ISBN 978 0 7546 2358 8

Globalisation and Business Ethics

Edited by

KARL HOMANN
University of Munich, Germany

PETER KOSLOWSKI
Free University Amsterdam, The Netherlands

CHRISTOPH LUETGE
University of Munich, Germany

Routledge
Taylor & Francis Group

LONDON AND NEW YORK

First published 2007 by Ashgate Publishing

2 Park Square, Milton Park, Abingdon, Oxfordshire OX14 4RN
52 Vanderbilt Avenue, New York, NY 10017

Routledge is an imprint of the Taylor & Francis Group, an informa business

First issued in paperback 2020

British Library Cataloguing in Publication Data
Globalisation and business ethics. - (Law, ethics and
    economics)
    1. Globalisation - moral and ethical aspects 2. Business
    ethics
    I. Homann, Karl II. Koslowski, Peter 1952 III. Luetge,
    Christoph, 1969-
    174.4

Library of Congress Cataloging-in-Publication Data
Globalisation and business ethics / edited by Karl Homann, Peter Koslowski, and
Christoph Luetge.
    p. cm. -- (Law, ethics and economics)
    Includes bibliographical references and index.
    ISBN-13: 978-0-7546-4817-8 1. Business ethics. 2. International
economic relations--Moral and ethical aspects. 3. Globalization--Moral and ethical
aspects. 4. Social justice. 5. Culture and globalization. I. Homann, Karl. II. Koslowski,
Peter, 1952- III. Luetge, Christoph, 1969- IV. Title: Globalization and business ethics.

    HF5387.G583 2007
    174.4--dc22

                                                                        2006034247

ISBN 978-0-7546-4817-8 (hbk)
ISBN 978-0-367-60372-4 (pbk)

Contents

List of Contributors

Silvia Bauer, M.A, Interdisciplinary Institute for Cultural and Gender Studies, München, Germany

Prof. Dr. Margo A. Bienert, Georg-Simon-Ohm University of Applied Sciences, Nürnberg, Germany

Dr. Michael Ehret, Marketing-Department, Freie Universität Berlin, Germany

PD Dr. Bernhard Emunds, Nell-Breuning-Institute for Economic and Social Ethics, Hochschule Sankt Georgen, Germany

PD Dr. Michaela Haase, Marketing-Department, Freie Universität Berlin, Germany

Prof. Dr. Dr. Karl Homann, Chair for Philosophy and Economics, Ludwig-Maximilians-Universität, München, Germany

Prof. Dr. Dr. Dr. h.c. mult. Klaus J. Hopt, Max Planck Institute for Comparative and International Private Law, Hamburg, Germany

Martin Kaluza, M.A., Department of Philosophy, Freie Universität Berlin, Germany

Prof. Dr. Dr. h.c. Peter Koslowski, Professor of Philosophy, especially Philosophy of Management and Organisations and History of Philosophy, Free University Amsterdam, The Netherlands

PD Dr. Christoph Luetge, Chair for Philosophy and Economics, Ludwig-Maximilians-Universität, München, Germany

Prof. Dr. Elke Mack, Institute for Christian Social Ethics, University of Erfurt, Germany

Prof. Dr. Georg Marckmann, MPH, Institute for Ethics and History of Medicine, University of Tübingen, Germany

Dr. Michael Neuner, Department of Business Studies and Economics, University of Applied Sciences Ludwigshafen/Rhine, Germany

Prof. Dr. Manfred Prisching, Department of Sociology, University of Graz, Austria

Dr. Frits Schipper, Department of Philosophy, Free University Amsterdam, The Netherlands

Dr. Eberhard Schnebel, Württemberger Hypo Bank, Stuttgart, Germany

Dr. Tatjana Schönwälder-Kuntze, Chair for Philosophy and Economics, Ludwig-Maximilians-Universität München, Germany

Matthis Synofzik, Institute for Ethics and History of Medicine, University of Tübingen, Germany

Introduction

Karl Homann, Peter Koslowski and Christoph Luetge

We are confronted with the problems of globalisation daily. Globalisation has become a common phenomenon, yet one that many people experience as a threat not only to their economic existence, but also to their cultural and moral self-image. Some join protest organisations like ATTAC and others. Their protests regularly lead to violence at international summits. Moreover, the current situation after September 11th can be seen as an indirect consequence of problems associated with globalisation. The terror could not have developed in such a way without an environment of people that feel threatened by globalisation.

It is the aim of this volume to differentiate the intuitive approaches to globalisation into different problem dimensions. These problem dimensions will then be worked on within different disciplines, namely philosophy, economics, sociology, social ethics, management and cultural studies, with the idea of ultimately re-integrating these different perspectives into an overall picture.

Globalisation, at first, is a development which increases the internationalisation of production and manufacturing, governing and financing processes. While international economic relations are nothing new, the global integration of production, governing and financing processes within the structures of multinational, globally operating corporations certainly is. Under conditions of globalisation, products are not manufactured any more in one country and then exported, rather, products are designed and produced in production sites in various locations around the world and financed by global investors and holding companies. Internationalisation is already present at the production stage, not only at the retail stage. Primary products are increasingly manufactured at different locations around the globe. The degree of division of labour increases. Division of labour takes place not only between manufacturers of final products at different locations, but already between manufacturers of primary products at different places. Internationalisation is thus boosted beyond traditional international division of labour both in vertical integration and in the supply chain.

This leads to an increased competition of workers, as corporations can sidestep into low-wage countries more easily than when the entire, highly differentiated product was produced in one country. The resulting global supply of labour for industrial production causes wages to fall in high-wage countries due to competitive pressure by low-wage countries. This development is seen by many workers as a threat to their existence.

A prerequisite of globalised production is the globalisation and liberalisation of financial markets, which enables or dramatically facilitates direct investment in foreign countries. A flood of mergers in the year 2000 is a good indicator both for the globalisation of financial investment as well as for the global integration of structures of production.

This development is also accompanied by ecological dangers and increased migration. Globally acting corporations often promote Western ideals and images of consumption in marketing and distribution, and they are supported in this role by the globally dominating position of Western mass media. Some authors regard 'consumerism' as the intrinsic *Weltanschauung* of the West, as its global ideology which, in other parts of the world, breeds counter-ideologies like Islamism.

Globalisation of markets and production, in another regard, greatly diminishes the efficiency of national politics, in particular, national economic and labour market policy, as these markets are not nationally organised any more and can only to a limited extent be controlled through national legislation and politics.

Globalisation also has normative and cultural dimensions. However, these dimensions are often discussed quite independent from – or even in direct opposition to – its economic dimensions. We have tried to avoid this fruitless split between normative and economic considerations in the present book, by choosing authors with competences in both domains.

The normative dimension of globalisation includes questions of the cultural self-images of man, the consequences of accelerating processes of modernisation on human identity, the increasing insecurity and the human capability to cope with it. It also includes the problem of winners and losers of globalisation – and the question how the winners might possibly compensate the losers for their losses or improve their situation.

A final question is how philosophical ethics can contribute to the processes described here. Can ethics set limits to global business, indeed, is this the task it has to fulfil? Or can the processes of globalisation, at least in principle, also be thought of as fulfilling the expectations that have been associated with the regulative ideas of universalistic ethics, like human dignity and solidarity? Could it be possible, in this way, to promote a constructive cooperation of philosophy and economics?

The present volume seeks to find answers to these questions. It is organised in four sections. The *initial section* deals with 'Concepts and Problems' and sets out the theoretical framework for globalisation, both systematically and historically:

The first contribution, by Karl Homann, can be seen as a programmatic chapter for the entire volume. Homann explains how globalisation can be judged both positively and negatively from a business ethics standpoint. He concludes that the chances outweigh the risks by far – both in a moral and in an economic sense.

The second chapter, co-authored jointly by Michael Ehret, Michaela Haase and Martin Kaluza, sets the conceptual framework for an analysis of globalisation in a more detailed way. The authors describe, from an economic viewpoint, how institutional structures have shaped the process of globalisation from Bretton Woods to recent developments.

Manfred Prisching, by contrast, tackles globalisation from a sociological standpoint. His chapter is a *tour de force* through 'diagnoses of our time' that have been made by writers of many eras since Antiquity. By offering such a broad overview on historical and contemporary approaches, the many faces of globalisation can be understood better against their historical and systematic background.

Silvia Bauer's and Tatjana Schönwälder's contribution concludes the conceptual section. Bauer and Schönwälder present a view on the process of globalisation from a gender perspective, offering new insights for its ethical dimension, in particular for the problem of equal opportunities.

After this conceptual groundwork, the *second section* of the book gets to core issues of business ethics under conditions of globalisation. The first chapter, by Klaus Hopt, sets the stage by taking on the legal framework of business ethics in the globalised world. Hopt concentrates on a particularly important aspect, the European legislation on Corporate Governance, which already incorporates a number of ethical aspects.

The next two chapters are concerned with ethical questions within corporations. Frits Schipper takes a closer look at the relation of two central concepts in management ethics: transparency and integrity. He shows that these two concepts are not necessarily in opposition to each other, but can also be considered as complementary.

Margo Bienert and Eberhard Schnebel analyse the role of commitments in large corporations. They show how social values form an important part in the functioning of multi-national enterprises. Bienert and Schnebel distinguish between different types of communication that are used, and they cite practical examples for this.

The *third section*, 'Global Justice,' is concerned with ethical problems related to developing countries. Here, the focus is not only on the relation between industrial and developing countries, but also on the relation between developing countries and multinational corporations.

The first chapter, by Elke Mack, aims at constructing an ethical theory that is adequate for dealing with the problem of extreme poverty. She discusses theories of justice by philosophers like Thomas Pogge and John Rawls as well as theological approaches. Mack envisages different scenarios in which different means of poverty reduction can be put to use, ranging from market interaction to transnational structures of governance.

Like Mack, Bernhard Emunds discusses ethical aspects of the institutional framework for international business. Emunds argues that international financial markets could serve the ethical purpose of achieving greater justice between industrial and developing countries, if certain institutional changes were made, especially in the banking sector.

In the final chapter of this section, Georg Marckmann and Matthis Synofzik focus on a particular detail of global justice that has been getting quite a lot of attention in recent years. Marckmann and Synofzik explore strategies for providing people in developing countries with essential medicines – both at fair prices *and* in a way compatible with the functioning of international markets.

The *closing section* of this volume, 'Globalisation, Philosophy and Culture,' comprises three chapters dealing with ethically relevant topics of globalisation that arise within a broader context of philosophy and culture. The first one, by Christoph Luetge, reaches deep into the philosophical domain. Luetge asks whether societies in the age of globalisation still need some kind of social glue. After critically examining how philosophers like Jürgen Habermas, David Gauthier and Ken Binmore have answered this question, Luetge argues in favour of a suggestion by the business ethics conception of order ethics.

Next, Michael Neuner's contribution looks at an ethical problem of the globalisation of culture: the question of the sovereignty of interpretation. Choosing the different images of the *Harry Potter* character as his prime example, Neuner shows how cultural pluralism can impoverish in the globalised age. He ends his chapter in a rather critical tone.

Finally, Peter Koslowski discusses key questions of ethics in globalised financial markets. In particular, Koslowski juxtaposes the German and the Anglo-Saxon system of governing stock corporations. Koslowski argues that while the Anglo-Saxon system holds a number of advantages, the German system can yield equally good results in many respects – for shareholders and other stakeholders.

Most of the contributions are revised and updated versions of papers presented at the 6th Annual Conference of the Forum for Business Ethics and Business Culture of the German Philosophical Association, which was held in Munich from 3rd to 5th December 2003. The editors would like to thank the Fritz Thyssen Foundation for the generous support of this conference.

PART I

GLOBALISATION: CONCEPTS AND PROBLEMS

Chapter 1

Globalisation from a Business Ethics Point of View

Karl Homann

It can be safely said that, despite all differences in detail, one important result of the ongoing discussion about business ethics is that the framework of both formal and informal rules is very important for the ethics of individual actors. The rules of a society have great impact on its members' behaviour. However, it is still a very controversial question how actors can be led to act in moral ways under conditions of competition.

The first part of this chapter will give an overview of the challenges that globalisation holds for the framework and for the implementation of ethical norms. The second part will deal with the role of corporations in the development of a framework of governance for the global society. The third part discusses the question of implementation of ethical norms.

The Problem Situation

Globalisation must now be regarded as a fact. But for business ethics, this fact poses a severe problem: a legal framework that would be able to govern the interactions within the global society in both an efficient *and* ethical way is only beginning to be developed. At best, first steps to this can be made out, namely the UN Charter, the World Trade Organization (WTO), the International Labour Organization (ILO), the International Chamber of Commerce (ICC), the Kyoto Protocol and others. In many parts of the earth, even these first steps have yet to be acknowledged or accepted.

At the same time, competition is becoming more and more intense. How can individuals act ethically under these conditions? It is beyond dispute that the social framework or social order is important for acting ethically, yet this question can be rephrased under conditions of globalisation in the following way: Who is going to develop the social framework for the global society? The nation states and their organisations of cooperation are mainly hindered by the fact that these states compete against each other, e.g., for investment and for the masterminds. Thus, the problem of competition and ethics recurs among states.

In trying to find a solution for this problem, a prominent school of philosophers has been referring to the thought of Immanuel Kant, who already saw the problem of defection, of free riding very clearly.[1] These philosophers propose either to commit

---

1 Kant: Kritik der Reinen Vernunft A 809f., B 837f. (Ak. – Ausg. Vol. 3, 525f.).

the actor categorically to what is 'her duty to do,' independent of what other actors do, or to use the state's power to enforce what is the law. Regarding duty, Kant himself left the question of implementation of duties open, and he saw this himself.[2] Regarding the law, it has to be acknowledged that under conditions of globalisation there is as yet no institution that could enforce the law on a global scale by sovereign means.

Do we thus need a 'global state'? How can the less developed countries be integrated into the global society? Is the theoretical model according to which we have to identify what is right or just and then enforce it via the law, adequate to the current problem situation? Has this model *ever* been adequate at all? Or do all cognitivist conceptions of ethics leave the problem of implementation unresolved?

Corporations and Global Governance

The process of globalisation leads to a decrease in the nation states' capability for governance. The main reasons for this are the rapid increase in the sheer number of interactions, the interdependencies resulting from this and the competition among states which leaves the actors with greater alternatives for evading a state's power. In both regards, no great changes can be expected for the future. While the differentiation of society into subsystems already caused the political system to lose a considerable amount of capacity for governance, this process is further accelerated by the emergence of a global society.[3]

New players enter into this vacuum. The two most important are non-governmental organisations (NGOs) and multinational corporations (MNCs). This chapter will focus on the role of corporations in designing the new social order for the global society. Which are the factors that force the MNCs – explicitly, in part, but in any case implicitly – into a political role?

With his 'Global Compact' initiative, UN Secretary General Kofi Annan has called on the MNCs to cooperate in the realisation and promotion of human rights, better working conditions and protection of the environment: It is clear that for Kofi Annan the community of nation states cannot do these jobs on their own. Thus he implicitly recognises the competence of corporations for efficient governing global processes of coordination. And he implicitly recognises too that to initiate a good development, it is futile to accuse MNCs of 'only' maximising shareholder value. By contrast, the three big players, governments, NGOs and MNCs, even today continue to each define themselves mostly in opposition to the other two, and the resulting self-perception leads them to act accordingly. But currently, the MNCs are probably the only ones to have the resources necessary to integrate those four billion people into the global society that are more or less still excluded today. Development aid provided by government and administration has, to a large extent, failed. The industrialised countries come nowhere near the promised 0.7% of the GNP for development aid, and their financial situation is not improving.

---

2   *Cf.* Patzig (1986/94, 1996); Förster (1992).
3   *Cf.* Luhmann (1997).

However, the MNCs still hesitate or even refuse to accept their new political role. From experience, I can speak of four reasons:

1. The call to take on political responsibility is often phrased in a semantics that forces MNCs into the role of opponents. 'Sacrifices' and 'taming of capitalism' are called for. But corporations cannot make sacrifices, and to tame self-interest is diametrically opposed to how the market economy works. And even morally sensitive CEOs have to abandon their attempts if the process of integrating developing countries is criticised in terms of normative redistribution theory. This semantics sees corporations as opponents, not as partners.

2. There is a growing number of corporations that have accepted their new public role and actively pursue it. But these activities are mostly of a regional nature (e.g., regional job opportunities), and in most cases, there is no coordination among the different corporations. As no corporation can initiate global development processes and social orders on its own, corporations do not really fully exploit their potential for governance. Corporations can bear this responsibility for the framework of governance only together. They seem not to be used to cooperating with other corporations in the area of global politics – in mutual interest – while still remaining rivals in markets.

3. Many politicians and NGOs make it harder for corporations to enter into their political role by reproaching them of having no democratic legitimacy. Two things can be said in response to this: First, practically none of the NGOs can be said to be legitimised democratically in *this* sense. Second, it is necessary to rethink the core concept of 'democracy'. Of course, corporations are not elected in a democratic way, but the people, by way of constitution, has given them an active role in fulfilling entrepreneurial tasks, because corporations can fulfil this role better than other actors. The same can be said of NGOs. So corporations should not let themselves be put off by this argument, but should rather develop and communicate a sustainable conception of democracy.

4. Transparency and communication are two central elements of democracy. Corporations are at the moment only *beginning* to live up to these elements. And chief executives are usually not trained for this task. In Germany, there are still only very few departments of economics which teach competence in business ethics.

Corporations have thus rather stumbled into bearing responsibility for the social order of global society. But why should they accept this task, which is laden with so many difficulties? Maybe they should rather resist this task, because it has to be fulfilled by other actors?

The Question of Implementation

In philosophy there have, since Greek antiquity, always been two paradigmatic answers to the question of how to implement normative claims: Insight and interests.

Both these answers recur in the ethical discussion about globalisation, mostly in certain mixtures, but sometimes also in 'pure' form:

1. If *insight* is to be the key to implementation, this can be called a *cognitivist* position, broadly speaking. This view has been held by Plato and Kant, and in contemporary theory by J. Rawls, J. Habermas, H. Jonas – and, with regard to globalisation, by Höffe (1999). In Höffe's argument, this view recurs with exceptional clarity:

   For Höffe, human beings enter society with certain fundamental, pre-social rights, i.e. human rights. Human rights need to be guaranteed by the state with its monopoly on the use of force. In a second step, the state is characterised as a 'qualified democracy,' which implies social policy. As the problems on the level of global society retain the same structure as those within the nation state, i.e. a prisoners' dilemma structure, a 'global state' ('Weltstaat') must be erected. This global state has – in Höffe's words – to be so powerful as to be able to stand up to multinational corporations and their strategic alliances as well as against the national interests of great powers, even superpowers.[4]

   Höffe calls this global state a 'legal-moral commitment' ('rechtsmoralische Verpflichtung'). The question of a state's *interests* is neglected. Rather, Höffe, reminding us of J.-J. Rousseau and the 'sober moralist' Kant, categorically states that an 'ought without compromise' like justice is 'not spoilt by bad reality'. Rather, reality has to justify itself before the ought, and not the ought before reality.[5]

   This model is made up of the following central elements:

   * What is legal, can be known in advance, in theory (cognitivism).
   * However, unlike others, Höffe does not lapse into moralising at this point.
   * Rather, he calls for the state, notably the global state, as an external power to enforce what has been identified as just.
   * His key aim is to 'tame' interests by means of government power, and not to find a way how interests may *cooperate*.

   These elements, plus the common moralising rhetoric which Höffe avoids, can be found in all conceptions of cognitivist ethics, in one mixture or another. The common idea is to have philosophy find out what is right and what is just, and then enforce this *against* interests, either by appealing to insight or by calling for legal power.

2. As opposed to Höffe, an order ethics approach tries to implement ethical norms by means of interests. Actors comply with norms from self-interest.

---

4 Höffe (1999, p.401).

5 'Im Gegenteil muss sich die Wirklichkeit vor dem Sollen und nicht das Sollen vor der Wirklichkeit rechtfertigen.' (Höffe, 1999, p.278.)

Their interests face up to scarce resources, and they conflict many times, of course. But still, actors also share *common* interests: They are interested in a social order. This problem can be modelled as a dilemma structure which can only be resolved by establishing a social order. This is the classic argument of social contract theory from Hobbes to Buchanan, which *refrains* from formulating normative prerequisites for a social order. Rather, social contract theory analyses the systematic conditions for complying with rules, and these conditions can only be non-normative, individual expectations of advantages and benefits. In other words: the process of *choosing* rules for global society cannot be seen within a framework of a) how to *comply* with rules, and especially not of b) *pre-established* norms, as those cognitivist approaches try.

But why might corporations be interested – or develop an interest in – the shaping of a social order for global society?

Corporations cannot be expected to make 'sacrifices,' but they can *invest* – in real or human capital, but also in the social order as a prerequisite of long-run benefit. At the moment, the lack of an adequate social order for global society still keeps two-thirds of humanity, four billion people, outside of productive interactions. An economist regards these four billion people as assets, as factors which can bring about wealth and prosperity, if conditions are set adequately. At the moment, these four billion people are regarded rather as a *threat* to the prosperity of the industrial nations. This way of thinking is clearly based in a zero sum paradigm, and it leads to political reactions which eventually *make* those people threats. It is in the corporations' vital interest to develop this potential, not by making 'sacrifices,' but by investing in the fundamental conditions of sustainable profits: the social order. This is a mutually beneficial activity, for the 'poor' as well as for the 'rich,' thus also for the corporations themselves.

It is therefore in the interest of corporations to open up potentials which currently lie idle. Managers are not only assigned to make profits on already existing markets, but in particular to open up new markets, to develop them, even to *create* them. Those who do not jump in now will have to make much greater efforts later to break into those markets. And these strategies can be argued for from the shareholders' view, as they can be expected to eventually lead to higher profits. Via stock prices, these expectations can already be capitalised now.

From a philosophical standpoint, the structure of this approach is quite interesting: There is no call for sacrifice, for redistribution or for taming the corporations' striving for profits. Rather, this striving for profits is to be unleashed. What is to be overcome, is the latent Manichaeism inherent in many conceptions of ethics and business ethics, which invariably condemns the striving for profits as the root of all evil. In the conception advocated here, the social order constrains the options for action not by external authorities, but from self-interest itself: Constraining the options for *action* produces *more and better* options in *interactions* for each individual, i.e. more individual freedom.

One major weakness of the Global Compact, in current opinion, is that the cooperation of corporations is voluntary and not enforced by the state. However, I would like to argue in favour of voluntary measures, by including in my argument the third major international player: NGOs.

Keeping measures voluntary guarantees that each player has to take into account the interests of other players, if he wants to realise his own ones. A voluntary process tends to safeguard the consideration of everyone's interest. Of course, no group will cooperate for *any* price, but only, if their vital and publicly justifiable interests are being accepted. The political authorities must respect the interests of corporations and NGOs, the NGOs must develop an understanding for governments and corporations, and the corporations themselves must be sensitised for political processes and the social and ecological consequences of their decisions.

This 'must' might be misinterpreted: However, it is not a moral 'must,' but a 'must' derived from the sustainable, long-run interests of the three players. For all three, there are incentives for changing their perspectives. Indeed, it is highly welcome to see that all three players currently are loosening their sometimes radical opposition against the other two. After all, they all share a common interest in the social order, and they are increasingly becoming aware of this. The 11 September 2001 has made it clear what costs the lack of a widely accepted, 'just' order entails.

Voluntary measures might also change the attitude of critics. There are many critics who regard the corporations' political engagement as a threat to the political culture, even as an official legitimisation of lobbying. They fear that the fox is put in charge of the henhouse, so that successful lobbyists can enforce their individual interests by government measures. But in networks based on voluntary cooperation, the sovereign force is left out. Networks are built on a principle of consensus. Consequently, the vital and justifiable interests of others will be taken into account, not by way of morals or of individual actors' personal properties, but by the structure in which these processes are organised.[6]

Final Remarks

Every morality needs to be based in interests, even for Kant. And every morality had such a basis as long as it was effective. I have no objections if, *in certain contexts*, morals become independent of this basis, such as during the process of education or in ethical theories. But if morals are turned against interests and are charged with taming them, then morals are turned against their own basis and consequently destroy themselves. Morals are made for man, not man for morals.

References

Apel, K.-O. (2001), Diskursethik als Ethik der Mit-Verantwortung vor den Sachzwängen der Politik, des Rechts und der Marktwirtschaft, in K.-O. Apel and H. Burckhart (eds.), *Prinzip Mitverantwortung. Grundlage für Ethik und PädagogikPrinzip Mitverantwortung. Grundlage für Ethik und Pädagogik* eds Apel, K.-O. and Burckhart, H., (Würzburg: Königshausen und Neumann), 69–95.

---

6   Cf. the interesting remarks by Apel (2001).

Förster, E. (1992), "Was darf ich hoffen?', *Zeitschrift für Philosophische Forschung*, **46**, 168–185.

Höffe, O. (1999), *Demokratie im Zeitalter der Globalisierung*, München: Beck.

Homann, K. (2004), Fakten und Normen: Der Fall der Wirtschaftsethik, in C. Lütge and G. Vollmer (eds.), *Fakten statt Normen? Zur Rolle einzelwissenschaftlicher Argumente in einer naturalistischen Ethik*, Baden-Baden: Nomos, 105–116.

Kant, I. (1781/87), *Kritik der reinen Vernunft*, 1st edn, 2nd edn, (Riga) (Riga 1787).

Luhmann, N. (1997), *Die Gesellschaft der Gesellschaft*, 2 Vols, Frankfurt am Main: Suhrkamp.

Patzig, G. (1986/1994), '"Principium diiudicationis" und "Principium executionis". Über transzendentalpragmatische Begründungsansätze für Verhaltensnormen', in *Gesammelte Schriften I: Grundlagen der Ethik* ed Patzig, G., (Göttingen: Wallstein), 255–274.

Patzig, G. (1996), Moralische Motivation, in *Die Rationalität der Moral* eds Patzig, G. et al., Bamberg: Verlag Fränkischer Tag, .39–55. (Translated by Christoph Luetge.)

Chapter 2

Concepts of Globalisation: The Institutional Prerequisites for the Integration of World Markets

Michael Ehret, Michaela Haase and Martin Kaluza

Introduction

Despite the current intensive and controversial debate, globalisation is anything but a recent phenomenon. Indicators support the view that by 1913 the world markets were much closer integrated than today (Micklethait and Wooldridge, 2000, pp.3–25, Wolf, 96–107). At the present time, the development of an institutional[1] order of an integrated world market has reached a critical phase. The failure of the World Trade Organization (WTO) to come to an agreement in the Cancún round in 2003 has thwarted the institutional integration of world markets.

Established economic theories maintain that the process of globalisation gives rise to advantages for all parties. However, these approaches often do not sufficiently consider the institutional prerequisites for the achievement of such a result. With our contribution we attempt to highlight the institutional conditions for a global governance structure which helps to generate the win-win potential promised by economic theory.

Efforts to establish a global governance structure date back to the first monetary and financial market conference of the UNO in 1944 in Bretton Woods. One consequence was the foundation of organisations able to take action on a global scale (like the World Bank and the International Monetary Fund) as well as the agreement on a set of world wide institutions. This post-war order was initially erected on the building blocks of a free trade regime among nations complemented by a welfare state within the respective nations, which was intended to manage the social costs of globalisation (Kapstein, 1999, p.94). It is important to realise that first the Bretton-Woods order was created by developed nations and designed to their needs, and second the aim was stability and the avoidance of depression, not the management of globalised relationships between developed and developing countries.[2]

---

1   We make a distinction between 'institutions' in the sense of rules and organisations. See North (1990, p.3).

2   Milner (2005, p.836) points out that all of the Bretton Woods organisations and institutions 'were created by the victors in World War II and were intended to help them to avoid another global depression. (…) They were designed to help the developed countries create a cooperative and stable world economy in a non-globalized world'.

Both principles – free trade and welfare state – have come under heavy pressure in the meantime. The design of a new order of international and global relationships is thus essential. In the same way as national economies can gain advantages from the establishment of pertinent institutional structures, a globalised economy is in need of pertinent institutions built on adequate knowledge and intentions. Knowledge as well as intentions are prerequisites for the creation of adequate institutions: intention is directed at the solution of dilemma situations or at the willingness to cooperate, whereas knowledge is required for the design of the 'right' institutions which support or accommodate cooperative efforts. In this regard, we can identify institutional deficits on the global scale, but also on the national arena.

Who talks about a need of *fairer* globalisation supposes deficits of fairness. In our contribution we describe these as deficits of participation. The political, cultural and social integration of developing countries in the process of globalisation is therefore a central aim of any endeavour to achieve a higher degree of fairness.[3] If and to what extent this aim can be realised is influenced by a couple of different factors. One outcome of development economics is that we cannot expect to find one clear defined path leading to success. Nevertheless, any successful path of globalisation needs to be built on legitimisation. This is hard to achieve without evaluating the process of globalisation by principles of fairness. In addition, even the existence of advantages for those who already participate in the course of globalisation do not give rise to sufficient legitimacy: Win-win situations are not necessarily fair.

Rhetoric of Globalisation, Political Interests and Economic Potential

Economic Arguments in Favour of Globalisation and their Perception in the Political Debate

From the perspective of economic theory all participating nations gain from liberalised trade. Based on David Ricardo's theory of comparative cost advantages, classical market theory emphasises efficiency effects accruing from liberalised trade. By participating in the world trade, a nation can focus on the production of those goods which it can produce at the comparatively lowest costs (Samuelson and Nordhaus, 1989, pp.898–910). Therefore, trade enables a nation to concentrate on those branches of the economy where it is more efficient than others. This is enabled by buying those products on the international market with respect to which the nation has relative cost disadvantages.

The argument above is based on opportunity costs. It has been enhanced by the new trade theory by integrating a value dimension. Specialisation gives rise to the development of 'core competencies' which can be translated into productivity advantages when used in world trade. Because of specialisation on particular branches of industry, nations can gain from positive external effects (Krugman, 1993). German manufacturers of investment goods, e.g., could establish themselves

---

3   This is no one-sided process, but a complementary one with respect to the developed countries. The expressions 'developed countries' and 'developing countries' designate relative positions which leave room for development for both groups of countries.

as 'hidden champions' in global business markets (Anderson and Narus, 1998, pp.16–17), whereas India has transformed itself into the software laboratory of the global market economy.

In economics, arguments for constraining world trade are hard to find (Krugman, 1993). This is in sharp contrast with the politics and rhetoric of world trade. On the political arena the process of trade liberalisation is experiencing a deep crisis following the failure of the WTO round in Cancún (2003). Whereas the developing countries have interrupted the process, the public debate in developed nations is affected by a growing scepticism concerning trade liberalisation (Milner, 2005, p.833; Sinn, 2006, p.7). Business strategies like 'outsourcing' and 'offshoring' are considered with growing suspicion and resentment. That notwithstanding, they are appropriate strategies for exploiting the potential gains from trade. How can we explain that the economic potential of globalisation is not reflected in the public political debate in developed nations?

Barriers for Productivity Effects of World Trade

As result of the economic analysis of world trade, it can be stated: All countries would take advantages from a liberalised world trade if they participated in it. Free trade allows for a focus on core competencies and the realisation of economies of scale by means of importing all those goods that the country cannot produce at a relative cost advantage. In the world of theory, world trade enables countries to specialise and realise economies of scale in an all-embracing manner.

Nevertheless, there are several areas of conflict which mainly result from a misfit between economies and institutions. At the present time, we perceive three central interfering factors which can be traced back to the realm of institutions:

1. Developed countries, in particular members of the OECD, can more easily profit from liberalised world trade than developing countries. However, the realisation of these advantages requires a change of internal structures even within developed countries, eventually eroding whole industries and devaluing complete branches of human capital. As Sinn (2006, p.6) comments with respect to Germany: 'The industrial workers displaced by Chinese workers, Polish Workers or robots, are not released for high-order jobs but for nothing.' ['Die von den Chinesen, Polen und Robotern verdrängten Industriearbeiter werden nämlich nicht für höherwertige Stellen freigesetzt, sondern für gar nichts'.] As a consequence, significant parts of the population face the threat of social decline (Micklethwait and Wooldridge, 2000, pp.246–270; Turner, 2001).

2. Both in developing and developed countries, the debate on economic policy does scarcely refer to the win-win potentials inherent in a liberalised word trade. World trade is not envisioned in the spirit of new trade theory, but in terms of 'international competitiveness' (Krugman, 1994). This leads to a selective participation in the world trade, pursuing the domination of world markets by 'national champions', on the one hand, and simultaneous safeguarding of large parts of industry and agriculture from worldwide

competition, on the other. It is to a large extent determined by the promise
of achieving national competitive advantages based on the performance of
particular national industries, accompanied by the protection of other national
economic branches against the exposition to global competition (Krugman,
1994). Against this background, the failure of Cancún can be understood
rather as a rejection of mercantilist policies and protectionist structures ruling
world trade than a rejection of economic gains from trade (Economist 2003).
3. To some extent, developing countries lack the institutional foundations
   enabling them to benefit from the world trade's economic potential. Insufficient
   legal systems and infrastructures provide a hindrance to the accumulation of
   capital, and they do not attract foreign capital in sufficient amount either. When
   investigating what is called 'dead capital,' De Soto highlighted an astonishing
   amount of hidden economic potential (Soto, 2000, pp.20–35). Concerning for
   example Lima, the capital of Peru, he estimated the value of real estate to
   which no property rights are assigned as equal to 74 billion US $ – the five-
   fold amount compared to the market capitalisation of Peru's publicly listed
   companies. The absence of market institutions hinders the registration of
   property, the organisation of its productive use and its selling on a market.
   As a consequence, entrepreneurs face prohibitive costs for establishing a
   business organisation. According to De Soto, institutional deficiencies are a
   substantial barrier to the development of many developing countries. Since the
   legal prerequisites for productive market activities are absent (Stiglitz, 2002,
   pp.23–52), the privatisation efforts issued or supported by the IMF and the
   World Bank have been often fallen short of one's expectations. In such cases
   the developing countries become *de facto* losers of the market integration
   whereas the developed countries can take advantage of it.

We arrive at the following conclusion: the present crisis of global integration is
merely caused by institutional deficits and not by a failure of substantial economic
integration in virtue of the ideas of comparative cost advantages and specialisation.
To put it in a slightly exaggerate form: the main problem is rather 'a too limited
market' than a 'too liberal market'. In this context it becomes evident that institutional
aspects cannot be left out of economic analysis, as obvious deficiencies in the world
market's governance structures block the generation of economic value.

Fallacies of the Win-Win Hypothesis with Regard to the World Trade

From the point of view of economics, market transactions realise economic potentials
for suppliers as well as for customers. Unreserved advocates of globalisation often
point out that those developing countries that have opened themselves to globalisation
are significantly better off since then. However, in certain cases it may turn out that it
would be a misconception to understand that as a win-win situation:

• In some cases it may appear that a country benefits from globalisation, but that
  the supposed win-win situation is merely superficial: While on an aggregate
  level the economy in question is better off, the improvement is dearly paid for

with the aggravation of the situation of particular groups within that nation. The question arises how to calculate the cost for the losers of globalisation. This also constitutes a problem of legitimacy for the institutions of world trade. In the long run, they can only be established if within the populations of the participating countries most people do not feel that globalisation leaves them worse off. The process of globalisation depends on the consent of the people on whose life and actions it has an influence. Their disapproval undermines the success of globalisation and therefore the generation of economic advantages. Such disapproval looms whenever the way in which globalisation is carried out is being perceived as unjust.

- Win-win situations do not necessarily amount to an increase in justice. A comparatively modest improvement of the situation of disadvantaged countries does not mean that they receive a just share of the potentially immense benefits of globalisation (see Sen, 2004, p.18). Globalisation may make the world more just. Or it may not. As long as claims for justice are systematically left out of consideration, globalisation will face a problem of legitimacy. A case in point is the access to world markets: Small benefits for developing countries on the one hand and huge benefits for those industrial nations able to exercise control on economic relationships on the other are not perceived as a just arrangement.

- In addition, the ascription of a win-win situation often leaves out one logical step: from the fact that a country which has opened itself to globalisation is now better off than before it cannot be concluded that the improvement was caused by globalisation.[4]

Current economic approaches like the theory of comparative cost advantages or the new trade theory tempt to produce such fallacies since they systematically leave out institutional questions. However, experience shows that market theories, in their treatment of global integration, have to face aspects of legitimacy.

Taking into account the institutional perspective, we find: Under the circumstances given, the developing countries' possibilities to participate in the positive effects of globalisation through integration in the world market are limited. However, this is not a necessary consequence within a deterministic process of economic globalisation (see Poser, 2003). It is rather an effect of a specific policy of globalisation that reflects particularly the interests of the leading industrialised nations (Krugman, 1994; Stiglitz, 2002). Thus, alternative – and arguably more just – forms of globalisation are not inconceivable. Such a perspective may serve as a point of departure for a more differentiated discussion of the phenomenon of globalisation and the processes it is composed of. It can help to qualify both the euphemistic economic promises

---

4   Thomas Pogge raises doubts about the validity of arguments that rest on comparisons over time: 'That the winds are benefiting you in your journey is not shown by your getting closer to your destination – your progress may be slowed badly by strong headwinds' (Pogge, 2002, 15). Likewise, it has to be admitted that a country worse off than before might have been even worse off without globalisation.

of unreflected globalisation rhetoric and the often undifferentiated criticisms of globalisation.

Before approaching a theoretical analysis of the role of institutions in the process of globalisation we shall briefly address the organisations and institutions that shape the current global market order.

The Development of Institutions of Global Market Integration – From Bretton Woods towards Washington and Cancún

Originally, designed in Keynesian spirit (Stiglitz, 2002), Bretton Woods can be seen as the starting point in the development of today's international economic order. With the integration of international markets as its central element, national states' policies and the newly founded international organisations like World Bank and IMF were designed in order to correct politically unwelcome market outcomes (or at least to help relieving its consequences). Later, with the Washington Consensus, which established the basic rules for the distribution of funds by IMF and World Bank, this policy was abolished. In light of the financial crisis in Latin America during the 1980s, US President Ronald Reagan and British Prime Minister Margaret Thatcher, above all, promoted the policy of liberalisation. Its centrepiece consisted in tying the granting of loans to those countries in need of support to the liberalisation of their financial markets, thus to reducing import restrictions and cutting back state deficits (Stiglitz, 2002, pp.1–22). The policy of world market integration put many developing countries in a situation of global competition they were not prepared for.

According to former chief World Bank economist Joseph Stiglitz, the problem does not lie in world market participation as such. After a series of institutional reforms, countries like Chile, for example, have been able to integrate in the world market and to participate in its economic potentials (Stiglitz, 2002, pp.18–19). However, in states that did not manage to create the necessary conditions in due time, complete industries died off and huge parts of the population fell into poverty. It is not surprising that developing countries consider the current conditions of world market integration not so much as an invitation to participate in fair competition, but rather as a game with loaded dice in that they can only lose ground. Therefore, it is necessary to create institutions that can promote world market integration in a constructive manner.

While the model of Bretton Woods aimed at multilateral market integration inwardly flanked by a social state, the model of the Washington Consensus was based on the trust in market forces and market dynamics. The 2003 WTO summit made it clear that both models failed. Nevertheless, the way back to the Keynesian order of Bretton Woods is blocked for the following reasons:

1. The alleged conflict between efficiency and justice: Bretton Woods was motivated by the thesis that efficiency and justice are two aims in conflict. Since the market gave rise to results that were economically efficient but politically unwanted, the state was prompted to use a part of the efficiency benefits to correct the market-based results by means of redistribution. As far as redistribution was meant to weaken inequalities, the relation of the aims

was understood as a trade-off between efficiency and equality (Gaertner, 1994). But this point of view has also been challenged. In further debates, doubts were raised about the assumption of a necessary conflict between the aims of efficiency and justice. Instead, it has been argued that the aims were rather complementary or interdependent (see Roth, 1999; Kubon-Gilke, 2002, Suchanek, 2002).

2. The erosion of the national states' autonomy of agency: As far as the options of national policy making are concerned, the idea underlying Bretton-Woods-based policy had to face an erosion in one of its major components, namely the inwardly directed social state policy (Sinn, 2003). On an international level, there are no means comparable to those of a social state. A worldwide tax collector is as inexistent (and it might be questioned whether it would be good to have one) as a world government. Instead, national states retrieved themselves within a new form of competition of systems that is owed to the globalisation process (Sinn, 2004). They are enforced to realise the possible benefits of globalisation by an efficient policy on the national level (Lachmann, 2006) which needs to be accompanied by the support of those in the developed countries that are left worse off by the national results of globalisation: These people need help to regain their competitiveness. In addition, international agreements sometimes put restrictions upon the options of national policy making. For its members, the European Monetary Union, for example, came along with a loss of action opportunities in policy making. After the liberalisation of capital flows, in particular for smaller states, it became more difficult to control their financial markets. National monetary policies and pertinent adjustments of exchange rates are no longer available as instruments to react on negative shocks of regional labour markets (HWWA, 2003, p.1). A case in point was the creation of an integrated European market of financial services completed in 2005 that obliged the German Government to realise the Financial Services Action Plan (FSAP).

3. The execution of national interests and playing off of national power: Those who argue that globalisation is not simply the consequence of 'universal structural constraints' or 'blind economic forces' (Sklair, 2001, p.5) usually stress the role of the actors of globalisation. Economic theory maintains that market transactions are carried out by equals. The assumption that both partners benefit from transactions which they freely agreed on (Kanbur, 2002) does not take into account the multiple characteristics of a transaction and the problems potentially emerging from those. The fact that a transaction is carried out voluntarily does not amount to anything more than that its expected utility exceeds its expected costs. In particular, it does not even mean that the transaction partners could not have been better off.

Problems resulting from differences in the opportunity to apply power to relationships are scarcely taken into account (De Geer, 2002; Kanbur, 2002, Rothschild, 2002). However, on the international level we are faced with actors who, apart from the different preconditions in institutions and human capital, dispose of very different opportunities to make use of power: Such actors are the nation states themselves, but also international organisations such as the Bretton-Woods organisations IMF and World Bank as well as NGOs, Epistemic Communities, companies and private households. The fact that actors have power is not negative as such since it does not say anything about how they use it. Power opens up possibilities of action; it can yield positive consequences if, e.g., it is used in order to provide global public goods. But it can also be used to take advantage of differences between two parties that formally share the same rights; in this case, power outlines the leeway for the enforceability of particularistic interests. Since the early 1990s, it is mainly the USA as a hegemonial state who plays a negative role in pursuing a foreign policy primarily determined by the short-term interests of domestic 'pressure groups' (Sautter, 1999, p.46).

To sum up: the idea embodied by Bretton Woods, namely that multilateral relationships[5] provide the basis for future development of the nation states, has suffered increasing erosion over the last years and decades. Multilateral organisations such as the WTO,[6] in which every member state has one vote, have lost in importance compared to associations like the Free Trade Area of the Americas (FTAA).[7] However, clubs cannot adequately replace the WTO with its rules binding upon all parties. From the viewpoint of economic theory, the question arises how we can develop a model of market integration that avoids the efficiency problem of the Bretton-Woods model and the legitimacy problem of the Washington Consensus as well.

Globalisation as a Consequence of Action

The process of globalisation is not a deterministic process, but one that is influenced by actors and institutions. Several levels of action are relevant for this process: the rules of the game, which are negotiated or issued by international organisations (with states or groups of states behind them), determine the highest level of global governance. Lower levels of action, like bilateral relationships between states, or relationships between states and organisations, are influenced by the highest level, too. An agreement on rules of the game requires cooperation which, independently of the respective level of action, will not have its starting point in harmonious interests. Most actors in the process of globalisation act with more or less diverse interests as well as on different opportunities of action which have an impact on the tasks or roles open to them in the process of globalisation (see Alger, 2003; Backer, 2003).

---

5   This is not tantamount to each state in a multilateral organisation having the same number of votes: in IMF and World Bank, the rights of participation in decisions depend on the share of capital contributed to the respective organisations.

6   The WTO is not among the original Bretton-Woods organisations; it emerged from the GATT agreement in 1994.

7   According to a DIE ZEIT chapter, the WTO listed 159 free trade areas in 2003 while another 70 are being currently negotiated, *Cf.* P. Pinzler and T. Fischermann: DIE ZEIT, 4.9.2003, 30.

Global governance is path and goal of the process of globalisation at the same time: its final goal is the construction and establishment of a global institutional order or framework of actions that promote cooperation on all levels of action. Intended consequences of the globalisation process like equitable participation of all states or humans, respectively, have been interpreted as 'global public goods'[8] (Kaul, Grunberg and Stern, 1999). The creation of these goods requires pertinent institutional presuppositions and global cooperative action (Sautter, 1999). The creation of an apt institutional structure can thus be interpreted as an 'intermediate global public good' (Kaul, Grunberg and Stern, 1999, p.13), the main goal of which is promoting the creation of global public goods.

Finally, actors and their knowledge about possible problem solutions are responsible for creating the necessary institutions of global governance. Dilemma structures are to be overcome in cases where the framework of actions has to be developed, since it does not exist or only in a limited manner. In general, there is a trade-off between the institutional structure and the moral presuppositions of actors: in this regard, their 'identity matters.' Possible consequences are conflicts which arise from both interest and identity.[9]

Even if all parties involved act for the best with respect to institutional design, mistakes and error, which put a burden on the tediously constructed coalitions of those willing to cooperate, are to be expected. Thus, all pathways towards greater justice in globalisation are accompanied by knowledge acquisition and learning processes. The essential knowledge refers to the recognition of social reality (and therewith to reasons and causes of states and developments) as well as to the opportunities to change it. In this context, the social sciences, including economics, are in charge.

As Kanbur (2002) remarks, developmental economics has its roots in neoclassical economics. The neoclassical mainstream, notwithstanding its advantages and merits, provides only in limited degree starting points for the conception of an institutional framework of action and its subsequent enforcement.[10] Institutional economics is the source of the idea that states (like individuals) have to learn governing their relationships, i.e., to learn behaving in a cooperative manner. In particular, the dynamic strand of the institutional economics approach analyses knowledge acquisition and learning processes in order to examine the impact of mental models (and the actions based upon them) on institutional change (Mantzavinos, North and Shariq, 2004).

---

8   The concept of public good does not imply any evaluation in the sense of 'good' and 'bad.' Thus, a public good might turn out to be a bad. Only in cases where there is or can be assumed a common understanding or consensus regarding the negative evaluation of a thing, we speak explicitly about a bad.

9   Identity is a possible attribute of individuals and organisations as well. Besides interest and identity, Engel (2002) points to emotions as possible sources of conflicts. Emotion, however, is an attribute that can not be assigned to organisations without reservations.

10 According to Kanbur (2003), developmental economics needs an interdisciplinary enhancement in order to analyse interrelations between ideas, beliefs and actions, on the one hand, and voluntaristic, informed action (including gender aspects and the role of institutions), on the other hand.

Knowledge and Learning

Basically, actors are assumed to be willing and able to participate in learning processes. Changes in activities and behaviour of several international organisations demonstrate that this vision cannot be fundamentally wrong. Although the Bretton-Woods organisations IMF and World Bank appeared as 'arrogant power' (Peter, 1994, p.316) ['arrogante Macht'] and as being unwilling to accept criticism until well into the 1970s, the World Bank has since then proven to be 'more communicative' and 'more inclined to take criticism' (see Peter, 1994, p.316) ['kritikfähiger und kommunikativer']. At least on a theoretical level, the position has been approved that there is a need for enhancing the participation of those parts of population which are affected by projects and politics (Peter, 1994, p.317), or that money transfers without any accompanying local development efforts are effective only to a limited degree (World Bank, 1998).

The prospects of success of any endeavour directed at the creation of institutional, political and economic presuppositions for the developing countries in order to improve their 'fitness,' their acceptability as cooperation partners of industrial countries, or their participation in the world market in general, are also affected by the self-commitment of developing countries regarding their compliance with agreements or necessary adjustment processes related to those. Adjustment processes cannot be ruled by decree but are in need of evolutionary, time-consuming processes. Formal institutions cannot simply be 'imported' and implemented without taking into account the extant system of informal institutions.[11] Informal institutions like conventions, customs, or norms, have an impact on child labour, security standards, or the payment of bribes; they also restrict or restrain the realisation of a company's self-commitment.[12]

Not only developing countries, but also industrial states need to relearn or to get rid of Samaritan-like behaviour, the consequences of which keep the receiver of alms in a position of continuing immaturity. Instead, developing countries have to be accepted as partners equipped with the same rights and obligations (nevertheless, one can imagine that there might be deviations from the principle of reciprocity which may have their reason in the opportunities of actions being available to the parties in a transaction). As illustrated by Sautter (1999), developmental cooperation instead of developmental aid requires the realisation of self-interest as well as of self-commitment by both developed[13] and developing countries.

---

11 See Werhane (2000, p.357f.) for examples. Risse (2003) mentions four prima-facie reasons against the transfer of institutions within the framework of developmental aid. These reasons, however, do not militate against a transfer of knowledge directed at the design of institutions.

12 Winstanley *et al.* (2002) report an example of child labour within a supply chain which demonstrates that there is role for activities of NGO's and other civil society organisations as well as a necessity of self-commitment by those companies part of the supply chain. The paper also shows how big the influence of culture, practices, and conventions actually is.

13 Sautter (1999, p.46) points out a need for additional self-commitment by the developed countries in the fields of foreign policy, structural policy, monetary policy, and fiscal policy.

As exemplified above by reference to the World Bank, detailed examples provide support for Risse's (2003) stipulation that organisations have the ability to learn. Nevertheless, with regard to learning processes, visible progress cannot be made out in every aspect: today, the three big players – governments, NGO's and companies – often base their actions on the idea of mutual demarcation from each other or apply a dominant position against each other (see Homann, 2007, p.9). A sizable number of international companies are endowed with a greater potential of resources than many developing countries (Zsolnai, 2002).[14] From this potential, opportunities of action result for companies to which their stakeholders may refer, or which may work as a basis for them to assert claims against a company. Organisations are thus assigned an elucidating role (Homann, 2007); they are addressed as 'moral actors' (Steinmann and Scherer, 1998), or challenged to base their conceptualisation of 'corporate identity' on organisational values (Morsing and Pruzan, 2002), or to make a socially responsible use of their opportunities for action in order to support the integration of those many humans who are socially, economically and politically excluded from the global economy (Geer, 2002; Homann, 2007).

Global social responsibility is not only a demand directed at international companies (as well as on the other actors mentioned above), but also at the citizens of the global civic society. This is the case if, for example, losers of globalisation emerge within a developed country – even if that country in general profits from globalisation. Changes in the competition of systems call for adapting the social security systems of nation states (Sinn, 2004). Finally, the acceptance of losses of consumer rent (see Lachmann, 2006) accruing from competition – not from abuse of power – as being legitimate is an important presupposition for the generation of an improved starting position for subsequent competition processes. The debate over global justice should refer not only to the changes in the opportunities for action of nation states, but should also emphasise the prospective achievement of global public goods. The shift of emphasis from restrictions to prospects might support the view that globalisation is not only a source of welfare losses but also of welfare gains. It might thus also foster its legitimisation.

'Team Production' of Cooperation

Non-governmental actors like international organisations, NGOs and their stakeholders take part in the acquisition of information, the supervision and realisation of agreements. Sautter (1999) emphasises that contracts between states, like those between individuals or organisations, have to be interpreted as relational contracts (Williamson, 1985). Uncertainty and a lack of opportunity to sanction defections increase the need for *ex ante* information and the execution of supervision throughout the transaction. Knowledge has its basis in the actor's mental models; information, however, is looked for in connection with problem solutions. Information can trigger change processes of actor's knowledge bases; in so far they are a source of both the creation of knowledge and its destruction – and thereby also of learning (Haase, 2004).

---

14 See the synopsis in Zsolnai (2002, p.239), Box 12.3: *Countries v Companies*).

The execution of every transaction requires the establishment of a more or less extensive transactional design which can be interpreted as an expression of the institutional and organisational governance of the respective relationship. Transaction costs result from the concrete transaction arrangement as well as from the institutional framework in which the transaction takes place. If the institutional framework is insufficient or hardly existent, then actors themselves can invest in the creation of pertinent institutions. This activity can be interpreted as an investment in the development of markets. The disposition to take over these costs is not guaranteed, however. Actors who invest in the development of new markets have to carry the burden of both specific information costs and transaction costs which accrue from this endeavour. Consequently, they should have an interest in reducing these costs. Therefore, those actors making the investment can hold an interest in activities of other kinds of actors who are not investors, but a kind of information transmitters such as, for example, NGO's or individual representatives of the civil society.

According to Mantzavinos, North and Shariq (2004), communication among actors is an important source for the creation of common *interpretations of reality* in thereby well-defined social realities. Socialisation, communication and learning processes provide the commonly worked out 'social borderlines' for possible institutions. Communication across borderlines might support the creation and enforcement of institutions which provide a framework of action broader than before. Actors participating in transactions can only indirectly support or improve the communication processes among the immediately involved actors; they can transfer information about transaction partners and their performance to the respective other immediate actors or can communicate goals, means and consequences of transactions to actors located more 'outside' of the transaction under discussion (as for example to members of the civic society). The idea of a global civil society clings to social movements, NGOs and networks of citizens across national borderlines as well. In that context, Peter (1994, p.325) ascribes to NGOs the possible role of a 'normative-discursive watchdog' ['normative-diskursives Wächteramt'] or of the 'conscience on behalf of the civil society' ['Gewissen im Auftrag der Zivilgesellschaft'].

From the perspective of a 'team production' of cooperation which includes not only the immediate involved parties but also the political stakeholders, De Geer (2002, p.67) characterises the difference between internationalisation and globalisation:[15]

> In contrast to internationalization, globalization indicates a structural change that reduces the role of national states. From above, national states are challenged by transnational organizations and business corporations, as well as by globally organized NGOs, often build as networks and able to allocate their actions anywhere. From below, national structures are challenged by a new individualism that recognizes the individual as the bearer of rights, which are not dependent on his/her belonging to specific nations, ethnic groups, religious beliefs or gender.

---

15 De Geer presents a list of characteristics of developmental phases.

Conclusions

The global order is underdeveloped but not necessarily inequitable (Risse, 2003). Inequity is less grounded in the existent than in the missing institutions as well as in the manner the parties make use of them: the most powerful national actors often refuse to follow multinational rules of the game. Organisations are not sufficiently involved in the creation of frameworks of organisational action at the present time. If frameworks are missing, the achievement of cooperative solutions requires an interplay of very different types of actors which have to engage in the exchange of information and learning processes. Finally, recognition, self-commitment and control are the main markers having an impact on the character and legitimisation of the process of globalisation.

That globalisation is accused of being inequitable results at least in part from our insufficient knowledge about the sources of the welfare of nations. Free trade is not an adequate target of criticism; it is furthermore the exclusion of many nations from it which is a consequence of the pursuit of particularistic interests and protectionist policies. But even in cases where economies do have access to the world market or participate in free trade, respectively, positive as well as negative consequences of this situation do not occur automatically: they are dependent on institutional prerequisites, on the one hand, and they result from efficient or inefficient policies, on the other.

The actors within the process of globalisation dispose of different opportunities of action based on different realms of responsibility which can be assigned to them. Against this background we can specify both scope and tasks of business ethics with respect to globalisation: i) business ethics should engage in interdisciplinary cooperation with economics in order to work out the theoretical knowledge necessary to the solution of problems of cooperation; ii) business ethics should support the social sciences in their endeavour to interpret, select and implement theoretical recognitions; iii) business ethics should help develop the presuppositions necessary for the communication (and thus for the flow of information and exchange of knowledge) between different actors or types of actors; iv) business ethics should provide support with respect to the formulation, realisation and monitoring of self-commitment of actors; v) finally, as empirical ethics, business ethics should help work out recognitions of local institutions – formal as well as informal ones.

References

Alger, C.F. (2003), Evolving Roles of NGOs in Member State Decision-Making in the UN System, *Journal of Human Rights*, **2**, No. 3, 407–424.

Anderson, J.C. and Narus, J.A. (1998), Business Market Management, *Understanding, Creating, and Delivering Value*, Upper Saddle River, NJ: Prentice-Hall.

Backer, D. (2003), Civil Society and Transitional Justice: Possibilities, Patterns and Prospects', *Journal of Human Rights*, **2**, No. 3, 297–313.

De Geer, H. (2002), Business and Society, in Zsolnai, pp.59–80.

De Soto, H. (2000), The Mystery of Capital, *Why Capitalism Triumphs in the West and Fails Everywhere Else*, London: Bantam.

Ebert, U., ed. (2006), *Schriften des Vereins für Socialpolitik* **228**, *Wirtschaftsethische Perspektiven*, Vol. VIII, Berlin: Duncker & Humblot.

Economist (2004), Behind the Mask. A Survey on Business in China, *The Economist*, March 18th 2004.

——, (2003); Flying on One Engine: A Survey on the World Economy, *September 18th* (2003).

Engel, C. (2002), Causes and Management of Conflicts, *Gemeinschaftsgüter: Recht, Politik und Ökonomie, Reprints aus der Max-Planck-Projektgruppe Recht der Gemeinschaftsgüter*, Bonn.

Gaertner, W. (1994), Pareto-Effizienz und normative Ökonomik, in Homann, K., pp.31–51.

Haase, M. (2004), Wissen und Information: Grundannahmen der Ökonomik und ihre Bedeutung für die Institutionenanalyse, in Held, M., Kubon-Gilke, G. and Sturn, R., pp.67–96.

HWWA Hamburg (2003), *Info* **10**, No. 2003; http://www.hwwa.de.

Held, M., Kubon-Gilke, G. and Sturn, R., eds. (2004), *Jahrbuch Normative und institutionelle Grundfragen der Ökonomik*. 3, Ökonomik des Wissens, Marburg: Metropolis.

—— (eds.) (2002), *Jahrbuch Normative und institutionelle Grundfragen der Ökonomik*, 1, Gerechtigkeit als Voraussetzung für effizientes Wirtschaften, Marburg: Metropolis.

Herder-Dorneich, P., Schenk, K.-E. and Schmidtchen, D., eds. (1995), *Jahrbuch für Neue Politische Ökonomie*, **14**; Band, Von der Theorie der Wirtschaftssysteme zur Ökonomischen Systemtheorie, Tübingen: J. C. B. Mohr/Paul Siebeck.

Homann, K., ed. (1994), *Wirtschaftsethische Perspektiven: Theorie, Ordnungsfragen, Internationale Institutionen*, Berlin: Duncker & Humblot.

——, (2007), 'Globalisation from a Business Ethics Point of View' in this volume, pp. 3–10.

Kanbur, R. (2002), Economics, Social Science and Development, *World Development*, **30**, No. 3, 477–486.

Kapstein, E.B. (1999), Distributive Justice as an International Public Good: A Historical Perspective, in Kaul, I., Grunberg, I. and Stern, M. A., pp.88–115.

Kaul, I., Grunberg, I. and Stern, M.A. (1999), Defining Global Public Goods, in Kaul, I., Grunberg, I. and Stern, M. A., pp.2–19.

– (eds.) (1999): *Global Public Goods: International Cooperation in the 21st Century*, New York: Oxford University Publishing.

Krugman, P.R. (1994), Competitiveness: A Dangerous Obsession, *Foreign Affairs*, **73**, 2 (March/April), 28–44.

—— (1993), The Narrow and Broad Arguments for Free Trade, *American Economic Review*, **83**, No. 2, 362–366.

Kubon-Gilke, G. (2002), Effizienz, Gerechtigkeit und die Theorie des guten Lebens, in Held, M., Kubon-Gilke, G. and Sturn, M., pp.329–357.

Lachmann, W. (2006), Die wirtschaftliche Globalisierung und ihre Kritiker – Eine alternative Sicht, in Ebert, U. (ed.), pp.173–200.

Le Monde Diplomatique, Atlas der Globalisierung, German Edition, Berlin: taz.

Mantzavinos, C., North, D.C. and Shariq, S. (2004), Learning, Institutions, and Economic Performance, *Perspectives on Politics*, **2**, No. 1, 75–84.

Micklethait, J. and Wooldridge, A. (2000), A Future Perfect, *The Challenge and Hidden Promise of Globalisation*, New York: Crown.

Milner, H.V. (2005), Globalisation, Development, and International Institutions: Normative and Positive Perspectives, *Perspectives on Politics*, **3**, No. 4, 833–854.

Morsing, M. and Pruzan, P. (2002), Values-based Leadership, in Zsolnai, L., pp.259–293.

North, D.C. (1990), *Institutions, Institutional Change and Economic Performance*, Cambridge: Cambridge University Press.

—— (1994), Zur ethischen Evolution von Weltbank und Währungsfonds, in Homann, K., pp.303–334.

Peter, H.-B. (1999), *Globalisierung, Ethik und Entwicklung*, Bern: Institut für Sozialethik.

Pogge, T. (2002), *World Poverty and Human Rights*, Cambridge: Polity.

Poser, H., (2003), Harmonie und Selbstorganisation, *fiph Journal* **2**, September, 3–6.

Risse, M. (2003), Do We Live in an Unjust World?, John F. Kennedy School of Government, Harvard University, Faculty Research Working Paper Series, http://ssrn.com/abstract=478923.

Rodrik, D. (2004), Growth Strategies, http://elsa.berkeley/edu/~chad/Handbook.html.

Roth, T.P. (1999), *Ethics, Economics and Freedom*, Aldershot: Ashgate.

Rothschild, K.W. (2002), The Absence of Power in Contemporary Economic Theory, *Journal of Socio-Economics*, **31**, 433–442.

Samuelson, P.A. and Nordhaus, W. (1989), *Economics*. Thirteenth edition, New York: McGraw-Hill.

Sautter, H. (1999), Entwicklungszusammenarbeit als gemeinsame Interessenwahrnehmung von Industrie – und Entwicklungsländern, in Peter, H.-B., pp. 31–53.

Sen, A. (2004), How to Judge Globalism?, in Lechner, F. and Boli, J., pp.16–21.

Sinn, H.-W. (2003), *'The Sick Man of Europe: A Desk Socialist's Diagnosis and Therapy (The German Speech)'*, Ifo Institute for Economic Research and Ludwig Maximilians University of Munich.

—— (2004), The New Systems Competition, *Perspektiven der Wirtschaftspolitik*, **5**, No. 1, 23–38.

—— (2006), Das Deutsche Rätsel: Warum wir Exportweltmeister und Schlusslicht zugleich sind, *Perspektiven der Wirtschaftspolitik*, **7**, No. 1, 1–18.

Sklair, L. (2001), *The Transnational Capitalist Class*, Oxford: Blackwell.

Steinmann, H. and Scherer, A.G. (1998), Corporate Ethics and Management Theory, *Lehrstuhl für Allgemeine Betriebswirtschaftslehre und Unternehmensführung an der Universität Erlangen-Nürnberg, Diskussionsbeitrag Nr.* **93**.

Stiglitz, J.E. (2002), *Globalisation and its Discontents*, London: Penguin.

Suchanek, A. (2002), Das Verhältnis von Effizienz und Gerechtigkeit aus vertragstheoretischer Perspektive, in Held, M., Kubon-Gilke, G. and Sturn, R., pp. 133–152.

Turner, A. (2001), *Just Capital: The Liberal Economy*, London: Macmillan.

Werhane, P.H. (2000), Exporting Mental Models: Global Capitalism in the 21st Century, *Business Ethics Quarterly*, **10**, No. 1, 353–362.

Williamson, O.E. (1985): The Economic Institutions of Capitalism. New York: Free Press, 1985.

Winstanley, D., Clark, J. and Leeson, H. (2002), Approaches to Child Labour in the Supply Chain, *Business Ethics: a European Review*, **11**, No. 3, 210–223.

World Bank (1998), *Assessing Aid: What Works, What Doesn't, and Why*, New York: Oxford University Publishing.

Zsolnai, L., ed. (2002), *Ethics in the Economy*, Oxford: Peter Lang.

Chapter 3

Diagnoses of Our Time: Theoretical Approaches to the Globalised Age

Manfred Prisching

The social sciences are becoming aware that their horizon has been limited, to a great extent, to a nation-state perspective. Economics, politics and culture have been objects framed in the constraints of national 'containers'. Economists took as the object of their studies the 'Volkswirtschaft,' the 'national economy,' and beyond these entities they located a kind of 'world economy' which consisted of relations between national units. Sociologists referred to the nation-state when dealing with the more abstract concept of 'society,' not least because their statistics were construed in these territorial categories. Cultural scientists were aware of the fact that, in the epoch of nation-states, the political unit was in most cases congruent with culturally integrated groups of people, and that problems arose wherever this congruency was compromised.

These economic, political, social and cultural pictures of the world are being dissolved in the process of globalisation. Economists are talking about a real 'world market,' even of the 'global market society;' sociologists recommend considering the 'world society' as the new essential object of their discipline; political scientists are pondering how a multi-layered global system of 'governance' could be imagined; and culturalists do not get by without regarding a possibly syncretistic 'world culture'. Globalisation dissolves traditional objects treated by the social sciences, and new approaches are needed to understand how societies are structured and how they are developing. This survey brings together two inventories of social science publications published within the last decades: studies about 'globalisation' and 'diagnoses of our time'. In both 'bundles' of analyses, numerous ethical questions are embedded.

First: Publications about the process of globalisation are partly affirmative, partly critical (Kurz, 1991; Agnew and Corbridge, 1995; Barber, 1995; Martin and Schumann, 1996; Greider, 1997; Boxberger and Klimenta, 1998; Forrester, 1998; Altvater and Mahnkopf, 1999; Bischoff, 1999; Dönhoff, 1999; Friedman, 1999; Jenner, 1999; Frank, 2000; Heuser, 2000; Theurl and Smekal, 2001; Held and McGrew, 2002; Safranski, 2003; Weinstein, 2005; Frieden, 2006). Actually, one does not get by without the concept of globalisation, in spite of all its fuzziness. There are almost no problems of the world that are not seriously touched by the new transnational constellation. The world has become flat (Friedman, 2005). For some people, globalisation means a breakthrough towards unlimited interconnectedness and peaceful universalism, and they embrace the entrance into the new era emphatically; for other people globalisation means an apocalyptic path causing all unpleasant, dangerous and repressive features of contemporary reality. The political and moral fight about the characteristics of the new 'great transformation' (Polanyi, 1978) is raging, and therefore 'globalisation' is a concept loaded with social-ethical questions and emotional strains (Lemert and Elliott, 2006).

Second: Comprehensive sociological studies of present society, beyond detailed studies of single phenomena, are flourishing (Pongs 1999, Kneer, Nassehi and Schroer, 2000, 2001; Reese-Schäfer, 2000, Schimank and Volkmann, 2000, Volkmann and Schimank, 2002, Prisching, 2003). Concise labels are used for grasping the essence of current developments, labels like 'risk society,' 'post-modern society,' 'society of adventure' or 'multi-optional society'. These studies focus on the whole of societal development, they paint the large canvas. They ask what it is all about, and, as they have to suggest comprehensive models of presence and future, they necessarily transcend restricted empirical findings and are, as the studies about globalisation, charged with ethical elements.

In the process of globalisation, special features of advanced societies are spread all over the world. Patterns of thought which have been developed for analysing the national state have to be adapted for applying them to the global level. The first step is to get a general idea of how to construe the more comprehensive models and to present a review which intends to give a crude orientation. A classification of the intricate approaches is needed to come to terms with the diversity of models, and to classify the conceptions I draw on some paradigms commonly used in history: models of decline, rise, stagnation, cycles, periodisations, and crises.

Global Paradigms of Decline

It is a reputed pessimistic tradition of western culture to insinuate that in the beginning there was an unhurt, beautiful world and to contrast this distant ideal with the story of decline which has taken place since then. Sometimes, the story of decline would even end in a forthcoming apocalypse. The paradigm of decline reminds us of stories of the Christian paradise; but there are also secular models which have suggested a continuous downhill movement of human civilisation, as presented in the works of Hesiod, Vergil or Ovid: 'Aurea prima sata est aetas, quae ....' The 'golden age' endowed with natural dignity and wisdom as well as representing true humanity has been described in glowing colours – and it has remained present in the modern world as a permanent critical option to play off a better past against an unsatisfying present. (The idea that men do not grow old and spring is an eternal condition, is an appealing picture for post-modern consumers clinging to youth and hoping for bio-technological advances that guarantee them eternity.) Romantic tendencies in present-day society ever again go back to the Garden of Eden, to untouched wilderness and true authenticity. Anti-hierarchical Christians refer to early Christian communities where solidarity feelings prevailed; Marxists adore the egalitarian communistic society of pre-history; and feminists follow the traces of theorists like Bachofen (1943) and Bornemann (1979) to explore imaginative conditions of a paradise-like society shaped by the matriarchat, a harmonious epoch destroyed merely by male power delusions (Dworkin, 1981).

The idea that societies have a core of authenticity and that earlier (or even primitive) communities have a more immediate access to the roots of human existence than modernised and industrialised societies has seduced many people to try to regain this kind of immediacy by a repertory of esoteric beliefs and practices. In the globalised world, the experience of cultural diversity does not only pose the problem of the relation of cultural relativism and tolerance *versus* self-assertion of identity and value system; a romantic discourse of authenticity sometimes seeks recipes for the improvement of mankind by appropriating attitudes of less developed – and therefore 'unspoiled' and 'authentic' – cultures.

Limits of Growth

Models of decline are not only pessimistic gestures based on 'feelings' or 'sentiments'. Computer models have drastically demonstrated what the global ecological consequences of economic and population growth would be, if wasteful life styles – as dominant in the rich countries – are maintained. There were some moments in the sixties and seventies when people became aware of their interdependencies, because pictures from the 'outside,' taken by new satellites, delivered strong impressions of the 'blue planet' in all its fragility. The world was called a 'common village'. At the time when these pictures were shared all over the world, the mathematical possibilities became available to simulate scenarios of global developments shaped by numerous variables and interdependencies. The studies of the Club of Rome (Meadows *et al.*, 1972) created an ecological apocalyptic consciousness; and the Club started a fiery appeal with a drum beat: There were absolute limits of growth and the time span until breakdown could be calculated by scientific scenarios. Even if one tried to manipulate the one or the other parameter of the model, the outcome was – because of the striking interdependence of the elements of the system – always the same: system collapse after the middle of the twenty-first century. This was a strong message; essentially it was one of the first truly global messages of the new era and it was the message of the possible self-destruction of mankind.

Later studies (e.g. Pestel, 1989; Giarini and Liedtke, 1998) showed that the limits of growth-study did not avoid all exaggerations; there would very well be possibilities for a determined social and environmental policy. In the seventies, versions of such policies were proposed in studies like *Global 2000* (1980), in the *Tinbergen report* (1977) and in other publications, often directed by international organisations. It is not in all cases their fault that we are still waiting for the implementation of suggested policies. The idea spread that the threatening situation was historically unique. It was the first time that mankind had entered the stage of its possible complete self-elimination (Jungk, 1977; Beck, 1986, Anders, 1987). But the initial panic was short, and it abated during the following years, when, as they were looking at the landscape, people realised that trees continued producing green leaves in spring. And the spring was not yet 'silent'. Many people were given the impression that some progress has been made: the water of European lakes and rivers became purer. Some recycling initiatives were started. The authorities put up stations for measuring air pollution.

The nuclear confrontation of the super-powers, which could have terminated the existence of mankind with a 'big bang' at any time, abated. And people got used to global warming, in spite of the flooding of islands, coasts and cities. At the turn of the century, everybody seems to be waiting for technological solutions in order to mitigate the scarcity of resources, especially fossil fuels; thereby technologically avoiding reconsiderations of life styles. In the meantime, advanced societies have adapted to other deteriorations of the environment, by developing devices to clean the air in apartments and by drinking bottled water. There is no 'green economy' (Jacobs, 1991). Therefore, the question whether mankind can resist the technology-driven and market-driven temptation to ruin itself is still open (Clapp and Dauvergne, 2005).

Globalisation Phobias

Woods are still green and the ecological discussion is crumbling. However, the current globalisation concerns sketch a more comprehensive picture of decline. According to the critics, globalisation ruins the achievements of prosperous countries, including social achievements, and it destroys the chances of the latecomers. It is not a model of wealth for all peoples, but at best a model for temporary 'winners'. Actually, critics contend that it is a model of exclusion leaving many countries before the door; a model of exploitation, favouring the rich countries and causing misery in many societies; a model of destruction spoiling nature and decreasing opportunities for future generations; a model of worldwide standardisation levelling cultural variety; and a model of speculation acclaiming the irrationality of financial markets. Therefore, globalisation has become the focus of a new protest movement emphasising the unpleasant features of the rising 'world society' (Albert, 1999).

The Asymmetrical World

The new world society is, according to critics, not integrated and not homogeneous. It exhibits evident power structures and the more powerful industrialised countries know how to use them. Power imbalances are converted into prosperity differences and the polarity of poverty *versus* luxury is rising. The relation of centre and periphery has already been described in classical theories of imperialism, by Rosa Luxembourg (1913) or John Hobson (1902). Later on, Johan Galtung (1975) added his theory of 'structural imperialism' and dependency theorists have added their view that underdevelopment is not the result of insufficient integration into the world market but just the outcome of more integration. Immanuel Wallerstein (1974) has elaborated on this view in his 'world systems theory'. These models come upon a polarised world which is not converging in its standards of living. Within countries income and wealth are polarised and the same takes place between the countries (Raffer and Singer, 2001). At the national and the international level, it is a winner-take-all society which produces rising cleavages (Frank and Cook, 1995).

Good intentions are not sufficient for promoting development in less developed countries and often even good intentions must not be presupposed, neither on the side of the industrialised countries and their international organisations nor on the side of political elites in less developed countries. Such elites are often corrupt and inefficient and have no interest at all in promoting social development which would threaten their domination. Joseph Stiglitz (2003), Nobel Prize winner in economics and former economist of the World Bank, has described some political mechanisms – and failures – of international organisations; and George Soros (1998) can also not be denunciated as a theoretician who does not know how the world works; he has emphasised the irrationality – and asymmetry – of global economic and political relations.

In the economy, the system produces luxury and poverty. In politics, it produces power and powerlessness. It is the model implemented by the most powerful empire in human history (Matzner, 2000; Tomuschat, 2003; Agnew, 2005; Bello, 2005; Merry, 2005), the imperial system of the USA and its vassals. Therefore, it is appropriate that the economic policy which is approved by international institutions is called 'Washington consensus'. Some observers forecast the 'end of the American century' (Hutchings, 1998), because of 'imperial overstretch' (Burbach and Tarbell, 2004), 'the eagle has landed' (Wallerstein, 2003); others would concede a second century (Bergner, 2003) – or, maybe, at least an 'Asian American century' (Cohen, 2002). There are a few publications celebrating the empire, and the question remains open whether the American empire is not yet the best solution for the Western world in order to avoid a global power vacuum as well as imperial aspirations of East-Asian nations. However, there are many people whose discomfort about the modes of interaction between the USA and its partners are growing (Eckes and Zeiler, 2003; Moore and Vaudagna, 2003).

Conflictuous World

There is still a more unpleasant version than the version of peaceful asymmetry of power: the 'pure' conflict model. Cultures are persevering and contacts do not always contribute to understanding and tolerance. Sometimes they evoke aversive reactions, as the tensions between the Islamic world and the Western countries demonstrate. Samuel Huntington (1998) has forecasted grand clashes. According to his cultural map of the world, there are eight civilisations and he is concerned about conflicts at the zones of their contact. It is not far-fetched suspicion to interpret some current events in Huntington's sense (Blankley, 2005). Fundamentalist movements (Davidson, 2002) are growing, sometimes as a reaction to modernisation, sometimes as an attempt to guard identity (Tibi, 1995), and they are a truly global phenomenon transcending borders.

After the Cold War, expectations arose that the world would enter a period of disarmament, de-militarisation and peace. However, these hopes were quickly dispersed. The 'new wars' managed by warlords are blazing up in numerous niches of the developing world and they are nourished by the global economy (Kaldor, 1999; Münkler, 2002; Gilbert, 2003). Global terrorism reminds modern countries that the essential function of the state, namely guarding law and order and securing their citizens, is by no means guaranteed (Enders and Sandler, 2006). The future of the global world cannot be taken to be peaceful and friendly. Perhaps it will have been the second half of the twentieth century that will be considered a 'golden age' when we look back from a condition of decline in the middle of the twenty-first century.

Global Paradigms of Advancement

The model of perpetual advancement is the counter-thesis to the model of decline. According to the progressive model, human society is developing in a favourable direction. There is an understandable path from raw, bestial beginnings to advanced cultures, with arts and sciences, sophisticated life-forms and general education. And the process of advancement could have a climax. Jewish religion hoped that one day the 'promised land' would be reached. Chiliastic movements in the Middle Ages expected a better future, a breakthrough to a renewed 'Eden', and millennial movements cling to the idea of the future paradise (Fenn, 1997; Stone, 2000). While most ecologists belong to the pessimistic camp Charles Reich's vision presented in his *Greening of America* (1971) that mankind could proceed to 'consciousness III' is close to millennial ideas.

After Ibn Khaldun's vision in the fourteenth century, ideas of progress (Bury and Beard, 1955) were revived at the time of renaissance and reformation when the mental framework of the modern world was established. Condorcet, for example, depicted the law of development in his 'outline of a historical representation of the progress of the human mind'. The 'big story' of intellectual human progress was fully deployed by several thinkers in the age of Enlightenment. Auguste Comte was convinced that the logic of history would guarantee permanent improvement and other cultural evolutionists like Herbert Spencer and Lewis Henry Morgan had no doubts about the favourable stages that the path of civilisation would follow. Georg Wilhelm Friedrich Hegel shared and supported their confidence, as did the Scottish Enlightenment thinkers, such as Adam Ferguson, John Millar and Adam Smith. Charles Darwin's theory confirmed the idea that even nature pressed inevitably towards general improvement. And of course Karl Marx, a classical-rationalistic conservative thinker, was convinced that 'historical laws' would turn the idea of progress into reality: an inevitable progressive movement of society, implemented by social revolutions and the mysterious forces of fate. Innumerable technocrats and ideologists dogged him, subscribing to the belief that the human spirit is about to achieve unimaginable progress in society.

According to the expectations of progressists of any ideological origin, modern society is an efficient machinery, producing beneficial innovations, year for year, without interruption. Everything becomes better: from scarcity to wealth, from barbarism to civilisation, from bad hygiene to general health, from physical uncertainty to social security, from tribulation to abundance, from superstition to knowledge; and recently: from human morbidity to the definite victory over cancer and heart attacks, advances that are only foreboding the final defeat of death. All these blessings are benedictory products of Western civilisation, especially of the progressive forces of free markets, and globalisation means the triumphal march of these achievements around the whole earth.

Technocracy and Golden Age

The universal panorama of progressivity has been transformed into detailed theories of modern age. In the sixties, models of technocracy were impressive for contemporaries who experienced the 'economic miracle' after World War II: Henceforth, scientific expertise would steer society and make the foolish projects of politicians obsolete (Mannheim, 1940; Young, 1959; Meynaud, 1969). In a loose connection to technocratic theories, economists constructed 'golden age' theories of growth: Only a few years of further research and some additional statistical studies would be needed and economists would be able to control and plan the most favourable economic growth path, 'fine tuning' the economic variables, like programmes on the radio (Middleton, 1998). Some years later, in the seventies, they had to admit that economic processes had demonstrated an unexpected and independent life of their own, that politics could not easily be replaced by calculations of optimality, and that ignorance is more likely to expand with the extent of knowledge. The oil crisis, for example, confused all seemingly reliable concepts by raising unemployment and inflation at the same time and thereby making Keynesian theories inapplicable. As it soon became clear, reasonable technocratic solutions did not eliminate all 'irrational' impulses in societies. Even 'atavistic' reactions, like nationalism, racism and tribalism, experienced unexpected upswings and contravened enlightened universalism. Nevertheless, ideas of technocratic omnipotence demonstrate a remarkable resistance to experiences of failure; today, a naive technocratic progressism seems to blossom primarily in management circles, disguised in new semantic gowns and, in an inconsistent way, reconciled with market paradigms.

Globalisation Euphoria

The idea of technocratic control was embedded in the framework of the nation state; and the question was: How can government be empowered to deal reasonably with economic and social processes? Afterwards, disappointment rose and the failure of government policies (Wallis and Dollery, 1999) was a fertile ground for neo-liberal policies of government retreat, non-intervention, deregulation and privatisation (Hovden and Keene, 2002; Saad-Filho and Johnston, 2005). Gaining strength in the eighties, images of the world started to change. Networks, interactivity, global communication – these are terms referring to 'world society' (Spybey, 1996) which is more and more becoming the comprehensive unit determining individual human life in all regions of the world. There is nothing left 'outside'. There are flows that transcend all borders. 'Flows' are persons, capital, drugs, fashions, goods, services, pictures, news, pollution. Cities and computers, clusters, ports and metropoles are nothing but 'knots' or 'nodes'. The *economy* becomes truly a 'world economy', a global 'network economy,' a huge apparatus which cannot be controlled by anybody, but which seems to have a life of its own. *Politics* is no longer enclosed into former 'containers', called nation-states, and the 'Westphalian system' (Rosenau, 1990; Robertson, 1998) is dissolving, while a new system of 'global governance' is blazing its trail (OECD, 2001). *Culture* becomes a new game shaped by concepts like multi-culturalism, diversity, glocalisation, hybridisation, and syncretism (Kraidy, 2005).

The global economy is the driving force. The (preliminary) success of the 'Western' model cannot be denied; even critics admit that the life of most people in wealthy countries has never been so secure, pleasant and long. But euphorics of globalisation maintain that they know even more: More global market economy effects faster development, growing prosperity, rising standards of living – for all people. Liberal economists like Carl Christian von Weizsäcker (1999) promise that the world-wide generalisation of unimpeded markets is the only way to success. According to the analyses of neoliberal economists, if something goes wrong it must be caused by the insufficient realisation of market society and, in most cases, the insufficiency is caused by irrational interferences and interventions of (populist) democratic politics. In contrast, a competitive market economy exerts a permanent pressure for delivering goods and services as efficiently as possible, as well as a permanent pressure for innovations, resulting in the superior efficiency of the market economy. If globalisation spreads the market system all over the world, the whole world will become innovative, efficient and wealthy – and, incidentally, it will improve its moral standards. So far the classic assumption that efficiency, social harmony and moral superiority would go hand in hand has survived in some groups until today. And the global promise is that all nations and regions will profit from growth. Problems like unemployment, socio-political dumping, financial instability, spirals of impoverishment, deficient environmental politics and processes of income polarisation do not result from the unhindered functioning of markets; quite the reverse is true. The stronger the market, the better – and neo-liberal hard-core theorists appeal to the European countries maintaining that their models of the 'social market economy' (Esping-Andersen, 1990; Pierson, 1995, Kaufmann, 1997) or of 'Rhenish capitalism' (Albert, 1991) are outdated and must be discarded as soon as possible (Kleinman, 2002; Clarke, 2004; Ellison, 2006).

Modernisation Euphoria

Can the European model simply diffuse all over the world? And will it be favourable for all regions of the world? In the visions of market globalisation, elements of a theoretical model which looks like familiar ideas of 'historical materialism' become visible. Paradoxically, these ideas seem to have migrated from the left to the right side of the political spectrum. Central assumptions are: First, if you look for determining forces of development, consider the circumstances of the process of production. Second, economic globalisation is a nomothetic process, it merely expresses technological and economic imperatives and there is no use for ethical considerations or deliberations of alternative ways. Third, the market is the lever which turns everything for the better.

This is the core of the strongest ideology of our time: neo-liberalism. Theorists of the 'modernisation school,' the predominant model in the sixties, were more cautious than the current market propagandists. The pure market model teaches that self-sustaining growth cannot fail to be triggered in less developed countries when money is pumped into a country and a few leading industries are established. It is the simple model of transformation recently revived for the post-socialist transformation process. And its shortcomings have again become obvious because the model, ignoring dimensions like 'economic culture,' failed in these countries. Classical modernisation theory (Almond and Verba, 1965, 1980; Binder *et al.*, 1971; Pye and Verba, 1972; Flora, 1974; Zapf, 1977, 1979), however, was more sophisticated because it described parallel and interdependent processes in the economic, political, social and cultural sphere; if an essential factor in any dimension was missing development would not take place. Take-off into self-sustained growth (Rostow, 1960, 1964) does not only depend on a single 'push' but needs a complicated process of development; and taking into account the complexity of the process, there may be no guarantee that the European model can be transferred into peripheral countries where several centuries of cultural development might be missing compared to Europe (Senghaas, 1982; Menzel, 1992). Islamic countries might, for example, need an epoch of intellectual 'enlightenment' to be prepared for modern economy and democracy.

Anyhow, even if this problem could be overcome whether there can be a generalisation of the European lifestyle is seriously questioned if ecological limits are regarded. If China continues its impressive and successful growth process (Moore, 2002), the world will be 'enriched' by hundreds of millions of consumers and polluters, and there is no doubt that this development will overload the sustainability of global eco-systems.

Euphoria of Democratisation

Optimists believe that in the current process the countries of the world do not only get rich, they become democratic too (and some of them even think that they become democratic *because* they get rich). Discussions about the relationship of capitalism and democracy that flicker up again and again belong to the context of societal paradigms of progress, and more attention has been paid to them since the 'third wave' of democratisation has taken place (Huntington, 1991). There have never been so many democracies in the world. Friedrich von Hayek (1976), Milton Friedman (1976), Peter L. Berger (1986) and other social scientists have described the affinity – as well as the mutual processes of reinforcement – of market economy and political democracy: Market society cannot only be justified by its promotion of wealth but also by its promotion of freedom (Dine and Fagan, 2006). When appreciating the expansion of democratic or at least half-democratic countries (according to the Freedom House index), one has to note, though, that Samuel Huntington's 'civilisations' are to a different degree deemed suited for establishing a democratic order. There is the following ranking from best to worst: Western civilisation (liberalism, Protestantism), Latin America (Catholicism), Japanese civilisation, Slavic-orthodox civilisation, Hindu civilisation, African civilisations, Confucian civilisation, and finally Islamic civilisation (Lipset, 2000). Huntington doubts that Confucianism and Islam are at all compatible with a democratic structure and the rule of law. These considerations limit the optimistic outlook of future progress and prosperity; perhaps we have already exhausted the potential of the 'third wave'.

The Convergent World

Bright messages about the blessed future world are combined in expectations of convergence. The globalised modernity eliminates differences and diversities, it shapes all societies uniformly – and proponents of globalisation consider the process to be favourable. It is a process of homogenisation encompassing technical, economic, political, moral and cultural dimensions. The strongest civilisation gains acceptance and there are signals that the American lifestyle seems to be strongest – because otherwise, as Americans used to argue, this lifestyle would not be accepted and appreciated by the younger generation all over the world. However, from the view of less developed countries, processes of CocaColonisation (Wagnleitner, 1994) are often viewed as burdening or degrading. It might seem amazing for Americans but the U.S. lifestyle is not convincingly superior in the view of all cultures of the world.

Convergence does not only refer to the *economic* sphere. In the *cultural* sphere, processes of hybridisation, the growth of transnational social spaces (Pries, 1998) and crossover cultures are observed. In the *political* sphere, some speculations that concern the existence of 'global citizens' (Albrow, 1998) or the possibility of 'world contracts' (Gruppe von Lissabon, 1987) are provided. The basic question is: Is there at all a common (cultural or ethical) basis for worldwide community? Otfried Höffe (1999) tries to justify a normative approach: the dangerous situation of the world will enforce the establishment of a 'world state' (Ruloff, 1988; see already Jünger, 1960). Hans Küng (1999, 2002a, 2002b) studies the question of whether the common ethical contents of world religions could be used to construct a common global 'core ethics'. It is certainly not impossible to imagine the core contents of these ethics: unity, peace, solidarity, understanding and global friendship. But the implementation of ethical goals is a different question.

Global Paradigms of Stagnation

Models of stagnation (Hansen, 1938, 1941; Steindl, 1952, 1979) are the alternative to models of decline and progress. They assume that dynamic and far-reaching changes come to an end. Of course, immutability was the predominant experience of traditional societies: history as repetition; always the same is happening. The phrase of the 'end of history' has staggered through the gazettes during the last few years: the countries of the globalised world would gather themselves around a trans-territorially and trans-culturally valid, timeless model of economy and polity. By depicting the future conditions in this way, Francis Fukuyama (1992) wanted to support his expectation that all countries of the world would take on the Western ideology. Actually, he did not mean that history comes to a halt but he forecasted an end of ideological conflicts about economic order and political constitution. There are no convincing alternative models left. However, the statement owed much to the good courage of a particular historical moment, the breakdown of the socialist empire; a few years after the publication of Fukuyama's book, it seems to be obvious that basic conflicts about political difference or uniformity are not yet finished.

Stagnation, additionally, means something else. Modern societies stand out due to their dynamic and innovative power. The modern market economy is – according to Joseph Schumpeter's (1952, 1961) often-quoted and often-misunderstood phrase – a society of 'creative destruction'. Untiringly, the system gives birth to new products, a process depicted in logarithmically explosive curves whatever the current topic of the statistical presentation might be. But mathematicians know that growth functions cannot be continued in all eternity. In the seventies, concerns about the slowing of the growth path were wide-spread: Some speculated about 'zero growth' (Sauvy, 1976) or the 'zero sum society' (Thurow, 1981), some considered a new 'ceiling' of growth paths necessary for ecological or anthropological reasons. But, in the end, most people regarded economic stagnation as a horror situation that has to be avoided and even the energy crisis of the seventies had only a limited effect on the long-term consciousness of the people.

Paralysis by Rationalisation

Is rationalisation dynamic or paralysing? Some social scientists argue that processes of rationalisation, technification and automation promote progress; but they also have another side. They contribute to the slowing of dynamics: Society becomes an apparatus, and man becomes a small wheel in the machinery. Innovative spirits are eliminated – an unpleasant perspective for societies which boast that they are founded on entrepreneurial innovation. This idea has influenced Friedrich Nietzsche, Max Weber, Joseph Schumpeter. Alfred Weber (1953) has described the fight of the *Homo europeensis*, who is born for freedom and inclined to transcendence, against the 'technological man,' who is but an element of a huge machinery. Arnold Gehlen (1986) has claimed that we stood at the end of an industrial 'late culture'. According to his observations, there was nothing left but 'cultural decay' and only 'technical civilisation' (with spreading processes of 'automation,' loss of experience and primitivisation) would spread further.

Peculiarities of modern civilisation enhance the necessity of rationalisation and of human self-disciplining. Norbert Elias (1979) has described the modern 'apparatus of self-coercion': in the network of modern society the individual must be made a reliably functioning element because otherwise he could cause too much damage. Spontaneity must be eliminated in contrast to the self-descriptions of modern individualistic societies. George Ritzer's McDonaldisation (1997) is an 'external' variant of this idea: the standardisation and automation processes of the modern world eliminate variety, not only variety in the production of burgers but also the diversity of hotel chains, media productions, and processes of education.

These observations suggest that we may be observing the last period of occidental dynamics. Western civilisation could possibly be suffocated by its own complexity. On the other hand, the removal of the predominance of the West may be a chance for less developed countries, for fresh, unspent people, taking the place of exhausted Western peoples. This transformation would undeniably mean a shift of global power potentials.

Paralysis by Maturity

A second version of the stagnation model uses the concept of maturity. The swivelling in of logarithmic curves can be described as a 'natural process'. Exponential equations are 'unnatural,' stagnation is more compatible with our knowledge about evolution, biology and anthropology. There are also romantic pictures: spring is better than fall, but somewhere along the way fall will arrive. Youth is better than old age but nobody can escape the latter. The blossoming of cultures has often been described in similar metaphors: rise and decline, blossoming and fading, imagined as the course of a year or the cycle of human life. There is no eternal youth or growth. In a global view, the industrialised countries are obviously the first candidates for future stagnation.

The classics could never imagine that the dynamic process of the modern economy would proceed without limits. We find sceptical remarks in the works of Adam Smith, John Stuart Mill or David Ricardo (Mill, 1913). In the 1970s theories of saturation were taken seriously and the question of whether the needs of the people were actually as unlimited as assumed on the first pages of economic textbooks was reconsidered (Falkinger, 1986). At that time, people had to hide behind developing countries in order to argue that their needs – and not the still unlimited needs of people living in luxury – required additional global growth; nowadays this strategy is no longer necessary because future growth has again become accepted as a matter of course in the rich countries. 'Zero growth theories' of the seventies are no longer given any attention. The Developed World has decided that its consumption needs are infinite and the conviction that all countries of the earth will experience decades of constant growth and prosperity in the twenty-first century prevails. Therefore, stagnation means threat, crisis, temporary weakness, the bursting of bubbles or some other unpleasantness; and it is not a condition for which one strives. Conscious constraint for having a higher quality of life is a minority program.

Global Paradigms of Cycles

Decline, advancement and stagnation – besides these three paradigms, there is a different model that is appreciated by managers and trend researchers all over the world: the cyclical model. Cycles might be irregular, like in Arnold Toynbee's (1934ff.) model of challenge and response: Historical entities face problems, and they have to stand their test. Their destiny is determined by their response: They might sustain or decline. Regular cycles, on the other hand, have a certain temporal structure of their ups and downs, like in the models of Oswald Spengler (1920ff) or Pitirim Sorokin (1937, 1941, 1953). These are comprehensive universal history pictures. But 'waves' have often been described as economic movements, like in models of 'long waves' or 'boom and recession' periods.

Long Waves

There is a rise and fall in the wealth of nations (Berry, 1991; Bornschier and Lengyel, 1992; Neumann, 1997). Many people are impressed by graphics using the idea of the Russian economist Kondratieff (Kondratieff, 1926; Mager, 1987). These cycles have something mysterious. Kondratieff thought that he could proof the existence of economic surges, in the length of 40–60 years, and Joseph Schumpeter has worked out the idea in more detail in his *Theory of Economic Development*. There are 'basic innovations' – like the steam-driven engine, chemistry, the automobile and the computer – which spread in a long-term process through all areas of economic life and transform it (Schumpeter, 1952). The present 'Kondratieff cycle' is obviously based on 'chips': the long wave of information technology (Atkinson, 2004). Speculations about the next cycle pushing the economy to further growth point to biotechnology and health as driving forces.

What happens in the Developed World is decisive for the whole global economic network. Cycles are global cycles. Technological innovations spread in a flash. The world market is a competitive challenge. The industrialised countries know that they can only maintain their position by constantly generating innovations. Studies about the 'new international economic order' (Fröbel, Heinrichs and Kreye, 1977; Matthies, 1980) have described characteristic 'product cycles': the industrialised countries produce high-technological products and, as soon as they enter the phase of their routine production, the production procedures are handed over to developing countries. Since the seventies, appeals for accelerating the process have been voiced again and again: the supply of innovations must become faster, more reliable, permanent. But in the future, the model of the product cycle will be doubted, since increasingly not only repetitive and routine activities are transferred to Developing World countries but also research, development and design functions. Some observers note that nothing but head offices and their staff could remain in the geographical area of the industrialised countries for the time being; and the service personnel for the highly-qualified staff that work there. But this would not be enough for securing mass employment.

Cultural Cycles

Sometimes cyclical models are used in the cultural sphere. Oswald Spengler (1920ff.), in his early bestseller about the decline of the Occident, has maintained that an advanced civilisation was a holistic entity and that it passed through the four 'ages' of childhood, youth, adulthood and old age, just like human life. According to his assessment, the twentieth century was in its late phase, and it was more and more determined by the dictatorship of money and the media. It was a time of dilapidation, shaped by a barren eclecticism (Farrenkopf, 2001). Pitirim Sorokin (1953, 1937, 1941) distinguished sensational and ideational cultural stages, alternating in history. According to his scheme, we have, since 1937, been in the period of 'late sensualism,' shaped by cynicism, normative relativism, anomie and protest movements. This period will necessarily be followed by a renewed ideational culture, determined by new faith and certainty, normative ligatures and solidarity. Walter Bühl (1987) does not derive his cyclical movements from speculating about mysterious surges but from correlating economic Kondratieff cycles with cultural movements: It would be strange if a far-reaching economic change would not express itself in a transformation of consumer habits, career paths and life styles, as well as in a change of more deep-seated motives and fears, appreciated or repressed meanings and expectations of salvation. However, with the exemption of economic long waves (being very popular at management seminars), cyclical paradigms do not get much attention nowadays.

Global Paradigms of Periodisation

Rise and decline, stagnation and fluctuation – some models add to these variants the idea of discontinuity, an old problem in history (Besserman, 1996; Koselleck, 2002). Time is continuous and periodisations are, to a certain degree, arbitrary. But the message of most current scholars is that we experience a break: disruption, discontinuity. We are passing a threshold. We enter a new epoch. There will not be only more or less of the same. A completely new social formation comes into existence and we have to decipher what its essential trends and features are. There are different proposals to name the new era; for instance many 'postisms,' or new brands, such as 'knowledge society'. Threshold assertions also serve as a means of dramatising the situation and legitimising the demand for change, adaptation or acceleration. It is more than the usual 'age of transition'. There is a 'future shock' (Toffler, 1970).

The Epoch of Postisms

The term 'globalisation' can be taken as the description of a threshold: the change from the particularised to the integrated world, from the limited to the global horizon, from the fragmented system to the world system, from nation-state society to world society. We are aware that late capitalism has been described as a 'post-industrial society' by Daniel Bell (1973) and Alain Touraine (1972). Bells far-sighted description, emphasising the axiomatic principle of knowledge, builds the bridge to newer models of the 'knowledge society'. Lately, semantic monsters like 'post-fordism' and 'post-taylorism' have been used to describe changes in the mode of production. The concept of 'post-modernism' has been used for characterising an epoch, while some proponents prefer to talk about 'post-modern elements' in an advanced phase of modernism (Lyotard, 1986; Welsch, 1987, 1988). 'Postisms' signal the wide-spread feeling that the 'modern age,' in the specific form it has taken from the end of the 19th until the beginning of the twenty-first century, has passed away – and how the new epoch we are entering can be described cannot be fully deciphered.

The New Modern Age

Among scholars devoted to diagnoses of our time a group proposes a shift from 'old modernity' to 'new modernity'. Ulrich Beck and Anthony Giddens have considered terms like 'second modernity' but have finally decided on 'reflexive modernity' (Beck, 1993, 1997; Giddens, 1995). Individuals in the modern world cannot solve their problems by stepping back into history reconstructing their consciousness as if the Enlightenment had not happened. That means: they cannot stop thinking and scrutinising everything. The signature of the time is 'reflexivity'. Richard Münch (1998) outbids others with the concept of the 'third modernity': according to his periodisation, first modernity produced capitalism and liberalism; second modernity combined the welfare state with democracy and the rule of law; henceforth, the push towards globalisation signifies 'third modernity,' exceeding the integrative power of the nation-state (Glatzer and Rueschemeyer, 2005). But in spite of these labelling attempts, the contours of the new constellation stand out only vaguely.

The Era of Knowledge

The propagandists of the 'knowledge society,' which is considered a new, distinguishable societal formation, occasionally also labelled 'information society' or 'communication society' (McLuhan, 1962), are influential because their claim that, in the new era, knowledge is the signature of the time, is backed by everyday experience (Böhme and Stehr, 1986; Stehr, 2001, 2005; Castells, 2002). Knowledge becomes the decisive economic necessity, research is the essential locational factor for firms, qualification is the adamant necessity for individuals. Sure enough, the conception of knowledge used in these models is a shrunken version of what the Occident has ever conceived when using the word. It is predominantly technological knowledge, economically useful knowledge, professional training for a better career and applied research for generating products: 'profitable' and 'marketable' knowledge. The message has reached politicians who are eager to make universities research laboratories for business. Regional consultants are fascinated by opportunities they associate with biotechnology, computer technology and nanotechnology. As Gibbons et al. (1994) have announced, knowledge assumes a completely new character; it has to get 'commercialised'. Managers and entrepreneurs are advised to implement 'knowledge management' in their organisations and to prepare intellectual 'balance sheets'.

Actually, in the global knowledge society a new map of the world is drawn along lines of technological competence. However, questions about the meaning of 'knowledge society' remain unsolved: questions about the discretionary 'educational malleability' of individuals, about the 'plannability' of innovations, about processes of polarisation observed between intellectual 'haves' and 'have-nots', about the accessibility of training and networks, and so on. Above all, the question of whether it would not be useful to provide residues of a kind of 'education' which is not bound to a technological purpose or to the generation of profits but which could be useful for developing a self-conscious personality and for understanding the world, is the ethical question lingering behind efficiency and growth considerations.

While trend researchers satisfy the curiosity of people by discovering lots of veiled 'trends' – or, even better: mega-trends or giga-trends (Naisbitt, 1990) – there are proponents of 'technological singularity' (Vinge, 1984) who claim that economic and social developments are progressing so fast that, from now on, nothing can be predicted and no future developments can be comprehended. We are rushing – very fast – into completely unknown territory.

The Post-biological Era

The periodisations mentioned in the preceding paragraphs seem to be totally unimportant if we compare them with a periodisation suggested by computer experts in the USA. Advances in computer technology, in biology and in cognitive sciences raise the question of how long it will take before robots can be built that are superior to human beings (or until these robots are able to evolve themselves towards higher levels). Should we try to keep pace by cyborgisation making ourselves combinations of human and technical beings? Or must the biological phase of the development of intelligent living organisms be regarded as nothing more than a period of transition, until a superior 'electronic species' will take over and populate the world. Possibly the world will look quite different, if we approach the post-biological phase in the evolution of mankind (Minsky, 1985, 1986; Moravec, 1988, 1999; Kurzweil, 1999; Warwick, 2002; et. al.): the new global era would be efficient, harmonious, rich, may be even ethical – but it will be a globality without human beings. Of course, in this situation common ethical considerations as we know them are no longer needed.

Global Paradigms of Crisis

Models of societal crisis assume that disturbances erupt in the 'interior' of advanced post-industrial societies because of 'faults' in the structure of the system. Therefore, by considering these paradigms we return, in a certain sense, to the stories of decline presented at the beginning of the survey. However, crisis paradigms do not analyse long-term changes based on something like 'historical laws'. 'Crises' are sudden stability problems in critical phases of societal development and they may, like crises in medical descriptions, end with the overcoming of the 'illness' or with the death of the 'patient'.

The System Fault Model

Some theorists maintain that the 'system,' especially the economic structure of industrialised market systems, has built-in defects, flaws or malfunctions causing excessive demands on the system or leading to a final breakdown. Endogenous flaws will cause the failure, so Western societies will not succeed in building a stable global model. Classical Marxist models belong to this type of reasoning and they have produced different versions of neo-Marxist thinking, such as paradigms of 'state monopolistic capitalism' (Dobb, 1966, 1970; Baran and Sweezy, 1973, Sweezy, 1974). But there are also other approaches: Encrustations, at the intermediary level for instance, effected by groups, associations and organisations, could produce inefficiencies, as James Coleman has described in his *Asymmetrical Society* (1982) or Mancur Olson (1985) has proposed in his analyses of sclerotising tendencies in the structure of modern societies. The inconsistency of subsystems could have a harmful impact: Daniel Bell (1979) has delineated a model of *Cultural Contradictions* resulting from tensions between distinctive rationality in the spheres of the economic-political system and a hedonistic and bohemian mentality in the spheres of leisure and consumption. Fatally, the system seems to need both dispositions which are, in the long run, incompatible.

An alternative approach assumes that the system works, but systematically produces exaggerated requirements towards itself, thereby stressing and finally destroying itself. The democratic structure could enhance populist appeals and the system could slither into ungovernability, as Michel Crozier and Samuel Huntington (1975) or Franz Lehner (1979) have presumed. It could fail economically because of a financial crisis, or it could politically fail because of its growth-addiction: Lester Thurow, in his *Zero Sum Society* (1981), has pointed to its inability to solve urgent problems because of a discrepancy between expectations of citizens and possibilities for action in a situation of deficient growth. There are some reasons why expectations about the excellent performance of the global market society might be deemed exaggerated.

The Model of Disorientation

Another version of the crisis contends that the system might not fail because of a constructive flaw but because of a simple confusion in the heads of people: because of its spawning of disorientation, confusion, indistinctiveness, deficit of meaning. 'Uneasiness' is spreading (Freud, 1930; Berger, Berger and Kellner, 1973). Individuals become 'one-dimensional' (Marcuse, 1964). First they lose their 'fathers' (Mitscherlich, 1965), then both of their parents. It is no economic crisis, because the structure continues working well; but it is a cultural crisis: a crisis of meaning – which will paralyse the system.

Some diagnosticians suggest the following model: the system depends on external resources, which it cannot produce itself, and these inherited (cultural) resources would be used up even while the system is working appropriately. The crisis stems from the overconsumption of 'cultural resources'. Joseph Schumpeter (1992) has described such a development in his book about *Capitalism, Socialism and Democracy*: a model of decline of capitalism because of its success, not because of its failure. Jürgen Habermas (1973) sketches a similar model in his theory of the *Legitimation Crisis*: the economic system is crisis-ridden, the state must stabilise it and in so doing it uses up the cultural heritage necessary for the continuance of the system. There is no administrative production of meaning. In addition to the detrimental political and administrative effects, the marketisation of all areas of life which, beyond doubt, is flourishing in all dimensions destroys cultural resources: There is a colonialisation of private life by the logic of the 'system' (Prisching, 2002).

Cultural pessimists have always found safety, security, tradition, anchorage, faith, embedding and so on in the past, while they have observed disintegration, destructuring, disembedding, and anomie in the modern era. All that is solid melts into air (Berman, 1983). Even goods disappear, they are substituted by access (Rifkin, 2000). The problem of how social cohesion can be maintained under modern (enlightened) conditions has already preoccupied Emile Durkheim and it is a common theme in the social sciences at the turn to the twenty-first century: Wilhelm Heitmeyer (1997) is dealing with the problem, as well as Francis Fukuyama (1995) and other theorists. Ulrich Beck (1986) tells us that the source of disorientation are processes of individualisation and pluralisation dissolving everything that seemed to be reliable. Richard Sennett (1998) narrates some life stories and shows what it really means for people when everything is flexible. Complete flexibility might look preferable at a first glance, but people can no longer get any hold; and they suffer. It is a 'weightless society' (Leadbeater, 2000), everything becomes 'liquid' (Bauman, 2000). Some models of 'value change' deal with similar problems, starting with the classic study by David Riesman (1956). He analysed the change from the inner-directed to the outer-directed man. Ronald Inglehart's empirical findings (1977, 1989, 1997; Abramson and Inglehart, 1995) measuring the change from 'materialist' to 'post-materialist values' are similar to Helmut Klages' (2001, 2003) more differentiated distinction of 'values of obligation' and 'values of self-actualization'. People want to 'have' more and more in order to 'be' – or how they understand it (Fromm, 1989). Ronald Hitzler (2001, 2003) contributes the idea of the awkward tinkering around that characterises modern attempts to get together personal identity. Most observers agree that people do not find their way any more.

The Model of Consumptionism

An influential version of cultural crisis takes up an old topic: the problem of wealth, prosperity and luxury. Wealth can be dangerous. It might endanger your psychological health. Prosperity may spoil people. However, the neo-liberal economy needs the insatiable consumer and therefore identifies 'good life' with the power to have goods and services at one's disposal. But there are serious doubts that, in the long run, the system can work on this basis. Consumistic societies (Campbell, 1987; Baudrillard, 1998; Cohen, 2003) are the ideal for the 'late-comers' all over the world, for all less-developed countries, and the process of globalisation is not only a process of the sprawl of the market system, but also a generalisation of the consumistic style of living prevailing in Western countries and ruining the eco-system.

It has to be emphasised that consumistic societies shaped by post-modernity are no longer 'materialistic' in a simple sense. They are post-materialistic, which means: They strive for experience, event, multioptionality, and fun. But individuals need a lot of money and a lot of goods and services (Prisching, 2006) to realise their goals of self-enrichment and self-actualisation. Rich people look for consumption in order to 'feel' themselves. They have no other ways to get to know that they are still alive. Years ago, Tibor Scitovsky (1976) argued that individuals want to avoid stress and boredom and to achieve a mental position in-between. The current prosperous society offers them an unbelievable wealth of goods and events, even too much; they get stressed and are overtaxed by the possibilities – and finally they are disappointed because, given limited time, growing possibilities mean rising renunciations. The 'society of adventure,' as described by Gerhard Schulze (1992), is characterised by the principle that in a rich world where individuals are exonerated from existential concerns life has to be designed so that emotional arousal can be kept on a satisfactory – and that means: a very high – level. This is a difficult task if one regards processes of satiation and hebetude.

Peter Gross (1994, 1999) has drafted the most comprehensive picture of the 'multi-optional society'. There are infinite options of how to spend time, money and life – working, loving, living, eating, praying, having fun, studying. The pressure to decide – without being supported by normative or ethical standards – challenges the individuals. It drives them into disappointment. People in rich countries are dissatisfied, under stress and in a bad temper.

The dynamic principle of permanent intensification and exaggeration, outbidding and outperforming is expressed in the global phenotype of post-industrial countries: the worldwide dominance of luxury, abandon, cultural trash, throwaway mentality, mass production mediocrity, a comprehensive entertainment economy (Franck, 1998; Wolf, 1999), strategic stupefication. Maybe the *Endgame of Globalization* (Smith, 2005). Therefore, the survey of models sketching decisive features of modern societies and forecasting trends of their development arrives at a classical, eternal question: the question of 'good life' (Jouvenel, 1999; Gomes, 2002; Rubin, 2004).

References

Abramson, P.R. and Inglehart, R. (1995), *Value Change in Global Perspective*, Ann Arbor: University of Michigan Press.

Agnew, J. and Corbridge, St. (1995), *Mastering Space. Hegemony, Territory and International Political Economy*, London: Routledge.

Agnew, J.A. (2005), *Hegemony. The New Shape of Global Power*, Philadelphia: Temple University Press.

Albert, M. (1991), *Kapitalismus contra Kapitalismus*, Frankfurt: Campus.

Albert, M. *et al.* (1999), *Die Neue Weltwirtschaft. Entstofflichung und Entgrenzung der Ökonomie*, Frankfurt a.M.: Suhrkamp.

Albrow, M. (1998), *Abschied vom Nationalstaat. Staat und Gesellschaft im globalen Zeitalter*, Frankfurt a.M.: Suhrkamp.

Almond, G.A. and Verba, S. (1965), *The Civic Culture. Political Attitudes and Democracy in Five Nations*, Princeton: Princeton University Press.

Almond, G.A. and Verba, S. (1980), *The Civic Culture Revisited*, Boston: Little Brown.

Altvater, E. and Mahnkopf, B. (1999), *Grenzen der Globalisierung. Ökonomie, Ökologie und Politik in der Weltgesellschaft. 4. Aufl*, Münster: Westfälisches Dampfboot.

Anders, G. (1987), *Die Antiquiertheit des Menschen*, 2 Vols., 7th edn, München: Beck.

Atkinson, R.D. (2004), *The Past and Future of America's Economy. Long Waves of Innovation that Power Cycles of Growth*, UK: Cheltenham/Northampton, MA: Edward Elgar).

Bachofen, J.J. (1943ff), *Das Mutterrecht. Eine Untersuchung über die Gynaikokratie der Alten Welt nach ihrer religiösen und rechtlichen Nature*, (Stuttgart); Gesamtausgabe, *Gesammelte Werke* (GW), ed. K. Meuli, 8 Bde. (Basel: Schwabe 1943-1967).

Baran, P.A. and Sweezy, P.M. (1973), *Monopolkapital. Ein Essay über die amerikanische Wirtschafts – und Gesellschaftsordnung*, Frankfurt a.M.: Suhrkamp. (*Monopoly Capital. An Essay on the American Economic and Social Order*, New York: Monthly Review Press 1966).

Barber, B. (1995), *Jihad versus McWorld*, New York: Ballantine.

Baudrillard, J. (1998), *The Consumer Society. Myths and Structures*, London: Sage.

Bauman, Z. (2000), *Liquid Modernity*, Cambridge: Polity Press.

Beck, U. (1986), *Risikogesellschaft. Auf dem Weg in eine andere Moderne*, Frankfurt a. M.: Suhrkamp. (*Risk Society. Towards a New Modernity*, London: Sage 1992).

Beck, U. (1993), *Die Erfindung der Politik*, Frankfurt a.M.: Suhrkamp.

Beck, U. (1997), Kinder der Freiheit: Wider das Lamento über den Werteverfall, in Beck.

Beck, U. and Kieserling, A., eds. (2000), *Ortsbestimmungen der Soziologie: Wie die kommende Generation Gesellschaftswissenschaften betreiben will*, Baden-Baden: Nomos.

Beck, U., ed. (1998), *Perspektiven der Weltgesellschaft*, Frankfurt a.M.: Suhrkamp.

Bell, D. (1973), *The Coming of Post-Industrial Society. A Venture in Social Forecasting*, New York: Basic Books.

Bell, D. (1979), *Die Zukunft der westlichen Welt. Kultur und Technologie im Widerstreit*, Frankfurt: Fischer. (*The Cultural Contradictions of Capitalism*, 2nd edn, London: Heinemann 1979).

Bello, W.F. (2005), *Dilemmas of Domination. The Unmaking of the American Empire*, New York: Metropolitan Bks.

Berger, P.L. (1986), *The Capitalistic Revolution. Fifty Propositions about Prosperity Equality, and Liberty*, New York: Basic Books.

Berger, P.L., Berger, B. and Kellner, H. (1973), *The Homeless Mind. Modernization and Consciousness*, New York: Random House.

Bergner, J.T., ed. (2003), *The Next American Century*, Lanham, Md.: Rowan and Littlefield.

Berman, M. (1982), *All That Is Solid Melts into Air. The Experience of Modernity*, New York: Simon & Schuster.

Berry, B.J.L. (1991), *Long-wave Rhythms in Economic Development and Political Behavior*, Baltimore: Johns Hopkins Press.

Besserman, L., ed. (1996), *The Challenge of Periodization: Old Paradigms and New Perspectives*, New York: Garland.

Binder, L., Coleman, J.S., LaPalombara, J., Pye, L.W., Verba, S. and Weiner, M. (1971), *Crises and Sequences in Political Development*, Princeton: Princeton University Press.

Bischoff, J. (1999), *Der Kapitalismus des 21. Jahrhunderts. Systemkrise oder Rückkehr zur Prosperität?*, Hamburg: VSA.

Blankley, T. (2005), *The West's Last Chance. Will We Win the Clash of Civilisations?*, Washington, DC: Regnery Publishing House.

Böhme, G. and Stehr, N. (1986), *The Knowledge Society. The Growing Impact of Knowledge on Social Relations*, Dordrecht: Reidel.

Bornemann, E. (1979), *Das Patriarchat. Ursprung und Zukunft unseres Gesellschaftssystems*, Frankfurt a.M.: Fischer.

Bornschier, V. and Lengyel, P., eds. (1992), *Waves, Formations and Values in the World System*, New Brunswick, NJ: Transaction Publishing.

Boxberger, G. and Klimenta, H. (1998), *Die Zehn Globalisierungslügen. Alternativen zur Allmacht des Marktes*, München: dtv.

Brosziewski, A., Eberle, T. and Maeder, C., eds. (2001), *Moderne Zeiten Reflexionen zur Multioptionsgesellschaft*, ed Konstanz: UVK.

Bühl, W.L. (1987), *Kulturwandel. Für eine dynamische Kultursoziologie*, Darmstadt: Wissenschaftliche Buchgesellschaft.

Burbach, R. and Tarbell, J. (2004), *Imperial Overstretch. George W. Bush and the Hubris of Empire*, London: Zed Books.

Bury, J.B. and Beard, Ch.A. (1955), *The Idea of Progress. An Inquiry into its Origin and Growth*, New York: Dover.

Campbell, C. (1987), *The Romantic Ethic and the Spirit of Modern Consumerism*, Oxford: Blackwell.

Castells, M. (2002), *Das Informationszeitalter*, 3 Vols, Opladen: Leske + Budrich.

Clapp, J. and Dauvergne, P. (2005), *Paths to a Green World. The Political Economy of the Global Environment*, Cambridge, MA: MIT Press.

Clarke, J. (2004), *Changing Welfare, Changing States, New Directions in Social Policy* (London-Thousand Oaks, CA: Sage).

Cohen, L. (2003), *A Consumer's Republic. The Politics of Mass Consumption in Postwar America*, New York: Knopf.

Cohen, W.I. (2002), *The Asian American Century*, Cambridge, MA: Harvard University Publishing.

Coleman, J.S. (1982), *The Asymmetric Society*, Syracuse: Syracuse University Publishing.

Crozier, M., Huntington, S.P. and Watanuki, J. (1975), *The Crisis of Democracy. Report of the Governability of Democracies to the Trilateral Commission*, New York: New York University Press.

Davidson, L. (2002), *Islamic Fundamentalism. An Introduction*, Westport, Conn.: Greenwood Press.

Dine, J. and Fagan, A., eds. (2006), *Human Rights and Capitalism. A Multidisciplinary Perspective on Globalisation*, UK: Cheltenham.-Northampton, MA: Edward Elgar).

Dobb, M. (1966), *Organisierter Kapitalismus. Fünf Beiträge zur politischen Ökonomie*, Frankfurt a.M.: Suhrkamp.

Dobb, M. (1970), *Entwicklung des Kapitalismus. Vom Spätfeudalismus bis zur Gegenwart*, Köln: Kiepenheuer & Witsch (*Studies in the Development of Capitalism*, New York: International Publishers 1947).

Dönhoff, M. (1999), *Zivilisiert den Kapitalismus. Grenzen der Freiheit*, München: Knaur.

Dworkin, A. (1981), *Pornography. Men Possessing Women*, New York: Putnam.

Eckes, A.E. and Zeiler, T.W. (2003), *Globalization and the American Century*, UK: Cambridge-New York: Cambridge University Press).

Elias, N. (1979), *Über den Prozeß der Zivilisation. Soziogenetische und psychogenetische Untersuchungen, 2 Vols*, 6th edn, Frankfurt: Suhrkamp. (*The Civilizing Process: Sociogenetic and Psychogenetic Investigations*, Oxford: Blackwell (2000)).

Ellison, N. (2006), *The Transformation of Welfare States?*, London: Routledge.

Enders, W. and Sandler, T. (2006), *The Political Economy of Terrorism*, New York: Cambridge University Publishing.

Esping-Anderson, G. (1990), *The Three Worlds of Welfare Capitalism*, Princeton, NJ: Princeton University Publishing.

Falkinger, J. (1986), *Sättigung. Moralische und psychologische Grenzen des Wachstums*, Tübingen: Mohr-Siebeck.

Farrenkopf, J. (2001), *Prophet of Decline. Spengler on World History and Politics*, Baton Rouge, Louisiana; State University Press.

Fenn, R.K. (1997), *The End of Time: Religion, Ritual, and the Forging of the Soul*, Cleveland: Pilgrim Press.

Flora, P. (1974), *Modernisierungsforschung. Zur empirischen Analyse der gesellschaftlichen Entwicklung*, Opladen: Westdeutscher Verlag.

Forrester, V. (1998), *Der Terror der Ökonomie*, München: Goldmann.

Franck, G. (1998), *Ökonomie der Aufmerksamkeit. Ein Entwurf*, München: Hanser.

Frank, R.H. and Cook, P.J. (1995), *The Winner-take-all-society. How More and More Americans Compete for Ever Fewer and Bigger Prizes, Encouraging Economic Waste, Income Inequality, and an Impoverished Cultural Life*, New York: Free Press.

Frank, T. (2000), *One Market Under God. Extreme Capitalism, Market Populism, and the End of Economic Democracy*, New York: Doubleday.

Freud, S. (1930), *Das Unbehagen in der Kultur*, Vienna: Internationaler Psychoanalytischer Verlag.

Frieden, J.A. (2006), *Global Capitalism. Its Fall and Rise in the Twentieth Century*, New York: Norton.

Friedman, M. (1976), *Kapitalismus und Freiheit*, München: dtv. (*Capitalism and Freedom*, Chicago: Chicago University Publishing (1982)).

Friedman, T.L. (1999), *Globalisierung verstehen. Zwischen Marktplatz und Weltmarkt*, Berlin: Ullstein. (*The Lexus and the Olive Tree*, Thorndike: Thorndike Press 1999).

Friedman, T.L. (2005), *The World Is Flat. A Brief History of the Twenty-First Century*, New York: Farrar, Straus & Giroux.

Fröbel, F., Heinrichs, J. and Kreye, O. (1977), *Die neue internationale Arbeitsteilung. Strukturelle Arbeitslosigkeit in den Industrieländern und die Industrialisierung der Entwicklungsländer*, Reinbek b.H.: Rowohlt.

Fromm, E. (1989), *Vom Haben zum Sein. Wege und Irrwege der Selbsterfahrung*, Weinheim: Beltz. (*To Have or to Be?*, New York: Harper & Row 1976).

Fukuyama, F. (1992), *The End of History and the Last Man* (New York: Free Press) (*Das Ende der Geschichte* Wo stehen wir? München: Kindler, 1992).

Fukuyama, F. (1995), *Trust: The Social Virtues and the Creation of Prosperity*, New York: Free Press.

Galtung, J. (1975), *Strukturelle Gewalt. Beiträge zur Friedens – und Konfliktforschung*, Reinbek b.H.: Rowohlt.

Gehlen, A. (1986), *Der Mensch. Seine Natur und seine Stellung in der Welt*, 13th edn, Wiesbaden: Aula-Verlag. (*Man. His Nature and Place in the World*, New York: Columbia University Press 1988).

Giarini, O. and Liedtke, P.M. (1998), *Wie wir arbeiten werden. Der neue Bericht an den Club of Rome*, Hamburg: Hoffmann und Campe.

Gibbons, M., Limoges, C., Nowotny, H., Schwartzman, S., Scott, P. and Trow, M. (1994), *The New Production of Knowledge. The Dynamics of Science and Research in Contemporary Societies*, London: Sage.

Giddens, A. (1995), *Die Konsequenzen der Moderne*, Frankfurt a.M.: Suhrkamp (*The Consequences of Modernity*, Cambridge: Polity Press 1990).

Gilbert, P. (2003), *New Terror, New Wars*, Washington, DC: Georgetown University Press.

Glatzer, M. and Rueschemeyer, D. (2005), *Globalization and the Future of the Welfare State*, Pittsburgh: University of Pittsburgh Press.

Global 2000, (1980), *Report to the President*. Ed. Council on Environmental Quality and the US Secretary of State (Washington).

Gomes, P.J. (2002), *The Good Life. Truths That Last in Times of Need*, San Francisco: Harper San Francisco.

Greider, W. (1997), *One World, Ready or Not. The Manic Logic of Global Capitalism*, New York: Simon & Schuster.

Gross, P. (1994), *Die Multioptionsgesellschaft*, Frankfurt a.M.: Suhrkamp.

Gross, P. (1999), *Ich-Jagd. Ein Essay*, Frankfurt a.M.: Suhrkamp.

Gruppe von Lissabon (1997), *Grenzen des Wettbewerbs. Die Globalisierung der Wirtschaft und die Zukunft der Menschheit*, Darmstadt: Luchterhand. (*Limits to Competition*, Cambridge: MIT Press 1995).

Habermas, J. (1973), *Legitimationsprobleme im Spätkapitalismus*, Frankfurt: Suhrkamp.

Hansen, A.H. (1938), *Full Recovery or Stagnation?*, New York: Norton.

Hansen, A.H. (1941), *Fiscal Policy and Business Cycles*, New York: Norton.

Hayek, F.A. (1976), *Der Weg zur Knechtschaft*, München: dtv. (*The Road to Serfdom*, London: Routledge (1944)).

Heitmeyer, W., ed. (1997), *Was treibt die Gesellschaft auseinander? Bundesrepublik Deutschland: Auf dem Weg von der Konsens– zur Konfliktgesellschaft*, Vol. 1, Frankfurt a.M.: Suhrkamp.

Held, D. and McGrew, A. (2002), *Governing Globalization. Power, Authority and Global Governance*, Cambridge: Polity.

Heuser, U.J. (2000), *Das Unbehagen Im Kapitalismus. Die neue Wirtschaft und ihre Folgen*, Berlin: Berlin Verlag.

Hitzler, R. (2001), Existenzbastler als Erfolgsmenschen, Notizen zur Ich-Jagd in der Multioptionsgesellschaft, in Brosziewski and Maeder.

Hitzler, R. (2003), *Die Bastelgesellschaft*, in ed Prisching.

Hobson, J.A. (1902), *Imperialism*, London/New York: Constable.

Höffe, O., 1(999), *Demokratie im Zeitalter der Globalisierung*, München: Beck.

Hovden, E. and Keene, E., eds. (2002), *The Globalization of Neoliberalism*, Houndsmill: Palgrave.

Huntington, S.P. (1991), *The Third Wave. Democratization in the Late Twentieth Century*, Norman: University of Oklahoma Press.

Huntington, S.P. (1998), *Kampf der Kulturen. Die Neugestaltung der Weltpolitik im 21. Jahrhundert*, München: Goldmann (Engl. *The Clash of*

Civilisations and the Remaking of World Order. New York: Simon & Schuster 1996.

Hutchings, R.L., ed. (1998), *At the End of the American Century. America's Role in the Post-Cold War World*, Baltimore: Johns Hopkins University Press.

Inglehart, R. (1977), *The Silent Revolution. Changing Values and Political Styles among Western Publics*, Princeton: Princeton University Press.

Inglehart, R. (1989), *Kultureller Umbruch. Wertewandel in der westlichen Welt*, Frankfurt a.m.: Campus. (*Culture Shift in Advanced Industrial Society*, Princeton: Princeton University Press 1990).

Inglehart, R. (1997), *Modernization and Postmodernization. Cultural, Economic and Political Change in 43 Societies*, Princeton: Princeton University Press.

Jacobs, M. (1991), *The Green Economy. Environment, Sustainable Development, and the Politics of the Future*, London: Pluto Press.

Jenner, G. (1999), *Das Ende des Kapitalismus. Triumph oder Kollaps eines Wirtschaftssystems?*, Frankfurt: Fischer.

Jouvenel, B., de (1999), *Economics and the Good Life. Essays on Political Economy*, New Brunswick, NJ: Transaction Publishing.

Jünger, E. (1960), *Der Weltstaat. Organismus und Organisation*, Stuttgart: Klett-Cotta.

Jünger, E. (1981), *Der Arbeiter. Herrschaft und Gestalt*, Stuttgart: Klett-Cotta.

Jungk, R. (1977), *Der Atomstaat. Vom Fortschritt in die Unmenschlichkeit*, München: Kindler.

Kaldor, M. (1999), *New and Old Wars. Organized Violence in a Global Era*, Stanford, CA: Stanford University Publishing.

Kaufmann, F.-X. (1997), *Herausforderungen des Sozialstaates*, Frankfurt a.M.: Suhrkamp.

Klages, H. (1985), *Wertorientierungen im Wandel. Rückblick, Gegenwartsanalyse, Prognosen*, Frankfurt a.M.: Campus.

Klages, H. (1988), *Wertedynamik. Über die Wandelbarkeit des Selbstverständlichen*, Zürich: Edition Interfrom.

Kleinman, M. (2002), *A European Welfare State? European Union Social Policy in Context*, Houndsmill: Palgrave.

Klingemann, H.-D. and Neidhardt, F., eds. (2000), *Zur Zukunft der Demokratie. Herausforderungen im Zeitalter der Globalisierung*, Berlin: Edition Sigma.

Kneer, G., Nassehi, A. and Schroer, M., eds. (2000), *Soziologische Gesellschafts-begriffe. Konzepte moderner Zeitdiagnosen*, 2nd edn, München: Fink.

Kneer, G., Nassehi, A. and Schroer, M., eds. (2001), *Klassische Gesellschaftsbegriffe der Soziologie*, München: Fink.

Kondratieff, N.D. (1926), Die langen Wellen der Konjunktur, *Archiv für Sozialwissenschaft und Sozialpolitik*, **56**, 573–609.

Koselleck, R. (2002), *The Practice of Conceptual History. Timing History, Spacing Concepts*, Stanford, CA: Stanford University Publishing.

Kraidy, M. (2005), *Hybridity, or the Cultural Logic of Globalization*, Philadelphia: Temple University Press.

Küng, H. (1999), *A Global Ethic for Global Politics and Economics*, New York: Oxford University Press.

Küng, H. (2002a), *Weltpolitik und Weltethos. Status quo und Perspektiven*, Vienna: Picus.

Küng, H. (2002b), *Wozu Weltethos? Religion und Politik in Zeiten der Globalisierung*, Freiberg: Herder.

Kurz, R. (1991), *Der Kollaps der Modernisierung. Vom Zusammenbruch des Kasernensozialismus zur Krise der Weltökonomie*, Frankfurt: Eichborn.

Kurzweil, R. (1999), *Homo sapiens. Leben 21. Jahrhundert Was bleibt vom Menschen?*, Köln: Kiepenheuer & Witsch.

Leadbeater, C. (2000), *The Weightless Society. Living in the New Economy Bubble*, New York: Texere.

Lehner, F. (1979), *Grenzen des Regierens. Eine Studie zur Regierungsproblematik hochindustrialisierter Demokratien*, Königstein: Athenäum.

Lemert, C.C. and Elliott, A. (2006), *Deadly Worlds. The Emotional Costs of Globalization*, Lanham, Md.: Rowman & Littlefield.

Lipset, S.M. (2000), Conditions for Democracy, *Klingemann and Neidhardt*.

Luxemburg, R. (1913), *Die Akkumulation des Kapitals*, Berlin: Sieger.

Lyotard, J.-F. (1986), *Das postmoderne Wissen. Ein Bericht*, Graz: Passagen.

Mager, N.H. (1987), *The Kondratieff Waves*, New York: Praeger.

Mannheim, K. (1940), *Man and Society in an Age of Reconstruction. Studies in Modern Social Structure*, New York: Harcourt, Brace & World.

Marcuse, H. (1964), *One-Dimensional Man. Studies in the Ideology of Advanced Industrial Society*, Boston: Beacon Press.

Martin, H.-P. and Schumann, H. (1996), *Die Globalisierungsfalle. Der Angriff auf Demokratie und Wohlstand*, 6th edn, München: Rowohlt.

Matthies, V. (1980), *Neue Weltwirtschaftsordnung. Hintergründe, Positionen, Argumente*, Opladen: Leske + Budrich.

Matzner, E. (2000), *Monopolare Weltordnung. Zur Sozioökonomie der US-Dominanz*, Marburg: Metropolis.

McLuhan, M. (1962), *The Gutenberg Galaxy. The Making of Typographic Man*, Toronto: University of Toronto Press.

Meadows, D.H., Meadows, D.L., Randers, J. and Behrens, W., III (1972), *The Limits to Growth*, New York: Universe Books.

Menzel, U. (1992), *Das Ende der Dritten Welt und das Scheitern der großen Theorie*, Frankfurt a.M.: Suhrkamp.

Merry, R.W. (2005), *Sand of Empire. Missionary Zeal, American Foreign Policy, and the Hazards of Global Ambition*, New York: Simon & Schuster.

Meynaud, J. (1969), *Technocracy*, New York: Free Press.

Middleton, R. (1998), *Charlatans or Saviours? Economists and the British Economy from Marshall to Meade*, UK: Cheltenham-Northampton, MA: Edward Elgar).

Mill, J.S. (1913/21), *Grundsätze der politischen Ökonomie, 2 Vols*, Jena (Principles of Political Economy, 1848).

Minsky, M. (1986), *The Society of Mind*, New York: Simon & Schuster.

Minsky, M., ed. (1985), *Robotics*, Garden City, NY.: Anchor Press/Doubleday.

Mitscherlich, A. (1965), *Auf dem Weg zur Vaterlosen Gesellschaft. Ideen zur Sozialpsychologie*, München: Piper.

Moore, L.R. and Vaudagna, M., eds. (2003), *The American Century in Europe*, Ithaca: Cornell University Publishing.

Moore, T.G. (2002), *China in the World Market. Chinese Industry and International Sources of Reform in the Post-Mao Era*, Cambridge: Cambridge University Publishing.

Moravec, H.P. (1988), *Mind Children. The Future of Robot and Human Intelligence*, Cambridge, MA.: Cambridge University Publishing.

Moravec, H.P. (1999), *Robot. Mere Machine to Transcend Mind*, New York: Oxford University Publishing.

Münch, R. (1998), *Globale Dynamik, Lokale Lebenswelten. Der schwierige Weg in die Weltgesellschaft*, Frankfurt a.M.: Suhrkamp.

Münkler, H. (2002), *Die neuen Kriege*, Reinbek b.H.: Rowohlt.

Naisbitt, J. (1990), Megatrends 2000, *Ten New Directions for the 1990's*, New York: Morrow.

Neumann, M. (1997), *The Rise and Fall of The Wealth Of Nations. Long Waves in Economics and International Politics*, UK: Cheltenham/Lynne, NH: Edward Elgar).

OECD (2001), *Governance im 21. Jahrhundert*, Paris: OECD.

Olson, M. (1985), *Aufstieg und Niedergang von Nationen*, Tübingen: Mohr. (*Rise and Decline of Nations*, New Haven: Yale University Press 1982).

Pestel, E. (1989), *Beyond the Limits to Growth. A Report to the Club of Rome*, New York: Universe.

Pierson, P. (1995), *Dismantling the Welfare State? Reagan, Thatcher, and the Politics of Retrenchment*, Cambridge: Cambridge University Publishing.

Polanyi, K. (1978), The Great Transformation, Frankfurt a. M.: Suhrkamp.

Pongs, A. (1999), *In welcher Gesellschaft leben wir eigentlich? Gesellschaftskonzepte im Vergleich*, 2 Vols, München: Dilemma Verlag.

Pries, L. (1998), *Transnationale Soziale Räume*, in Beck.

Prisching, M. (2002), Vermarktlichung – ein Aspekt des Wandels von Koordinationsmechanismen, *Ökonomie und Gesellschaft: Jahrbuch*, **18** (Marburg), 15-38.

Prisching, M. (2006), Die zweidimensionale Gesellschaft. *Ein Essay zur neokon-sumistischen Geisteshaltung*, Wiesbaden: V S Verlag für Sozialwissenschaften.

Prisching, M., ed. (2003), *Modelle der Gegenwartsgesellschaft. Reihe Sozialethik Der Österreichischen Forschungsgemeinschaft*, 7 (Vienna: Passagen).

Pye, L.W. and Verba, S. (1972), *Political Culture and Political Development*, Princeton: Princeton University Publishing.

Raffer, K. and Singer, H.W., (2001), *The Economic North-South Divide: Six Decades of Unequal Development* (Cheltenham (UK)-Northampton (US): Elgar).

Reese-Schäfer, W. (2000), Die seltsame Konvergenz der Zeitdiagnosen, Versuch einer Zwischenbilanz, in Beck and Kieserling.

Reich, C.A. (1971), *The Greening of America*, New York: Bantam.

Riesman, D. *et al.* (1956), *Die einsame Masse. Eine Untersuchung des amerikan-*

ischen Charakters, Darmstadt: Luchterhand (*The Lonely Crowd. A Study of the Changing American Character*, New Haven: Yale University Press 1950).

Rifkin, J. (2000), *Access. Das Verschwinden des Eigentums. Warum wir weniger besitzen und mehr ausgeben werden*, Frankfurt a. M.: Campus (*The Age of Access. The New Culture of Hypercapitalism, Where All of Life is Paid-for Experience*, New York: Tarcher-Putnam 2000).

Ritzer, G. (1997), *Die McDonaldisierung der Gesellschaft*, Frankfurt a. M.: Fischer (*The McDonaldization of Society. An Investigation into the Changing Character of Contemporary Social Life*, Thousand Oaks: Pine Forge 1996).

Robertson, R. (1998), Glokalisierung: Homogenität und Heterogenität in Raum und Zeit, in Beck.

Rosenau, J.N. (1990), *Turbulence in World Politics. A Theory of Change and Continuity*, New York: Wheatsheaf.

Rostow, W.W. (1960), *Stadien wirtschaftlichen Wachstums. Eine Alternative zur marxistischen Entwicklungstheorie*, Göttingen: Vandenhoeck & Ruprecht (*The Stages of Economic Growth*, Cambridge: University Press 1960).

Rostow, W.W. (1964), *The Economics of Take-Off into Sustained Growth*, London New York: Macmillan.

Rubin, J.B. (2004), *The Good Life. Psychoanalytic Reflections on Love, Ethics, Creativity, and Spirituality*, Albany: State University of New York Press.

Ruloff, D. (1988), *Weltstaat oder Staatenwelt? Über die Chancen globaler Zusammenarbeit*, München: Beck.

Saad-Filho, A. and Johnston, D., eds. (2005), *Neoliberalism. A Critical Reader*, London: Pluto Press.

Safranski, R. (2003), *Wieviel Globalisierung verträgt der Mensch?*, München: Hanser.

Sauvy, A. (1976), *Zero Growth?*, New York: Praeger.

Schimank, U. and Volkmann, U., eds. (2000), *Soziologische Gegenwartsdiagnosen I, Eine Bestandsaufnahme*, Opladen: Leske + Budrich.

Schulze, G. (1992), *Die Erlebnisgesellschaft. Kultursoziologie der Gegenwart*, Frankfurt: Campus.

Schumpeter, J.A. (1952), Theorie der wirtschaftlichen Entwicklung, *Eine Untersuchung über Unternehmergewinn, Kapital, Kredit, Zins und den Konjunkturzyklus*, 5th edn, Berlin: Duncker & Humblot (erstmals 1912). (*The Theory of Economic Development. An Inquiry into Profits, Capital, Credit, Interest, and the Business Cycle*, Cambridge: Harvard University Press 1934).

Schumpeter, J.A. (1961), *Konjunkturzyklen. Eine theoretische, historische und statistische Analyse des kapitalistischen Prozesses*, 2 Vols, Göttingen: Vandenhoeck & Ruprecht (*Business Cycles. A Theoretical, Historical and Statistical Analysis of the Capitalist Process*. New York/London 1939).

Schumpeter, J.A. (1992), *Capitalism, Socialism and Democracy*, 6th edn, London: Routledge.

Scitovsky, T. (1976), *The Joyless Economy. An Inquiry into Human Satisfaction and Consumer Dissatisfaction*, New York: Oxford University Press.

Senghaas, D. (1982), *Von Europa Lernen. Entwicklungsgeschichtliche Betrachtungen*, Frankfurt: Suhrkamp.

Sennett, R. (1998), *Der flexible Mensch. Die Kultur des neuen Kapitalismus*, Berlin: Berlin Verlag. (*The Corrosion of Character: The Personal Consequences of Work in the New Capitalism*, New York: Norton 1998).

Smith, N. (2005), *The Endgame of Globalization*, New York: Routledge.

Sorokin, P.A. (1937), *Social and Cultural Dynamics*, New York: American Book.

Sorokin, P.A. (1941), *The Crisis of Our Age. The Social and Cultural Outlook*, New York: Dutton (*Die Krise unserer Zeit. Ihre Entstehung und Überwindung*. Frankfurt a. M. 1950).

Sorokin, P.A. (1953), *Kulturkrise und Gesellschaftsphilosophie. Moderne Theorien über das Werden und Vergehen von Kulturen und das Wesen ihrer Krisen*, Stuttgart: Humboldt Verlag.

Soros, G. (1998), *The Crisis of Global Capitalism. Open Society Endangered*, New York: Public Affairs.

Spengler, O. (1920ff), *Der Untergang des Abendlandes. Umrisse einer Morphologie der Weltgeschichte*, München: Beck (*The Decline of the West*, New York: Knopf, 1947).

Spybey, T. (1996), *Globalization and World Society*, Cambridge, UK: Polity Press.

Stehr, N. (2005), *Knowledge Politics*, Boulder: Paradigm Publications.

Stehr, N. (2001), *Wissen und Wirtschaften. Die gesellschaftlichen Grundlagen der modernen Ökonomie*, Frankfurt a. M.: Suhrkamp.

Steindl, J. (1952), *Maturity and Stagnation in American Capitalism*, Oxford: Blackwell.

Steindl, J. (1979), Stagnation Theory and Stagnation Policy, *Cambridge Journal of Economics*, **3**.

Stiglitz, J.E. (2003), *Globalization and Its Discontents*, New York: Norton.

Stone, J.R., ed. (2000), *Expecting Armageddon*, London/New York: Routledge.

Sweezy, P.M. (1974), *Theorie der kapitalistischen Entwicklung. Eine analytische Studie über die Prinzipien der Marxschen Sozialökonomie*, 4th edn, Frankfurt: Suhrkamp (*The Theory of Capitalist Development. Principles of Marxian Political Economy*, New York: Oxford University Press 1942).

Theurl, T. and Smekal, C., eds. (2001), *Globalisierung. Globalisiertes Wirtschaften und nationale Wirtschaftspolitik*, Tübingen: Mohr-Siebeck.

Thurow, L.C. (1981), *Die Null-Summen-Gesellschaft. Einkommensverteilung und Möglichkeiten wirtschaftlichen Wandels*, München: Vahlen (*The Zero-Sum Society: Distribution and the Possibilities for Economic Change*, New York: Basic Books 1980).

Tibi, B. (1995), *Krieg der Zivilisationen. Politik und Religion zwischen Vernunft und Fundamentalismus*, Hamburg: Hoffmann and Campe.

Tinbergen, J. (1977), *Wir haben nur eine Zukunft. Reform der internationalen Ordnung. Der RIO-Bericht an den Club of Rome*, Opladen: Westdeutscher Verlag (*Reshaping the International Order: A Report to the Club of Rome*, London: Hutchinson (1977)).

Toffler, A. (1970), *Future Shock*, New York: Random House.

Tomuschat, C. (2003), Der selbstverliebte Hegemon Die USA und der Traum von einer unipolaren Welt, *Internationale Politik*, **58**, No. 5, 39–47.

Touraine, A. (1972), *Die postindustrielle Gesellschaft*, Frankfurt: Suhrkamp (*The Post-Industrial Society. Tomorrow's Social History. Classes, Conflicts and Culture in the Programmed Society*. New York: Random House 1971).

Toynbee, A.J. (1934/1963ff) *A Study of History*, New York: Oxford University Publishing.

Vinge, V. (1984), *True Names*, New York: Bluejay Books.

Volkmann, U. and Schimank, U. (2002), *Soziologische Gegenwartsdiagnosen* II. *Vergleichende Sekundäranalysen*, Opladen: Leske + Budrich.

Wagnleitner, R. (1994), *Coca-colonization and the Cold War. The Cultural Mission of the United States in Austria after the Second World War*, Chapel Hill: University of North Carolina Press.

Wallerstein, I. (2003), *The Decline of American Power. The U.S. in a Chaotic World*, New York: New Press.

Wallerstein, I.M. (1974), *The Modern World System, Capitalist Agriculture and the Origins of the European World Economy in the Sixteenth Century*, New York: Academic Press.

Wallis, J. and Dollery, B. (1999), *Market Failure, Government Failure, Leadership and Public Policy*, New York: St Martin's Press.

Warwick, K. (2002), Cyborg 1.0, www.wired.com/wired/archive/8.02/warwick. html.

Weber, A. (1953), *Der dritte und der vierte Mensch. Vom Sinn des geschichtlichen Daseins*, München: Piper.

Weinstein, M.M., ed. (2005), *Globalization: What's New?*, New York: Columbia University Publishing.

Weizsäcker, C.C., von (1999), *Logik der Globalisierung*, Göttingen: Vandenhoeck & Ruprecht.

Welsch, W., (1987), *Unsere postmoderne Moderne* (Weinheim: VCH).

Welsch, W., ed., (1988); *Wege aus der Moderne. Schlüsseltexte der Postmoderne-Diskussion*, Weinheim: VCH.

Wolf, M.J. (1999), *The Entertainment Economy. How Mega-Media Forces Are Transforming Our Lives*, New York: Random House.

Young, M.D. (1959), *The Rise of the Meritocracy*, Baltimore: Penguin Books.

Zapf, W., ed. (1979), *Theorien des sozialen Wandels*, 4th edn (Königstein/Ts.: Athenäum et.al.).

Zapf, W., ed., (1977), *Probleme der Modernisierungspolitik*, Meisenheim a.G.: Hain).

Chapter 4

Globalisation as a Gendered Process: A Differentiated Survey on Feminist and Postcolonial Perspectives

Silvia Bauer and Tatjana Schönwälder-Kuntze

When we addressed ourselves to the task of writing an chapter about *globalisation* and *gender* within the context of *business ethics* we immediately encountered the difficulty of reaching an agreement on what we actually mean by those very terms and concepts. We reasoned that it is impossible to provide clear definitions or to summarise the current debates and reach a clear disambiguation of the concepts in question, but that at the same time we deemed it necessary to start with some working propositions on these three topics. Therefore, we will begin with a brief review of the notions of business ethics, globalisation and gender, and comment on common usages and established definitions of those terms, even though we are well aware that this also means to neglect myriad important aspects, insights and considerations.

In our contribution to this book on business ethics we hope to point out the deeply complex interconnectedness of gender, globalisation and business ethics and highlight the deplorable fact that the vast majority of current discourses on globalisation and business ethics is still profoundly gender blind. We share the belief that thinking about gender as a crucial category in (the context of) evaluating business ethics within the parameters of globalisation can pave the way towards more global justice, gender equality, and individual well-being, as well as more fairly distributed wealth and worldwide prosperity.

We consider *business* and *ethics*, the two terms that make up the compound *business ethics*, not as antagonistic terms and, therefore, understand *business ethics* not as an oxymoron or a *contradictio in adiecto*. In our perspective, *business ethics* provide a framework for doing business in such a way that common welfare increases hand in hand with corporate profits. *Business ethics* in this sense aspires to formulate *obligatory* rules and laws that should be applied world wide for the benefit of all. So one of the aims of *business ethics* as theoretical work is seen in enabling *global players* to work also on staging political, democratic justified institutions so that they can choose and give those rules for the world. Therefore, we understand our contribution to this reader not as a discussion of *gendered* views on *business ethics* but as a focusing on some perspectives on globalisation that are informed by *gender* or *feminist* theory. We are convinced that these positions could help *theorise* global problems in a more suitable manner, and consequently could improve our understanding of what shape the rules have to have to ensure equal conditions at the start of our lives.

Thus, theorising globalisation in terms of economics means to see the problem in establishing such rules, that 'the production of the material conditions to satisfy (our) basic needs must be treated as an independent economic problem and as a prerequisite for the *establishment* of human liberty' (Madöring, 2005, p.39), so that human rights and liberty are at least a goal of economics because they are their necessary preconditions.

Definitions for *globalisation* are numerous; they vary in their degree of differentiation as well as in their focusing on diverse features that are considered to be the most significant characteristics of the complex processes of globalisation. Hirsch and Vom (1998) point out four different aspects of globalisation: a political, an economical, an ideological respectively cultural one, and a technical aspect. The *political* aspect refers to the end of the Cold War and the end of the binary division of the world between the USSR and the USA and aims at the prospective idea that there might be one day a world government. The *economic* aspect concerns the boundless flows of money and goods; the *ideological* aspects refers to the (Western) ideal of universalising human rights and individualism; and the *technical* aspect mentions the possibility of new technologies which – theoretically – connect each person with the whole world in no time. Crane and Matten (2004) argue that these attributes do not single out the really *new* aspect that distinguishes the globalisation of today from the globalisation of former times, so they prefer to focus on the technical possibilities and define the notion as 'the progressive eroding of the relevance of territorial bases for social, economic, and political activities, processes, and relations' (Crane and Matten, 2004, p.16).

Others like Teusch (2004) distinguish between a perception of globalisation as 'fate', as an uncontrollable, unstoppable and unshapeable evolution of world economics and, on the other side, a critical analysis of globalisation that maintains its fundamental openness to dynamic change and perpetual reorganisation. Therefore, he argues, it is not so much a matter of controversy between proponents and opponents of globalisation, but rather a debate among advocates and critics of certain developments and effects of specific globalisation processes. Globalisation is neither a process of linear progression leading towards complete globality, nor an unambiguous development, but, quite the contrary, is characterised by a multidimensional dialectics of globalisation-localisation, integration-fragmentation, and liberalism-fundamentalism producing ambivalent effects. The four principal actors of globalisation, according to Teusch, are the national states and their governments, and, more importantly, transnational corporations and international institutions like WTO, IMF, World Bank, etc., and last not least, transnational non-governmental organisations (NGOs) like Attac, Transparency International, Greenpeace, Amnesty International, etc.

To answer the pivotal and recurring question 'What is new about globalisation?' we would argue, that while today's globalisation processes may have a new quality and intensity, especially in regard to the opening up and almost neutralisation of spatial and temporal categories by means of new communication technologies, it is nevertheless indispensable to position present-day developments in a historical perspective of colonialism and postcolonialism, imperialism and neo-imperialism. Schroeter (2002), for instance, detects the beginnings of globalisation in the time of explorations during the fifteenth and sixteenth century. The newly discovered regions and the newly established colonies provided crude materials and cheap labour as well as new markets that could be exploited. The nineteenth century was characterised by industrialisation and a liberal free trade policy that supported an ever-increasing internationalisation. New technologies rapidly revolutionised transportation and communication, production and labour conditions. By the end of the nineteenth century imperialism reached its peak and the world powers, driven by an ideology of nationalism, competed for 'free' territories overseas, especially in Africa, Asia and the Middle East.

Considering globalisation in the context of its historical predecessors is important because it broadens the perception towards alternative perspectives and new possibilities for action or intervention. Often we get the impression that debates on globalisation and business ethics are reduced to the economic principles of neoliberalism, the maximising of profits or the changed relations between the nation state and transnational corporations. In view of the historical heritage of colonialism and imperialism the effects of globalisation on social relations and especially on gender relations and gender regimes become visible more easily.

This brings us to the third and probably the most controversial term. Definitions of the notion of *gender*, seem to be the most difficult because in fact there are many different understandings and ways of using this concept in theory, politics and – business. The historian Joan Wallace Scott, who proclaimed gender as 'a useful category for historical analysis' in 1986, and whose influential chapter helped to get the sex/gender distinction widely accepted as a basis for analysis, recently turned away from using the term *gender* because to her 'gender seemed to have become routinized, contributing to, rather than unsettling the stability of the man/woman opposition. I got tired of finding myself cited in books and chapters that simply took for granted the transparency of physical differences between the sexes, that raised gender to the status of a theory, when in fact it served merely as a synonym for the uninterrogated categories of "women" and "men"' (Scott, 2001, p.29). Scott continues that

> [...] gender has acquired exactly that allure of social scientific neutrality that is meant to distinguish it from the politically engaged project of feminism and that guarantees its academic respectability. It has become a way of taking (or not taking) a position on the question of feminism, which is the contested term these days. Gender can be a means of distinguishing one's work from the special pleading associated with feminism, or it can serve to disguise the explicit feminist aims of scholarly projects – in either case it is feminism, not "gender" that is at issue. (Scott, 2001, p.31)[1]

---

1   We hope that the readers of this chapter will notice that we, too, use the term *gender* in the title of this chapter to disguise our feminist position.

We want to continue with another quotation to make clear from the beginning what we are thinking about the roles of theory *and* feminism:[2]

> Feminism is about the social transformation of gender relations. Probably we could agree on that, even if "gender" is not the preferred word for some .... We may have very different ideas of what social transformation is, or what qualifies as a transformative exercise. But we also must have an idea of how theory relates to the process of transformation, whether theory is itself transformative work that has transformation as one of its effects.

If 'ideas matter' one of our aims as academics must be to avoid that our concepts and investigations – with recourse to however 'scientifically founded' knowledge – reinforce and re-naturalise those differences that are used to justify and maintain disadvantaging social hierarchies and which need to be transformed – and this highly concerns gender(ed) relations.

After we have sketched preliminary our position within the multidimensional and versatile field that is specified by the concepts of *business ethics, globalisation,* and *gender* we will now continue with a short outline of different issues that could be considered if the *gender aspect* were already an integral part of a *theory* of *globalisation* and *business ethics*. In the then following second part of our chapter we will present two selected perspectives on globalisation, one referring to feminist philosophy (Sandra Harding), and the other to transnational feminist networks (Valentine Moghadam) and the concept of solidarity (Chandra Mohanty). The third and last part sums up what is to be learned from feminist or gender theories and which advice or consequences we can draw from that.

What Kind of Perspective Does the Gender Aspect Bring up in Theories?

As we said before *gender* is adapted to different subjects and is used in different ways in theories. Again, we selected three distinct approaches we want to present: a) *essential* approaches to *gender*; b) obvious *gender effects* and c) *gender* as a *category of analysis*. Seeing this preview, it becomes clear already that we are going from the apparently 'natural' or naturalised usage to an obvious use of gender as an empirically given subject to the more implicit, more complex, and disguised functions that can be discovered by using gender as an analysing instrument.

Essential Approaches to Gender

Essential approaches take place if the direction of theory building goes from apparently empirical 'facts' in the behaviour of some human 'groups' to apparent 'essences' as (natural) given that are subsequently perceived as unchangeable. One of the best known examples is the study of the psychologist Gilligan *In a Different Voice* (1982)

---

2   We will use the notions *gender* and *feminist* as if they were synonyms because given a certain type of theory in fact they are considered as synonyms. The main difference is that *gender* seems to be more indifferent to activist engagement and *feminist* has the political aim of overcoming hierarchic structures; this common goal, of course, unites these theories.

based on Piaget's studies of three-level-model, respectively on Kohlberg's more elaborated six-level-model of moral development, where she points out, that women have essentially different ideas of being moral than men.[3] The findings of her study provided the basis for developing her ideas of an *ethics of care*, which does not build on 'male' conditions and values like, e.g., autonomy, abstract rights or fairness, but on interdependent familial structures, concrete situations and responsibility.[4]

The trouble we have with such a naturalising attribution is the idea that individuals belong from the beginning of their lives to a special group, and are defined by their essence that determines their behaviour and, even worse, that sets the frames for their normality. We will come back to this point at the end. Furthermore, such a view restricts the perspectives of investigation on typical themes that seemingly belong to women: reproduction labour, household, care, etc. We can also see this type of investigation in the work of Hartmann, a pioneering feminist economist[5] whose work analyses the problems of balancing work and family, and who fights for changing social inequity. She rose a debate about women's places in our society and was sometimes read as if she fought for bringing women back home. The problem with these investigations is, that there is a need for them to be done in order to make hierarchic social differences obvious, but at the same time they can be misunderstood and abused to legitimate certain 'lifestyles' as unchangeable nature.[6]

Obvious Gender Effects

Another kind of investigation does not strive to naturalise and universalise behaviour by essences, but presupposes that there *are* by nature two different genders – men and women. Then, based on this uninterrogated presupposition, these studies explicate what impact the social construction of gender has on the embodied existence of the

---

3   Despite all the sound criticism Gilligan's thesis had to endure, we deem it important to note that her study originally had the purpose to dissent from Kohlberg's assumption that girls on average were only able to reach a lower level of moral development than boys. In Kohlberg's model girls only arrived at the fourth level of his six-levels-model. Gilligan contradicts Kohlberg's idea that women normally are only able to reach the conventional level, since, according to his view, they rarely develop a real, autonomous idea of morality that is orientated towards absolute principles. Gilligan formulates an alternative scheme, which does not intend to not limit liberty and thereby maintain autonomy, as Kohlberg's seemingly Kantian adaptation suggests, but rather to preserve integrity. She argues for a model of (female) morality, which is not based on principles but on relations. – for an extensive discussion of the ethics of care *vs.* the ethics of justice and different feminist stances on the Gilligan controversy, *Cf.* Gilligan 1982.

4   Cf. e.g. Crane and Matten (2004), 98.

5   She is also the founder of the *Institute for Women's Policy Research* (IWPR) in Washington, DC.

6   There are a lot of feminist critiques on economic mainstream thinking; see, e.g., Meyer (2003) who especially refers to Gary S. Becker's gender(ed) division of labour, who argues in a strong Hegelian way that the most efficient form of labour is the one, in which the male specialises in labour outside of the home while the female specialises in housework; therefore social institutions should support this kind of 'differentiated labour' as good as they can; see also Fineman and Dougherty (2005).

gendered subjects, on which the research is based – especially on women. Thus, with *obvious gender effects* we refer to analyses of globalisation that study the outcomes of the various processes of globalisation on one specific gender. Usually these studies investigate aspects that concern women, and typically women are seen as the 'losers' of globalisation and as 'victims' of gender relations. At a second glance, however, it becomes apparent that the situation is more complex, and unequivocal conclusions with clear winner/loser distinctions are hard to find.

Concepts like *feminisation of labour* or *feminisation of poverty* point towards the importance of gender-aware approaches to globalisation, and, furthermore, show the significance of gender discourses. Many of these surveys deal with post-Fordist forms of informal and precarious labour economies, with working conditions of women in *Maquiladoras* or *sweatshops*, or with the situations of migrant women as domestic workers. Others examine the sexual exploitation of women in a global economy by inspecting the situation of sex workers in the sex tourism industries or by exploring the global routes and networks that sustain trafficking in women and children. Some issues of reproduction are considered in the discourses on *missing women* in India or China that refer to selected abortions of female fetuses.[7]

Generally speaking, the gendered oppositions between public and private spheres, between productive, formal economies and reproductive economies of the household are still prevailing in contemporary analyses of globalisation and business ethics that see the private and the public as complementary spheres, thereby neglecting the embedded interconnectedness and interdependence of those two spheres, especially when it concerns women. Many feminist scholars have pointed out that this gendered antagonism of economic markets and social structures like the family is full of ambiguities and contradictions.[8] For instance, with increasing privatisation of child care or care for the elderly, mainly women have found new jobs in professional service industries. At the same time, reproductive activities that, at least in Europe, have for a long time been supported by public institutions, have now once again become an 'economic and social externality' (Young 2002, 40) and thus have been rendered invisible. Another effect is that the disparity among well-educated, socially privileged women and low-paid, often migrant, women workers increases and reintroduces a 'mistress'-'maid' structure of dependence and exploitation along the lines of class, ethnicity, and gender.

As the last example illustrates, it is not sufficient to reflect on the effects of globalisation on gender alone. Such an approach would assume that these effects were the same for all women and that women all over the world somehow shared the 'universal' experience of *being* 'woman'. But constructions of gender are contingent on historical, cultural, political, social, or economic conditions, and therefore categories of difference as class, ethnicity (race), age, but also residence permit status, health, educational status and so on have to be taken into account. If these kinds of investigation are not perceived and reflected as analyses of the *status quo*, but instead seen as consequences of somehow given essences, there is a danger that

---

7   Cf. the demographic studies by Sen (1990) or Klasen and Wink (2003).
8   Cf. Becker-Schmidt (1993, p.44); Young (2001, p.39).

these findings might re-formulate and re-stage *gender* again as naturally given, and thereby they are most likely thwarting their original goals.

Gender as a Category of Analysis

As we mentioned above, gender was introduced as a category of analysis into the feminist academic discourse by Scott (1986). She defines gender in four different ways: 1) as a constitutive element of social relations, 2) as a way of giving relations of power their meaning, 3) in its relation to politics and social institutions and, finally, 4) gender as the subjective identity of an individual person.[9] In this respect, gender becomes a category – not only in historical investigation, but in philosophical, social, psychological, etc. as well – which can be put to use to make social differences obvious as well as the categories of 'race,' class, sexual preference or, more recently, age and religion. Therefore, *gender* appears as a life-shaping category of relations and not as a property of individuals. Furthermore, gender functions as a border or boundary that makes a difference referring to the possibilities and chances a person will get to lead his or her life.

Even though gender remains a valuable category of analysis, in recent years its precision has been diluted, and, as we already mentioned, many feminist scholars today prefer the terms *feminism* or *sexual difference* when talking about gender inequalities or gendered differences. *Gender* was also a highly controversial term at the United Nations Fourth World Conference on Women held in Beijing in September 1995 precisely because the term highlights the constructedness, contingency, and changeability of gender and gender differences, while calling the alleged 'normalcy' of a biological definition of 'natural' gender into question. The clarification that was achieved in Beijing agreed on 'the commonly understood meaning of "gender"' (Scott, 2001, p.32), even though there obviously was no 'generally accepted usage' to agree upon. Nevertheless, one of the conservative outcomes of the Beijing conference was, that now *gender* has become 'just another way of referring to women and men' (Scott, 2001, p.33).[10]

The Program of Action called on governments to 'mainstream a gender perspective in all policies and programmes, so that before decisions are taken an analysis may be made of their effects on women and men, respectively' (UN Report, 1995).[11] This strategy became the basis for the Gender Mainstreaming programmes of the European Union that have been laid down in the treaty of Amsterdam in 1996. Many feminists by now criticise the missing impact of this strategy which mainly leads to reliable statistical data that is disaggregated by sex. Since the Beijing

---

9 *Gender* as a concept has been developed by Simone de Beauvoir (1949) to name the difference between our given biological body, i.e. *sex*, and the social structures and conditions that make *a woman*. A short overview over the shifts of this notion give, e.g. Harding (1996, p.274) or Schönwälder and Wille (2003).

10 Mostly it is used as a synonym for women: 'The 200 or so mentions of "gender" in the Program of Action from Beijing are often simply substitutes for the word "women"' (Scott, 2001, p.33).

11 Cf. United Nations. *Report on the Fourth World Conference on Women*, Beijing, 4-15 September. Chapter IV, D, Section 123.

Conference many other transnational institutions like the World Bank or the World Economic Forum have also incorporated gender approaches into their strategies and programmes. In 2005 the WEF published a report on *Women's Empowerment: Measuring the Global Gender Gap* which compared the extent to which women have achieved equality with men in five crucial areas: economic participation, economic opportunity, political empowerment, educational attainment, and health and well-being. Again, *gender* is used as a synonym for *women* and does not consider more abstract dimensions like *difference* or *relation*. And, again, men are seen as the unmarked norm or the measure of full 'human social development' (WEF Report, 2005, p.1) to which women have to aspire, if they are seeking *equality*. Variations from this norm suggest female deficiency or 'lack'.

Any analysis of *globalisation* and *gender* has to take into account not only women and men (if *gender* should be used as a mere synonym for *women* or *men*), but also other categories of difference, like (race) ethnicity, or class, that are interconnected with the category of gender. The history of feminism, women's studies and gender theory is characterised by an ongoing debate on differences between women, on ethnocentricity and heterosexism, to name but two examples. Feminist and gender discourses benefited enormously from interventions by black feminists, queer theorists, and 'Third World' scholars. Crenshaw (1989) coined the term of *intersectional analysis* that takes the interconnectedness of different relational categories like gender (race), and class into consideration. An intersectional analysis is much needed in order to do justice to the social, economic, and political inequalities and the cultural differences that can be found among women on a global scale. Collins (1998) called for a *both/and-strategy* to allow for a consideration of a multitude of categories:

> We cannot study gender in isolation from other inequalities, nor can we only study inequalities "intersection" and ignore the historical and contextual specificity that distinguishes the mechanisms that produce inequality by different categorical divisions, whether gender, race, ethnicity, nationality, sexuality, or class. (Risman, 2004, p.443.)

Summing up this first part we could say, that every view on our social life presupposes theory as a mostly implicit decision on how to formulate the problem, how to reduce the point of view by focusing this and not that aspect of human beings, and by producing new distinctions. There is nothing to do against it, because we need to differentiate if we want to know something about how our social life is constructed and if we want to solve the problems we have with it. But we have to consider that every standpoint, every theorising is an answer to a question which is itself the result of a theorised and theorising perspective on our world. Subsequently if we are talking of a feminist or gender perspective on globalisation or on any other topic we have to reflect the differences we use for analysis and the impact this usage might have which we may not have intended. Furthermore, we have to take care of the frames and the presuppositions we are making.

Feminist Perspectives of Globalisation

As we mentioned before, feminist philosophers and scientists in general found themselves in the situation that 'minority' scientists who lead or prefer another lifestyle, criticised the constricted point of view that usually characterises the 'normal' lives of heterosexual middle class citizens. This critique came also from others parts of the world – especially from the South – additionally describing this kind of thinking as Eurocentric, i.e., as a white, academic, 'enlightened' women's standpoint which excludes a lot of other women's experiences throughout the world. Feminist theory was asked to globalise itself to answer these rejections respectively exclusions in an adequate manner. We have selected two different ways of answering this global challenge which we will present below: at first we take a look on global feminism(s) in terms of philosophy of science; then we turn to postcolonial and sociological perspectives and present a concept of decolonisation and solidarity that, among others, can be put to use in transnational feminist networks.

Sandra Harding: The Challenge of Global Feminism(s)

Harding is a philosopher of science and analyses globalisation referring to required Post-Enlightenment concepts, because she argues that there can be seen a 'complicity of Enlightenment philosophies of science with failures of Third World development policies and the current environmental crisis' (Harding and Narayan, 2000, p.240). She starts by showing how the gender, environment and sustainable development (GED) debates link criticism of global development thinking to a critique of epistemology and philosophy of Enlightenment. Her next step is to discover how Post-Enlightenment and postcolonial science studies can support, in turn, the challenges of GED.

Under the title 'Is development gendered?' (Harding and Narayan, 2000, p.242), she points out that at first the development of women stood in the focus, because in many ways economic growth for women – and peasants – in the so called 'Third World' meant de-development for them, because of 'increasing women's unpaid domestic labour, enticing or forcing women into the lowest-paid manufacturing and agricultural labour, and appropriating their inherited land' (Harding and Narayan, 2000, p.242). So the idea that growth or development belongs immediately to everybody related to his or her abilities – and not to his or her 'gender' or 'class' – was discovered as a mistake. The second step in analysing development was to conceive gender as a category of relations which made obvious that women were excluded 'from Enlightenment standards of the human, the good, progress, social welfare, and economic growth as well as of objectivity, rationality, good method, and what counted as important scientific problems' (Harding and Narayan, 2000, p.243).[12] The third gendered moment of development (programs), mentioned by Harding, consists in the daily, implicit use of gender based prejudices by people who

---

12   From our point of view one has to reformulate this point in a negative way: The Philosophy of Enlightenment *was not able to refuse* and *avoid* that women and others were excluded instead of assuming that the concepts of Enlightenment intended to do so – we can

were involved in the international, national and local development agencies as well as their thinking. She concludes the first part with the statement that development *is* gendered and sums up that the 'feminist origins of Enlightenment re-evaluations were strengthened and expanded in the GED accounts through their link to criticisms of development economism and ignorance about nature's limits.' (Harding and Narayan, 2000, p.244.)

Her second question is 'Is Enlightenment Philosophy Economistic?' in the sense that economistic values and interests permeate it. From a feminist point of view and as it was mentioned above, the problem here is not so much that 'development was initially conceptualised as economic growth' (Harding and Narayan, 2000, p.245), but that economic growth – and the theory which belongs to it – does not realise that one of the conditions of economic growth exists in housework, which is 'usually' done by women; or, if economists think about this problem, they legitimate this labour division, as it has been done by Becker. Another aspect Harding points out is that the relations between different factors of growth and development or non-development are conceptualised in a false manner: 'it is poverty that causes population growth, not the reverse' (Harding and Narayan, 2000, p.246), even if the relation has been seen in reverse for a long period. Thirdly, she is naming the limits of growth which include that we cannot just go on consuming as much of our environmental goods as we do to this date, and at last she touches the problem of all the other 'goods' that make life worth while living and which are not mentioned in classical development theories. She concludes:

> Such considerations lead to the suspicion that rational man, who seeks information always in order to maximize his own benefit, ensures the destruction of the very conditions necessary for his survival when those benefits are conceptualized solely as economic.' (Harding and Narayan, 2000, p.246.)

Therefore, she gives in the second part of her paper some very short ideas which do not refer to Enlightenment conceptualisations, but to what she calls Post-Enlightenment philosophy of science. She thinks, e.g. of substituting the ideal of 'universality' in knowledge to local knowledge systems; she looks for imperfect knowledge systems which include the unforeseeable daily life and which are made for 'smart knowers'; she insists in resting the dichotomy between relativism and idealism and wants a rationality which is internalising democratic ethics and politics in sciences, because 'Enlightenment notions of rationality locate ethics and politics outside the borders of rationality' (Harding and Narayan, 2000, p.256).

We want to add two more remarks on this way of thinking globalisation by feminist philosophers (of science). First, to make Enlightenment philosophy *responsible* for not having avoided 'bad' developments mixes up two very different forms of investigation: theories can be seen as a picture of our realities and therefore they can be qualified as good if the relation between significant and sign is properly adequate. But if we consider theories as theoretical attempts to give an answer to problems we want to have solved, i.e. as a way of thinking solutions, we cannot blame on them

---

find this more careful formulation in the introduction to the reader (Harding and Naranyan, 2004, viii).

responsibility for what people – even if they are scientists or philosophers – have made out of these ideas or concepts. That would be like blaming our languages for the possibility of getting used as 'hate speech' – we have to see, that every notion has at least two sides which could be used with very different *intentions* – so the responsibility must be attributed to the contexts or circumstances and not to the notions themselves.

The second comment is to understand which meaning of 'Enlightenment Philosophy' is used here. Harding connects it with the beginning of the Modern times,[13] i.e. with the late sixteenth century when Europeans started to 'discover' and explore the world. This was a condition for modern sciences but subsequently it were new discoveries and developments by the sciences which only made many of the travels and expeditions possible at all. So her point of view on Enlightenment comes from the 'hard' empirical sciences. But Enlightenment as a philosophical term has also a meaning of discovering, or – to formulate it more clearly – of *creating theoretically* the basis and the conditions to make all the people able to live *their* lives as they want to. If we consider, e.g. the most famous theory of Enlightenment of Kant, we see, that he conceptualised rationality the way he did it in order to make blissfulness possible for everybody. Therefore, theory has a real and practical aim within the Kantian thinking and rationality itself has two parts: a theoretical, epistemological or knowledgeable part and a practical one. Furthermore, rationality does not exclude ethics and politics, but the other way round rationality's theoretical parts are build to serve them!

To sum up the feminist interventions in theory building mentioned here, we want to say that we do highly agree with the diagnosis of what effects globalisation can have on women's – and others' – lives, but that we cannot affirm whether Enlightenment philosophy has caused this development nor subsequently that we need Post-Enlightenment notions or concepts to rule globalisation in a more feminist way. What we need is trying to understand adequately the Enlightenment conceptualisations as an attempt to set us free to choose our rules and the ways we want to live together, all of us – as existing human beings! This conceptualisation must be understood as the presupposition of every concrete analysis of situations and by no means as an empirical description of human beings, because it constructs the conditions and possibilities of being different: Kant tells us that the only inborn right is the right of liberty and that there can be only one restriction to it – the restriction to not disturb the liberty of others.[14] That does not mean that the liberty of others is the boundary of everyone's own liberty, *but that the distortion of liberty* is my and everyone's boundary of free acting and therefore the boundary we are not allowed to cross – and everyone means everyone. If there were many ways of intended misunderstandings and misinterpretations of these notions, it is now time

---

13 In Harding (1990) she considers that the names 'Enlightenment' and 'Humanism' do not really describe what she wants to discuss, although she uses these two again and again in the same way throughout her work, see e.g. Harding (1986).

14 *Cf.* Kant (1797, p.237) (quoted after the German Akademie Ausgabe).

to see the radical intent Kant put into his theory, even if some of our colleges and contemporaries might not accept it.[15]

Decolonising Theory, Feminist Solidarity, and Transnational Networks (Chandra Mohanty's Feminism without Borders and Valentine Moghadam's Globalising Women)

In the first part of our chapter we presented several approaches how the inclusion of gender aspects into the research on globalisation can lead to interesting new insights and perspectives and how these aspects make topics, that are usually excluded from mainstream globalisation theory, more accessible. What happens when we now shift the focus to the question of how globalisation also influences feminist theory and feminist activism respectively organisations? What are feminist perspectives or concepts to better understand and deal with the issues globalisation holds ready? And how does this interaction with globalisation reflect developments within feminist thinking? New challenges require new concepts as well as new organisational forms to manage those very challenges.

The transnationality of globalisation processes therefore can be answered with the formation of transnational feminist networks which are based on a concept of strategic solidarity that replaces an older notion of global sisterhood. Two crucial foundations for the development of an attitude of solidarity are (1) a critical awareness of interconnectedness that acknowledges differences while it envelopes common interests, and (2) a self-reflexive critical stance that is aware of its own socio-historical embeddedness. Especially for white, Western feminist academics, a thorough examination of how Eurocentric ideas inform one's own thinking seems indispensable.

Critical whiteness studies, postcolonial theory and criticism of Eurocentrism are but three approaches that currently inform feminist and gender theories on economic, political, cultural, social, or ecological globalisation. The majority of contemporary analyses of globalisation ignore both, aspects of gender as well as the postcolonial continuum of exclusion, exploitation, and discrimination (Randeria, 2000, p.19). Yet, this is more than just a 'bad epistemic habit' (Shohat and Stam, 1994, p.10). The West's disproportionate power today is a direct result of colonialism, slave-trading, and imperialism. At the same time indigenous achievements in non-Western regions are often denied or played down in political or economic discourse.[16] Cultural theorist Ella Shohat explains:

15　Because we can only touch the feminist discussion of Kantian philosophy and ethics here, we just give references to some of the most important interpretations, *Cf.*, e.g. O'Neill (1985); Benhabib (1992), Nagl-Docekal and Pauer-Studer (1995), Schott (1998), Friedman (2000).

16　'Eurocentrism sanitizes Western history while patronizing and even demonizing the non-West; it thinks of itself in terms of its noblest achievements – science, progress, humanism – but of the non-West in terms of its deficiencies, real or imagined.' (Shohat and Stam, 1994, p.3.)

'Eurocentrism first emerged as a discursive rationale for colonialism, the process by which the European powers reached positions of hegemony in much of the world. (…) As an ideological substratum common to colonialist, imperialist, and racist discourse, Eurocentrism is a form of vestigial thinking which permeates and structures contemporary practices and representations even after the formal end of colonialism. Although colonialist discourse and Eurocentric discourse are intimately intertwined, the terms have a distinct emphasis. While the former explicitly justifies colonialist practices, the latter embeds, takes for granted, and "normalizes" the hierarchical power relations generated by colonialism and imperialism, without necessarily even thematising those issues directly. Although generated by the colonizing process, Eurocentrism's links to that process are obscured in a kind of buried epistemology.' (Shohat and Stam, 1994, p.2.)

The so called 'neoliberal discourse' is full of Eurocentric assumptions: while claiming to be the advocate of Enlightenment values and rationality, bringing free trade and liberal democracies to the non-Western parts of the world, it is indeed 'the West' who restricts free trade and unhindered access to its own home markets. Western officials accuse non-Western governments of violating human rights, while at the same time Western administrations or corporations find lame excuses why they themselves are violating basic human rights. And while Western feminists accuse non-Western countries for discriminating against women, they themselves are still a far way from gender equality. For example, the WEF report on *Women's Empowerment* lists the USA on rank 17, and Costa Rica on rank 18; China can be found on the 33rd rank, and Switzerland made it to 34th, Bangladesh is 39th, whereas Italy is only 45th of a total of 58 measured nations.

Especially postcolonial feminists like Mohanty or the sociologists Randeria and Moghadam propose a reconsideration and reconceptualisation of solidarity as a means of feminist resistance to and interference with globalisation processes.[17] Randeria calls for a transnational and transcultural solidarity among women (Randeria, 2000, p.28). Together with Mohanty and many others, Randeria sees common interests as the motivating basis for joined interventions, that respect the complex web of diverse differences like class, 'race', etc. It is obvious that amid the wide diversity of visions of gender equality and gender justice at a global as well as local scale, feminist endeavours can not aim at reaching a universal or global answer to the challenges of globalisation.

While it is hard to tell which woman or man individually counts as winner or loser of globalisation processes – women working in *Maquiladoras* or sweatshops gain economic self-determination and independent income, while they are also encountering potential dangers of being exploited, getting sexually harassed or harming their health – yet, the feminist movement as such can surely be considered a winner of globalisation. Technologies of globalisation like transnational organisational forms, communication networks and increased mobility offer new possibilities for feminist theory and activism. While gender theory has often been criticised for losing touch with gender activists or the women's movement, transnational feminist networks can obtain a renewed interconnectedness of theory and activism, a complex

---

17 For a history of female solidarity from a German feminist perspective, *Cf.* Praetorius (1995), 74–84.

association of women from all different backgrounds who nevertheless retain their individual differences. Instead of 'global sisterhood', Mohanty favours the concept of solidarity that does not presuppose a common interest due to a supposed common ground based on being a woman.[18] Agarwal calls it 'strategic sisterhood' (Agarwal, 1996, p.88), a concept which recalls Spivak's notion of 'strategic essentialism'.[19]

Mohanty's concept of solidarity is an explicit counterstrategy to and criticism of Robin Morgan's construction of 'global sisterhood'. Mohanty criticises Morgan for assuming to much homogeneity among women, seeing women as a 'cross-culturally singular, homogeneous group with the same interests, perspectives, and goals and similar experiences' (Mohanty, 2003, p.110). This notion of universal sisterhood seems to eradicate differing historical experiences, for instance experiences of the colonisers *versus* those of the colonised, by trying to situate women outside contemporary world history. Mohanty argues that this is 'a model with dangerous implications for women who do not and cannot speak from a location of white, Western, middle-class privilege' (Mohanty, 2003, p.111). By contrast, Mohanty's proposed concept of solidarity involves 'mutuality, accountability, and the recognition of common interests as the basis for relationships among diverse communities. Rather than assuming an enforced commonality of oppression, the practice of solidarity foregrounds communities of people who have chosen to work and fight together. Diversity and difference are central values here – to be acknowledged and respected, not erased in the building of alliances' (Mohanty, 2003, p.7).

To counter the long-term effects of colonialism and Eurocentrism, Mohanty argues for a thorough process of *decolonialisation*. This concept, which was coined by Fanon in his classic text on colonisation, *The Wretched of the Earth* (1963), involves in Mohanty's words 'profound transformations of self, community, and governance structures. It can only be engaged through active withdrawal of consent and resistance to structures of psychic and social domination' (Mohanty, 2003, p.7). Mohanty illustrates her idea of decolonialisation more clearly, when she presents her evaluation of contemporary approaches of teaching Comparative Feminist Studies in the U.S. university classroom. In recent years, differences of race, class, and sexuality as well as international perspectives have been incorporated into the feminist curriculum. Mohanty supports a 'pedagogy of dissent' that links the global with the local in such a way that prevailing hierarchies and power structures are challenged. She discerns three distinct approaches:

1. *The Feminist-as-Tourist Model*, which Mohanty criticises as merely additive and Eurocentric, since non-Western women are usually stereotyped as victims

---

18 'I outline a notion of feminist solidarity, as opposed to vague assumptions of sisterhood or images of complete identification with the other. For me, such solidarity is a political as well as ethical goal.' (Mohanty, 2003, p.3.)

19 Gayatri Spivak proposed a 'strategic use of essentialism in a scrupulously visible political interest'. (Spivak 1987, 205) To affirm a political identity Spivak suggests that minority groups could use essentialism as a short-term strategy, as long as this identity does not get fixed as essential by the minority or the dominant group. Strategic essentialism is a context-specific strategy, it has to be tailor-made for specific purposes and can not provide long-term political solutions.

of 'exotic' or 'barbaric' cultures.The effects of this strategy are that students and teachers are left with a clear sense of the difference and distance between the local (defined as self, nation, and Western) and the global (defined as other, non-Western, and transnational). (Mohanty, 2003, p.239.)

3. The *Feminist-as-Explorer Model* originated in the field of area studies and, compared to the first model, this one 'can provide a deeper, more contextual understanding of feminist issues in discreetly defined geographical and cultural spaces' (Mohanty, 2003, p.240). Yet, for Mohanty it is still a profoundly inadequate approach which is defined by cultural relativism. This attempt to globalise knowledge is characterised by a 'separate-but-equal' attitude: 'international' here stands for 'outside' of the U.S. nation state and no connections are drawn between the unmarked 'own' culture and the 'other'. Mohanty dismisses this approach because

> [...] globalization is an economic, political, and ideological phenomenon that actively brings the world and its various communities under connected and interdependent discursive and material regimes. The lives of women are connected and interdependent, albeit not the same, no matter which geographical area we happen to live in. (Mohanty, 2003, p.241.)

Clearly,

3. *The Feminist Solidarity or Comparative Feminist Studies Model* is the only one that answers Mohanty's demand for transformation and the one that stimulates self-reflexive processes while at the same time questioning political and social structures of power, agency, and justice.

> This curricular strategy is based on the premise that the local and the global are not defined in terms of physical geography or territory but exist simultaneously and constitute each other. It is then the links, the relationships, between the local and the global that are foregrounded, and these links are conceptual, material, temporal, contextual, and so on. (Mohanty, 2003, p.242.)

Mohanty's comparative feminist studies model accentuates the interconnectedness and interdependence of – sometimes even contradictory – processes as well as experiences of globalisation, and therefore is itself an example of intersectional analysis. She also foregrounds structural inequalities or possibilities for collective action, while paying attention to individual differences, thereby allowing for strategic formations of solidarity.

Feminist sociologist Valentine Moghadam, who is also Chief of the UNESCO Gender Equality and Development Section, explains how transnational feminist networks (TFNs) work and organise themselves to oppose both growing inequalities that are caused by globalisation processes and the increasing impact of patriarchal fundamentalisms on the lives of women. Moghadam combines an analysis of globalisation not only with studies on the growing importance of NGOs for a global civil society and for global social movements but also with an examination of international women's movements and organisations. She shows that globalisation is a multidimensional and gendered process that leads to economic, political, social, and cultural changes and transformations.

> In the 1980s, women began to be disproportionately involved in irregular forms of employment increasingly used to maximize profits; at the same time, they remained responsible for work related to the family. This is to say their growing labor-market participation was not accompanied by a redistribution of domestic, household, and childcare responsibilities, in part due to cutbacks in social services. The changing nature of the state vis-à-vis the public sector meant the withdrawal, deterioration, or privatisation of many public services used by working-class and middle-class women and their families. (Moghadam, 2005, p.7.)

According to Moghadam 2005 was a turning point for the international women's movement. Before the third UN World Conference on Women in Nairobi there was no sense of a 'collective identity'. During the preparations for the conference new forms of 'bridge building and consensus making across regional and ideological divides' developed (Moghadam, 2005, p.6) and gave rise to a global consciousness of women for structural injustices and gender inequality. In *Globalizing Women*, Moghadam focuses on six transnational feminist networks: three TFNs deal with economic and development issues like structural adjustment programmes and are engaged in the global justice movement, namely DAWN (Development Alternatives with Women for a New Era), WIDE (Women in Development Europe), and WEDO (Women's Empowerment and Development Organization). WLUML (Women Living Under Muslim Law) and SIGI (Sisterhood Is Global Institute) promote women's human rights and oppose fundamentalism. AWMR (Association of Women of the Mediterranean Region) is a regional network that engages in peace and demilitarisation. It becomes clear that TFNs are 'structures organized above the national level that unite women from three or more countries around a common agenda, such as women's human rights, reproductive health and rights, violence against women, peace and antimilitarism, or feminist economics' (Moghadam, 2005, p.4). Moghadam claims that the TFNs share common attributes: the reach out beyond 'feminist sisterhood' to practise transnational solidarity; this political solidarity transcends boundaries of differences like class, race, ethnicity, or religion; and, as a movement, they rely on the idea of networks interacting with other networks rather than on forming a single, unified movement and they use network structures to improve their methods of communication and self-organisation.

The interconnectedness of 'First World feminists' and 'Third World feminists' is pointed out by the following development of central issues. In the late 19th and during the twentieth century the feminist movement of 'the West' originally focused on legal equality rights, political participation, and reproductive rights, whereas women in the 'Third World' engaged primarily with economic issues and postcolonial questions. With contemporary globalisation however the situation changed.

> The new economic and political realities led to a convergence of feminist perspectives across the globe: for many First World feminists, economic issues and development policy became increasingly important, and for many Third World feminists, increased

attention was now directed to women's legal status, autonomy, and rights. (Moghadam, 2005, p.8.)

In her study, Moghadam presents the close working relations of transnational institutions and organisations, transnational NGOs, and TFNs. The TFNs are acting globally but are connected to various feminists movements that act locally. Transnational feminist networks contribute to globalisation and collective activism by developing alternatives for economic globalisation that are not synonymous with neoliberal capitalism, and by enhancing democratisation processes and global governance while supporting the welfarist nation-state as key institutional actor. To sum up the interconnectedness of TFNs and globalisation, Moghadam states:

> I argue that global feminism and transnational feminist networks are the logical results of the existence of a capitalist world-economy in an era of globalization, and the universal fact of gender inequality. (Moghadam, 2005, p.20.)

Summary and Outlook

A central insight of feminist theory is the utmost importance of one's awareness of one's own position and of one's embeddedness in a very specific socio-historical, cultural, and political context. Thinking and reasoning therefore always has a specific place from which it starts, it is rooted in a certain socio-geographic locality. For instance, while *business ethics* in Europe is very much engrained in philosophical and economic theory, in North America *business ethics* have a more applied focus. This pragmatic primacy of praxis over theory, respectively theory over praxis in the European context, can be best understood if the different philosophical traditions and dominant schools of philosophical thinking, but also different structures of educational institutions are taken into account. To think about universal goals and values therefore always is confined by one's own situatedness and at the same time, often unwillingly, has the danger of excluding others. Economic theory (as any theory) is never purely descriptive, but always based on the recognition of its inherent, but unmentioned values; theory always serves certain interests, while disguising this very fact as 'disinterested objectivity'. The main aim of feminist interventions is to include the perspectives of women into these claims to universality respectively to radically call the legitimacy of this very claim to universality into question.

It is the end of feminist theory and gender theory to broaden the perspectives of those theories and approaches that still take the white, 'male', heterosexual, Western subject as its main point of reference, and to point out the inherent discriminatory practises. Feminists demand a fair share of 'the good life' that is based on justice, equality, participation, liberty, and well-being. We have shown that due to the manifold internal differences among women and the controversies resulting thereof, feminist thinking had to adopt multiperspectivity and (self-)reflexivity as crucial methods of feminist criticism, and by necessity, had to become interdisciplinary. This opening up of new perspectives, the praxis of constant self-reflexivity of one's own decision-making processes and processes of attribution of meaning is a most significant contribution gender theory and feminist ethics has to offer to theories of *globalisation* in the context of *business ethics*.

To sum up our chapter and to give an outlook of what *gender aspects* mean in connection with *globalisation* and *business ethics* we can surely say that we cannot describe or give an idea of one *singular* perspective on women, feminists or gendered human beings that could become a topic on the to-do-list of any kind of global player to be 'checked off'. Even worse, we cannot formulate more than the one and only goal that consists in preparing the (economic) conditions for everyone in that way that s/he can live her/his life as s/he wants to – within the boundaries we mentioned above – and that means to have the same chances and opportunities to participate in, to lead and to create our social life.

With Judith Butler we are deeply convinced that theory *is* a practical part of shaping, arranging and organising not only our views on the world but the world itself.

> Thus, if 'Feminism is about the social transformation of gender relations ... we must ... have an idea of how theory relates to the process of transformation, whether theory is itself transformative work that has transformation as one of its effects .... But one must also understand that I do not think theory is sufficient for social and political transformation. Something besides theory must take place, such as interventions ...., sustained labour, and institutional practise, which are not quite the same as the exercise of theory. I would add, however, that in all of this practices, theory is presupposed. (Butler, 2004, pp.204–205).[20]

In this context we want to take a look at the meaning of *norms* and *normativity*; two notions whose signification depend on the *theory* and the *context* in which they are used – so, as Butler claims, they have to be seen in their theoretical and practical context to be understood in an adequate manner. Butler argues that she has difficulties to lay out some simple ideas of what *gender* should be, 'in what equality and justice would exist' (Butler, 2004, p.205), because norms and normativity have a double meaning: 'although we need norms in order to live, and to live well, and to know in what direction to transform our social world, we are also constrained by norms in ways that sometimes do violence to us and which, for reasons of social justice, we must oppose.' (Butler, 2004, p.206.) In other words, if we are talking about norms and normativity we face the paradoxical situation that we need norms and normativity, because we cannot do without them, but at the same time 'we do not have to assume that their form is given or fixed' (Butler, 2004, p.207). In addition to this we also have to analyse very clearly and very carefully what kind of norms are needed and are to be conserved – even if norms as social categories are always a kind of violence, because they are at first not chosen, but have enabling functions as, e.g. the languages we are forced to learn – and what kind of norms we want to disrupt, because of their disabling consequences. Gender norms are often used to violate, punish or even kill people who do not fit in, so these norms are to be

---

20 Judith Butler became very famous for her book *gender* Trouble (1990) which has been widely *misunderstood* as a constructivist appeal to change and re-define *sex* and *gender* as you like it – even daily.

opposed without any doubt (Butler, 2004, p.214). That does not mean that people were not allowed to live in different manners, to feel themselves belonging to this or that group of human beings, but that states, rules and normativity are not allowed to prescribe in any way *what kind of differences must be observed* to be respected as a full member of our societies: with or without 'sexual identity', 'sexual orientation', 'racial identity', etc.

In so far as theories are not only built to make descriptions but to find solutions we want to give some advice from a philosophical/theoretical point of view:

- Differences are necessary to reduce complexity and to make propositions about *our* social reality which is mostly binary divided in 'male' and 'female' professions, qualities, properties, etc. But they are to be seen as presuppositions which must be reflected *as* presuppositions: as moral, social, academic, emotional presuppositions which sometimes make sense – e.g. as analytical instruments to make the *status quo* obvious – and sometime make no sense, especially if they are used to describe political goals or to reach aims.
- Differences or concepts that describe and name differences must not be seen as natural essences which preshape the forms of social life unchangeable. Nobody belongs necessarily to this or that group and behaves subsequently in this or that manner.
- Therefore, we *always* have to ask ourselves while using differences: Why do we need them here? What kind of context makes them useful, and which one does not? Whose aim do they serve? Does it really make a difference for the solution looking at the problem using that difference?
- Accordingly we have to ask the same questions using norms and speaking of normativity: What is the reason for norms in the given context? What kind of context makes it necessary to formulate norms? Do we really need them here? What would happen, if we reformulated that norm into its contrary?

In one sentence: Nothing prevents us from using a reflective and critical attitude[21] especially in relation to our own implicitly presupposed differences that shape our perceptions and our ways of thinking. Considering *globalisation* we might say that it belongs to the things 'we' cannot stop – even if we wanted to do so. We could and maybe also should see a chance for equal *conditions* for everybody in the current transformation of the economic conditions world wide, and we should realise that feminist aims cannot be enforced *against* economic change but only *with* it. As scientists and philosophers we have to work on theories that are built to give answers to the problems as we see them, as we 'create' them as a problem and that means that they are not only an image of our reality but also an image of our dreams! If we want to overcome the world's division in better and worse people because of their apparently 'natural essence,' we have to put this as a goal in our theorising and must avoid theoretical reinforcement that provides practical legitimisation.

---

21 *Cf.* Foucault (1984, pp.38–39).

References

Agarwal, B. (1996), From Mexico 1975 to Beijing 1995, *Indian Journal of Gender Studies*, **3**, No. 1, 87-92.

Becker-Schmidt, R. (1993), „Geschlechterdifferenz – Geschlechterverhältnis: soziale Dimensionen des Begriffs ‚Geschlecht", *Zeitschrift für Frauenforschung* no.1-2, 37-46.

—— (2002), *Gender and Work in Transition: Globalization in Western, Middle and Eastern Europe*, Opladen: Leske +Budrich.

Benería, L. (2003), Gender, Development, and Globalization, *Economics as if All People Mattered*, New York: Routledge.

Benhabib, S. (1992), *Situation the Self*, Cambridge: Polity Press.

Butler, J. (2004), *Undoing Gender*, New York: Routledge.

Collins, P.H. (1998), Fighting Words, *Black Women and the Search for Justice*, Minneapolis: University of Minnesota Press.

Crane, A. and Matten, D. (2004), *Business Ethics*, Oxford: Oxford University Press.

Crenshaw, K. (1989), Demarginalizing the Intersection of Race and Sex: A Black Feminist Critique of Antidiscrimination Doctrine, Feminist Theory and Antiracist Politics University of Chicago Legal Forum 1989, 139-67.

FAM, ed. (2005), Better Business – Creating a Gender-Equal Europe!, *Proceedings of the Conference held*, 29–30 October 2004 *in Munich* (Berlin: Copyprint).

Fineman, M.A. and Dougherty, T., eds. (2005), *Feminism Confronts Homo oeconomicus: Gender, Law and Society*, Ithaca: Cornell University Press.

Foucault, M. (1984), What is Enlightenment?, in Rabinow, ed. pp.32-50.

Fraser, N. (2003), Redistribution or Recognition?, *A Political-Philosophical Exchange*, London: Verso.

Fricker, M. and Hornsby, J., eds. (2000), *The Cambridge Companion to Feminism in Philosophy*, Cambridge: Cambridge University Press.

Friedman, M. (2000), Feminism in Ethics: Conceptions of Autonomy, in Fricker and Hornsbyeds , pp.205-224.

Gilligan, C. (1982), *A Different Voice*, Cambridge: Harvard University Press.

Hankinson Nelson, L. and Nelson, J., eds. (1996), *Feminism, Science, and the Philosophy of Science*, Dordrecht: Kluwer Academic Publisher.

Harding, S. (1986), *The Science Question in Feminism*, Ithaca: Cornell University Press.

—— (1991), Whose Science?, *Whose Knowledge? Thinking from Women's Lives*, Ithaca: Cornell University Press.

—— (1996), *Feminist Philosophies of Science, in Hankinson and, Nelson (eds.),* 263-85.

——, and Narayan, U., eds. (2000), *Decentering the Center: Philosophy for a Multicultural, Postcolonial, and Feminist World*, Bloomington, Indiana; University Press.

Harding, S. (2000), *Gender, Development and Post-Enlightenment Philosophies of Science*, in Harding and Naranyan eds, (2000), pp. 211-240.

Hartmann, H.I. (1994), *The Family as the Locus of Gender, Class and Political Struggle: The Example of Housework*, in Herrmann, C. *et al.*, pp.171-197.

Herrmann, C. and Stewart, A.J., eds. (1994), *Theorizing Feminism: Parallel Trends in the Humanities and Social Sciences*, Boulder, Colo.: Westview Press.

Hirsch, J., (1998); V*om Sicherheitsstaat zum nationalen Wettbewerbsstaat*, (Berlin: ID Verlag).

Hobuß, S., Schües, C., Zimnik, N., Hartmann, B. and Patrut, I., eds. (2001), *Die andere Hälfte der Globalisierung: Menschenrechte, Ökonomie und Medialität aus feministischer Sicht*, Frankfurt am Main: Campus.

Honegger, C. and Arni, C., eds. (2001), *Gender – Die Tücken Einer Kategorie*, Zürich: Chronos Verlag.

Jaggar, A. and Young, I., eds. (1998), *A Companion to Feminist Philosophy*, Oxford: Blackwell Publishers.

Kelly, R.M., Bayes, J.H., Hawkesworth, M. and Young, B., eds. (2001), *Gender, Globalization, and Democratization*, Oxford: Rowman & Littlefield Publishers.

Klasen, S. and Wink, C., (2003), 'Missing Women: Revisiting the debate', *Feminist Economics*: Taylor and Francis Journals, 9:2-3, 263-99.

Klingebiel, R. and Randeria, S., eds. (1998), Globalisierung aus Frauensicht, *Bilanzen und Visionen*, Bonn: Dietz.

Kreisky, E., (2001), ‚Die maskuline Ethik des Neoliberalismus – die neoliberale Dynamik des Maskulinismus', in *femina politica* 2/2001, 76-91.

Lemoine, M. (1998), 'Die Arbeiter Zentralamerikas als Geiseln der "maquilas", in *Le Monde diplomatique*, (March), pp.14–15.

Madöring, M. (2005), Economic and Social Policy: Old Patterns of Thinking and New Perspectives, FAM (ed.).

Meyer, M. (2003), 'Moderne Ökonomik und Gender-Analysen,' in Schönwälder-Kuntze *et al.*eds, pp.148-156.

Moghadam, V.M. (2005), Globalizing Women, *Transnational Feminist Networks*, Baltimore: The Johns Hopkins University Press.

Mohanty, C.T. (2003), Feminism without Borders, *Decolonizing Theory, Practicing Solidarity*, New York: Routledge.

Morgan, R. (1984), *Sisterhood Is Global: The International Women's Movement Anthology*, New York: Anchor Press.

Nagl-Docekal H. and Pauer-Studer, H. eds., (1995), *Jenseits der Geschlechtermoral: Beiträge zur feministischen Ethik*, (FaM: Fischer).

Narayan, U. (1997), Dis/locating Cultures, *Identities, Traditions, and Third World Feminism*, New York: Routledge.

O'Neill, O. (1985), Between Consenting Adults, *Philosophy and Public Affairs* 14:3 (Princeton: Princeton University Press).

Pieper, A. (1998), *Gibt es eine feministische Ethik?*, München: Wilhelm Fink Verlag.

Praetorius, I. (1995), *Skizzen zur feministischen Ethik*, Mainz: Matthias-Grünewald-Verlag.

Rabinow, P., ed. (1984), *The Foucault Reader*, New York: Pantheon.

Risman, B.J. (2004), 'Gender as a Social Structure: Theory Wrestling with Activism,' in, *Gender and Society*, August, 2004, 429-451.

Sassen, S. (1998), *Globalization and its Discontents: Essays on the New Mobilities of People and Money*, New York: New Press.

Schönwälder-Kuntze, T. and Wille, K. (2003), 'Einleitung,' in Schönwälder-Kuntze *et al.*eds , pp.13-23.

Schönwälder-Kuntze, T. *et al.*, eds. (2003), Störfall Gender, *Grenzsdiskussionen in und zwischen den Wissenschaften*, Wiesbaden: Westdeutscher Verlag.

Schott, R. (1998), Kant, in Jaggar and Youngeds , pp.39-48.

Schroeter, T. (2002), *Globalisierung*, Hamburg: Europäische Verlagsanstalt.

—— (2001), Millennial Fantasies: The Future of "Gender" in the 21st Century, in Honegger *et al.*eds , pp.19-37.

Scott, J.W. (1986), Gender: A Useful Category of Historical Analyses, in American *Historical Review* 91:5 (Dec. 1986), 1053-75.

Sen, A. (1990), Gender and Cooperative Conflicts, in Tinker eds , pp.123-149.

Shohat, E. and Stam, R. (1994), Unthinking Eurocentrism, *Multiculturalism and the Media*, London: Routledge.

Spivak, G. (1987), *Other Worlds. Essays in Cultural Politics*, New York: Methuen.

Teusch, U. (2004), Was ist Globalisierung?, *Ein Überblick*, Darmstadt: Primus Verlag.

Tinker, I., ed. (1990), *Persistent Inequalities*, New York: Oxford University Press.

United Nations (1995), *Report on the Fourth World Conference on Women*, Beijing, 4-15 September 1995. http://www.un.org/esa/gopher-data/conf/fwcw/off/a--20.en.

Wichterich, C. (1998), Die globalisierte Frau, *Berichte aus der Zukunft der Ungleichheit*, Reinbek: Rowohlt.

World Bank (2002), Integrating Gender into the World Bank's Work: a Strategy for Action. http://siteresources.worldbank.org/INTGENDER/Resources/ strategypaper.pdf.

World Economic Forum (2005), *Women's Empowerment: Measuring the Global Gender Gap*, http://www.weforum.org/pdf/Global_Competitiveness_Reports/ Reports/gender_gap.pdf.

Young, B. (2001), Globalization and Gender: A European Perspective, in Kelly, R. M. *et al.*, pp.27-47.

PART II

GLOBALISATION, BUSINESS AND CORPORATE GOVERNANCE

Chapter 5

Globalisation of Corporate Governance: The Difficult Process of Bringing About European Union Internal and External Corporate Governance Principles

Klaus J. Hopt

International Concepts of Corporate Governance: Internal and External Corporate Governance

Concepts and Phenomenon of Corporate Governance

Corporate governance is a problem area that is discussed today globally. The word – and indeed the concept – is Anglo-Saxon. In the European continent, both the word and the concept were more or less unknown until the middle of the 1990s. In Germany there is not even a German word for it: the term is used in its original English version. It is the same in many other countries, with the exception, for example, of France, which has always been more conscious of its own language and uses the term '*le gouvernement de l'entreprise*'. In Germany the English term is not only used in economic and legal publications[1] but even the official 'German Corporate Governance Code' of 2002[2] and indeed the German Stock Corporation Act as amended in 2002, use the term. The German Corporate Governance Code is a voluntary code that is based on the work of the Governmental Commission Corporate Governance of 2001[3] and was formulated by the Governmental Commission Corporate Governance Code. It was backed by the legislature in a mandatory provision prescribing the 'disclose-or-comply' principle for German listed companies.[4] Neither the Code nor the legislature tries to define what is meant by corporate governance, but the Code mentions in the foreword that it contains 'internationally and nationally recognised

---

1 See the comprehensive references in Hommelhoff (2003) with contributions from economics, law, and business practice.

2 Deutscher Corporate Governance Kodex, Düsseldorf 26.2.2002, in the meantime in its 2005 version.

3 Baums (2001).

4 § 161 of the German Stock Corporation Act as modified by Chapter 1 of the Law on Transparency and Disclosure of 19.7.2002, Official Gazette I 2681.

standards of good and responsible governance of corporations.'[5] Indeed, corporate governance reaches far beyond what is covered in traditional stock corporation law. It is a short term for the totality of the legal and factual rules for the management and control of the enterprise.[6] This concept is more economic than legal, unless legal is understood in a functional comparative law understanding, and the spreading of the concept illustrates well that corporate governance has been international from its very beginning, and that today it is a global phenomenon.

The problem of corporate governance as such is not new; it reaches back to the beginning of the modern stock corporation. The latter is characterised by the fact that the persons who manage and govern the corporation and those to whom the corporation 'belongs' are not the same. This is the well-known Berle-Means phenomenon of the separation of ownership and control, but it was already described by Adam Smith in his famous work of 1776, *An Inquiry into the Nature and Causes of the Wealth of Nations*:[7]

> The directors of such companies,[8] however, being the managers rather of other people's money than of their own, it cannot well be expected, that they should watch over it with the same anxious vigilance with which the partners in a private copartnery frequently watch over their own .... Negligence and profusion, therefore, must always prevail, more or less, in the management of the affairs of such a company.

This problem of the negligent or even unfaithful management of others people's money concerns primarily the internal affairs of the corporation, i.e., the management and control by the board, whether it is a unitary board as in Anglo-American countries, or a two-tier board where management or its delegation lies with the management board while control stays with the supervisory board (as, for example, in Germany). Accordingly, in the USA the corporate governance movement is concerned with the position, duties, and responsibility of the directors of the corporation.[9] The same is true for the Code of Conduct movement, which has its origin in the United Kingdom and has its focus on the board of directors, its committees, and the control over its action by the auditors of the corporation. The same is true, for example, for the German Corporate Governance Code. Apart from some recommendations concerning the rights of the shareholders and the general assembly, the German Code deals primarily with the two boards and the cooperation between them.

Internal and External Corporate Governance

The German Corporate Governance Code contains a final section which deals with the annual report and the auditing. This is indeed important and illustrates that corporate governance is more than traditional stock corporation law. It is not just

---

5   Cromme, G., Chairman of the Governmental Commission German Corporate Governance Code in the Preface to the Code.

6   Von Werder (2003a), 4.

7   Adam Smith (1789).

8   I.e., public companies.

9   See the pathbreaking contribution of Eisenberg (1994).

concerned with the internal affairs of the corporation, but with its appearance to and impact on the investing public and the capital markets. However, as mentioned before, corporate governance reaches further, comprising the totality of the legal and factual rules for the management and control of the enterprise. This means that the market and its disciplining function for the corporations and their boards cannot be disregarded. Accordingly, the modern international and interdisciplinary discussion covers both internal and external corporate governance. As to the latter, the market for corporate control is of prime importance. It is regulated in the 13th European directive on takeovers, which will be dealt with in the last part of this report.

The International Development of the Corporate Governance Discussion

The International Corporate Governance Discussion

As mentioned previously, corporate governance is a concept and a movement that stems from the USA. This is hardly surprising, for the problems of corporate governance were first observed and became pressing in the country with the most shareholders and the broadest capital market in the world. Similarly, in Europe corporate governance was first discussed and developed in the United Kingdom. There the stock corporations are typically not family owned or controlled by blockholders as in most countries on the European continent; instead, the shares are held by a multitude of small shareholders who are not in a position to control the management by themselves, but must rely on the board of directors to do this for them.

Starting from the USA and the United Kingdom, corporate governance has made a triumphant march into the modern industrial states of the New and the Old World.[10] In a collection edited by a Belgian colleague Eddy Wymeersch and myself in 1997[11] only the most important contributions were presented: documents from seven countries, starting with the USA and Canada, continuing with the United Kingdom, France, Belgium, and the Netherlands, and finishing with Germany. In the meantime, contributions and research projects can be found all over the world[12] *inter alia* in Scandinavia, Switzerland, the Commonwealth countries, Japan, and the formerly socialist transformation countries in Middle and Eastern Europe. Parts of the *Comparative Corporate Governance* volume of 1998 have been translated into Chinese, and in China there is an acute interest in the corporate governance developments in the USA and Europe. In 1993, a specialised international English-language review called *Corporate Governance* was founded[13] and since 1995 there has been a European Corporate Governance Network with its seat in Brussels. More

---

10 As to II 1 und 2, see in more detail Hopt (2000) with further references.

11 Hopt and Wymeersch (1997) and the comprehensive review by Zimmer (1999).

12 A bibliography of international and interdisciplinary contributions can be found in Hopt et al. (1998) at 1201-1210. See also in Hopt and Wymeersch (2003), Hopt et al. (2005), and Gillan (2006).

13 *Corporate Governance: an international review*, Hong Kong (since 1992); furthermore, for example: *Corporate Governance International* (CGI), Hong Kong (since 1998); *Journal*

recently, this institution was transformed into the European Corporate Governance Institute (ECGI). Members include academics of various disciplines, in particular economists and lawyers, and practitioners from many countries who are striving to better understand and improve corporate governance. The ECGI advises the European Commission and organises for it the Transatlantic Corporate Governance Dialogue in cooperation with the American Law Institute. Two annual meetings of the Transatlantic Corporate Governance Dialogue have already taken place, one in Brussels in 2004 and another in New York in 2005. Both have attracted great attention and have contributed to an easing of the transatlantic supervisory cooperation which can be politically difficult at times, in particular after Enron and the U.S. Sarbanes-Oxley Act. The Institute has a website with comprehensive information and edits two working paper series.[14] Today corporate governance is also of great concern to stock exchanges, banks, industry associations, and even the parliaments of many countries. In the aftermath of the crises at Enron, WorldCom, Parmalat and others, far-reaching legislative reforms concerning corporate law, auditing, stock exchange regulation, and capital market law have been enacted or initiated. Many of them name better corporate governance as their aim, while some contribute to it at least in substance.

The International Corporate Code of Conduct Movement

Codes of conduct are not statutory or other legal norms but are non-legal, more or less voluntary, standards of behaviour. Their rules and recommendations are usually elaborated by the specialists of the profession concerned, either at their own initiative because they care for the reputation and the future of their profession and are simultaneously acting out of ethical considerations, or by official mandate of the government and the legislature which, for one reason or another, are not (yet) prepared to go forward with binding legal norms.

The code of conduct movement – i.e., the attempt to improve corporate governance not by law with continually new law reforms, but by voluntary codes of good conduct, in particular for the board of directors – has its origin in the United Kingdom. Its beginning can be traced to the Report of the Committee on the Financial Aspects of Corporate Governance, the so-called Cadbury Report of 1992. Its key recommendations have been made binding for all corporations listed at the London Stock Exchange. The recommendations of the report concerned, *inter alia*, the inclusion of non-executive directors, the majority of whom should be independent of management; a mere 3-year term for contracts of executive directors unless agreed upon differently with the shareholders; transparency of the remuneration of the directors (with disclosure of the total amount of remuneration for all of them together, of the chairman and of the highest paid UK director); and the formation

---

of Management and Governance, Kluwer (since 1997); *Corporate Governance Newsletter* (since 1998) and many others.

14 'Law Series' und 'Financial Series': <http://www.ecgi.de>. Contact: <admin@ecgi.org>. See in the Law Series the early contribution on the impact of Enron on European corporate governance by Hopt (2003).

of an audit committee with at least three independent directors. Furthermore, the recommendations also covered certain tasks and responsibilities, a report on the effectiveness of the internal control system, the relationship between the board and the auditors, and many other matters. The Cadbury Code was followed in 1995 by a report of the same committee on 'Compliance with the Code of Best Practice' which had a high impact in the City of London, and in the same year by the Greenbury Report on 'Directors' Remuneration: The Code of Best Practice', and in January 1998 by the Final Report of the Committee on Corporate Governance, the so-called Hampel Report. Since 1998 the recommendations of these three reports on corporate governance have been consolidated in the Combined Code of the London Stock Exchange, named 'Principles of Good Governance and Code of Best Practice'. It was added to the Listing Rules as an annex. The Combined Code was reformed in July 2003.

After the Enron crisis, the corporate governance work continued, not only in the USA, but also in the United Kingdom and in many other countries.[15] This is true in particular for the New York Stock Exchange. There the requirements for corporate governance, and in particular for the independence of the directors and the composition of the audit committees, have been stiffened considerably.

Most of the countries on the European continent experienced a similar code of conduct movement as in the United Kingdom. This movement continued with the OECD Principles on Corporate Governance, which have been revised and considerably improved but are more relevant for Middle and Eastern European countries, Asia, and Latin America than for the Western countries where detailed corporate governance codes already exist. The development in the member states of the European Union has been described in detail by the report for the European Commission of January 2002.[16] This report found corporate governance codes in 13 out of then 15 member states. Most of those came into existence in and after 1997. In the meantime, Austria also has such a code. In several of these member states there are not only one but several such codes. *In toto* the report covered around 40 codes and analysed them as to their content, reach, effect, and other relevant parameters. Key questions concern, *inter alia*, labour codetermination (here there are the greatest differences); protection of the shareholders only or also of the creditors (i.e., social and stakeholders issues); shareholder rights; the board, namely, the management board and the supervisory board; the independence of directors; and the functioning of the controlling organ, board committees, and transparency.

---

15 As a result of the post-Enron initiatives, several final reports were presented in the UK: in June 2002 the Higgs Report on the role of the non-executive directors, in December 2002 the Smith Report on improving the work of the audit committees, the Report of the Coordinating Group on Audit and Accounting Issues and of the Team at the Department of Trade and Industry on the Review of the Regulatory Regime of the Accountancy Profession, the two latter in January 2003.

16 Weil, Gotshal and Manges (2002).

Building Blocks of a System of Internal and External Corporate Governance

Corporate governance is the topic of contributions by very different disciplines and of many different countries. Many of them concern particular aspects of governance or the impact of the market conditions in the particular country on corporate governance. More recently, special attention has been focused on the diversity and/or the convergence of corporate governance systems. This research area is now globally named 'comparative corporate governance.'

It is obviously difficult or even impossible to grasp the highly heterogeneous approaches and aspects of this international and interdisciplinary discussion. One attempt to look into it has been made in the book *Comparative Corporate Governance: The State of the Art and Emerging Research*, published in 1998 by Oxford University Press.[17] This work isolates six building blocks of a system of corporate governance: 1) the board, 2) labour and labour codetermination, 3) the banks, 4) the stock exchange and the capital market, 5) the market for corporate control, i.e., takeovers, and 6) transparency and auditing. These building blocks can be found in all national corporate governance systems in various combinations and intensity. Each particular combination is a product of history and the unique conditions prevailing in the given country. This is called path dependence.[18]

The Board

The most important building block of each corporate governance system is the organ of the corporation to which management and control is entrusted by the shareholders. In the German stock corporation, the shareholders have mandated the management board with running the corporation and the supervisory board with the task of controlling the management board. This fundamental division between the two organs has been mandatory for more than a century and has never been seriously called into question by legislative reform. Only most recently has the German legislature been required by the European Union to provide for a one-tier board choice in the European Company, the so-called Societas Europaea. But this choice is confined to this new corporate form and not open to the traditional German stock corporation. Internationally, the two-tier board system is not as common as the one-tier board system, which prevails in the Anglo-Saxon countries as well as Switzerland and many other states.

There is much controversy as to the advantages and disadvantages of both systems.[19] In the City of London, the unitary board is generally thought to be better. The findings of the Cadbury Commission make this very clear. In contrast, in Germany the predominant opinion both in theory and in practice holds that the obligatory division between governing body and control institution is preferable – even though the practice shows intermediate or 'gray' situations, such as when a

---

17 Hopt *et al.* (1998).

18 The following considerations on the six building blocks are elaborated in more detail in Hopt (2001).

19 See the impressive transnational dialogue of Lutter (2001) and Davies (2001).

weak management board faces an overpowering supervisory board (as in the case of a majority stockholder) or, on the other hand, when a publicly owned company with diversified shareholdings has such a powerful management board that it practically chooses its own supervisory board. Some countries – for example, France and Italy – have drawn their consequences from this and allow their companies to choose between a one-tier system and a two-tier system. In Italy, corporations can choose from even more than two options. This could actually be the best solution because it would be the responsibility of the corporations to choose the system that fits them best; for example, a smaller company might choose only one institution which is more flexible and less costly, while larger or international corporations could decide on giving the control to a separate organ.

Labour and Codetermination

Corporate governance is also affected by the workforce of the enterprise, the trade unions and the labour markets. This is particularly so if there is a mandatory system of labour codetermination in the corporate board, as in Germany. Labour codetermination has been questioned vigorously in economic theory, especially by economists and legal academics from the USA and Great Britain. At an international level, co-determination is strictly opposed in the Anglo-American countries. And even on the European continent, it appears in its full parity and *quasi*-parity form only in the Netherlands and in Germany. It is telling that in the Netherlands, multinational companies were never required to have full-fledged labour codetermination, and most recently the Netherlands are even moving away from their *quasi*-parity co-optation system and are going for a mere one-third parity model. More rights for the plant council under workplace codetermination and only a one-third parity in the board is indeed the most common pattern on the European continent. Furthermore, it is well known that the question of labour codetermination has been the main obstacle for a European harmonisation of company law for decades. A compromise solution was finally found for the European Company: a special codetermination directive provides for initial bargaining between capital and labour. Yet in the case of a deadlock, the strongest form of codetermination valid for one of the partner companies prevails, and this will nearly always be the German one. Though labour codetermination at parity seemed not to have been called into question by German business for decades, this has definitely changed since 2003. In a more and more globalised world, German business leaders are afraid to be at a competitive disadvantage by this far-reaching codetermination system, which is clearly not liked or even imitated abroad. Yet their call for legislative reform[20] has little chance to be heard, certainly not by a coalition government that comprises the Social Democratic Party as well as the Christian Democratic Party. But even the latter alone is afraid of a fundamental clash with the trade unions. The economic evaluation of labour codetermination is difficult, both on the microeconomic theoretical level and even more empirically. The German model is certainly path dependent: it was introduced in the years 1920 and 1945–49 as a result of the lost wars and with the goal to begin anew with combined strength,

---

20 Cf. von Werder (2003).

as an institutional determinant to uphold a climate of confidence and collaboration between investors and employees.

The Banks

The influence of German banks, in particular the large private banks, on corporations has traditionally been significant when compared with other countries, especially the USA and the United Kingdom. What has been criticised most often is the combination of four means of influence by the banks: providing credit; holding block participations in large corporations; deputising bank representatives onto the boards of large corporations, sometimes even as chairman of the supervisory board; and the depository vote, i.e., the practice of representing the shareholders in the general assemblies and exercising their votes according to their instructions. In addition, German investment company business is usually in the hands of the banks, investment companies being their subsidiaries. All this has led to criticism in legal and economic literature and from politicians and the press, and the 'power of the banks' has been denounced as an obstacle to good corporate governance in Germany.

In the meantime, it has become clear that the situation must be seen in a much more realistic and nuanced way.[21] First there is the fact that economic concentration of the German banking sector and the market share of private banks are rather small compared to the situation in the European Union. Quite the contrary, there is now a vivid discussion about how the private banking sector could be strengthened by more merger activity, both in the private banking sector itself and between the private and the larger public banking sector, particularly the savings institutions and their head institutions in the various German *Länder*. Most recently, there has even been growing concern as to whether the large German banks will be able to improve their cost-profit situation, to come to grips with combining credit banking and investment banking, and not to fall back further in the rank of the largest international banks. Otherwise they face the danger of being taken over like the Munich HypoVereinsbank by the Italian Unicredito.

The Stock Exchange and the Capital Market

Corporate governance is also a matter for stock exchanges and capital markets. This fourth building block clearly concerns external corporate governance. As to the influence of the capital markets on corporate governance, it suffices to say that a functioning equity market – above all the assessment of the company and its shares on the stock market – continuously affects the control of the company and its management most objectively and efficiently. The Anglo-American system, with its controls through the equity market, is often contrasted with the traditional German and Japanese systems, which are characterised by the role of their banks. Indeed, a scale might be drawn with the German system and its strongly bank-orientated financing, concentrated ownership relations, and not overly liquid equity markets

---

21 See Hopt (1999).

at one end of the scale, and the American and maybe the British system with strong market-orientated financing, diversified holding instead of block holdings, and highly liquid equity markets at the other end of the scale.[22] This scaling – as it is rather crudely maintained by some – corresponds to the German Stock Corporation Act, which is adjusted to the needs of the company and its stakeholders, as compared to the USA and to a lesser degree Great Britain, where company law and practice are orientated toward the shareholders and shareholder value. However, more important than such scaling and typologies is more empirical research as to the relevance of national capital markets and corporate governance.[23]

The Market for Corporate Control

Traditionally, a functioning market for corporate control has been lacking in Germany, while in many other European states – such as the United Kingdom, but also France and Belgium – such a market has existed for a long time. Hostile takeovers in particular were practically unknown in Germany until recently and are still rare, though the famous Krupp/Thyssen case and more recently Vodafone/Mannesmann have signalled a turning point in Germany, with each being followed by hectic political and legislative activities. Since 2002, Germany also has its takeover statute.[24] This statute was enacted as a clear reaction to European developments and global influence. During the legislative process, there was a discussion on whether to wait until the 13th directive on takeovers was enacted or to go ahead and respond proactively to the international takeover movement and the changes in the takeover market. The latter was held to be unavoidable. In the meantime, the 13th directive was finalised in April 2004. This will necessitate considerable modifications in most member states, including Germany, though one of the main decisions of the German statute – on the permissibility of frustrating actions by the board of the target – will remain as it stands. In spite of this, the 13th directive will have an impact on the market of corporate control and on external corporate governance, as will be shown in the last part of this report.

Transparency, Disclosure, and Auditing

In all countries, transparency, disclosure, and auditing play a key role in corporate governance. Transparency and disclosure in their various forms are particularly relevant if they are audited by independent auditors. In this way, the market participants receive reliable information about the corporations and their investment in them; from a regulatory standpoint, disclosure is a less intrusive interference that is more compatible with market processes than legislation, particularly mandatory rules. Apart from the periodic disclosure, in particular via the annual report, there is now the European rule on instant disclosure of a great number of market-relevant

---

22 See Berglöf (1997).

23 See, for example, Barca and Becht (2001).

24 Cf. the survey by Hopt (2002). In the meantime there is a host of commentaries and contributions in academic and professional journals.

events concerning the enterprise as prescribed by the Market Abuse Directive. The reporting duties concerning block holdings should also be mentioned. Under European law they start at the level of 10 percent, in most countries at 5 percent, and in the United Kingdom already at 3 percent. Under the impression of the growing influence of hedge funds on corporations, there is a tendency in Germany and some other countries to lower the level down to 3 per cent in order to give the corporation the chance to know about the building up of voting blocks of a possibly hostile bidder at a very early stage. In the aftermath of Enron and the other spectacular corporation breakdowns, it is clear that in the future there will be an increased emphasis, nationally and internationally, on disclosure, and as a consequence on auditing and more independence of the auditors.

Internal Corporate Governance and the European Union

The Action Plan on Company Law and Corporate Governance of 21 May 2003:
Development, Reactions, Implementation, Further Consultation

On 21 May 2003 the European Commission presented its Action Plan on 'Modernising Company Law and Enhancing Corporate Governance in the European Union'.[25] With this plan, the European Commission started a completely new chapter of European company law and corporate governance in the European Union. The Action Plan is bound to influence the discussion surrounding corporate practice in the coming years.

In nearly all relevant issues, the Action Plan followed the second report of the so-called High Level Group of Company Law Experts[26] on 'A Modern Regulatory Framework for Company Law in Europe' of 4 November 2002.[27] This group of experts was mandated by the European Commission to relaunch the discussion between the Commission and the European Parliament on the 13th directive on takeovers, a decision which had come to a full stop when the Parliament voted down the Commission proposal of 2002. The Group considered the controversial takeover issues in its first report, which will be discussed *infra*. The second report of around 150 pages dealt with a number of general company law issues, such as formation and maintenance of capital, groups of companies and corporate pyramids, restructuring enterprises and corporate mobility, and new European corporate forms (such as the

---

25 European Commission (2003). The Action Plan and its aftermaths are analysed by Hopt (2005).

26 Chairman: Jaap Winter (at that time) chief legal counsel of UNILEVER and professor at the University of Rotterdam. The other members were: J. M. Garrido Garcia, chief legal counsel of the Spanish supervisory authority and professor, Madrid; K. J. Hopt, Max Planck Institut for Comparative and International Private Law, Hamburg; J. Rickford, counsel of the Department of Trade and Industry, London; G. Rossi, fomer president of the Italian supervisory agency CONSOB, professor and attorney in Milan; J. Schans Christensen, professor and attorney in Copenhagen; as well as J. Simon, director for legal affairs at the French employers organisation MEDEF, Paris.

27 High Level Group of Company Law Experts (2002b).

European Private Company, a sort of European limited liability company, or the European foundation). Yet its main focus was on corporate governance questions. Four of these stand out: 1) the role of the non-executive directors viz. the members of the supervisory board in a two-tier system; 2) the remuneration of board members; 3) the responsibility of the board for financial information to the public; and 4) auditing practices.

After presenting the Action Plan, the European Commission opened a public consultation for all those concerned. The result was predominantly positive, though obviously the details were controversial (and remain so). In the meantime, many of the actions planned for the first period (short term 2003–2005) have already been realised, including the directive on cross-border mergers of limited liability companies of 26 October 2005,[28] the recommendations on remuneration of 14 December 2004[29] and on independent directors of 15 February 2005,[30] and draft directives on capital maintenance and alteration of 29 October 2004[31] and on shareholder rights of 5 January 2006.[32]

Before entering the second phase of implementation of the Action Plan, the new Commissioner McCreevey started a second consultation on the Action Plan which culminated in a public hearing in Brussels on 3 May 2006. Around 300 participants took part in this hearing and followed the presentation and discussion in four panels: 1) shareholders' rights and obligations, 2) modernisation and simplification of European company law, 3) responsibility of directors and internal control, and 4) corporate mobility and restructuring. For the written consultation, more than 250 responses from all major stakeholders were received, not only from member states but also from the U.S., Switzerland, and Japan. The European Commission announced that a detailed report on the answers received would be published shortly. The overall impression is that, while deregulation and better regulation are important goals and there is a call for slowing down the regulatory activity in general, there are a number of actions which the European Commission is encouraged to follow up soon, in particular the 14th directive, the European Private Company Statute, the European Foundation Statute, and certain actions concerning corporate governance and the rights of shareholders, in particular mandatory special investigation. It remains to be seen how the European Commission will proceed in the near future. Even if certain actions of the Action Plan are not followed up on, they remain on the agenda of the discussion on company law reform and better corporate governance in Europe and in the member states.

The Content of the Action Plan Concerning Corporate Governance

For the purposes of the present chapter, it is sufficient to present the summary of the original Action Plan of the European Commission as summed up in its Annex 1.

---

28 European Parliament and Council (2005).
29 European Commission (2004a).
30 European Commission (2005).
31 European Commission (2004b).
32 European Commission (2006).

This summary shows clearly that corporate governance is the most important topic on the agenda. This corresponds to the global relevance and discussion of corporate governance.

Table 5.1   Corporate Governance: Short-Term Actions (2003-2005)

Description of action	*Preferred type of initiative*
Enhanced corporate governance disclosure amending requirements (including confirmation of collective responsibility of board members for key non financial statements)	legislative (directive existing legislation)
Integrated legal framework to facilitate efficient shareholder communication and decision-making (participation to meetings, exercise of voting rights, cross-border voting)	legislative (directive)
Strengthening the role of independent nonexecutive (recommendation) and supervisory directors	non legislative
Fostering an appropriate regime for directors (recommendation) remuneration	non legislative
Confirming at EU level the collective amending responsibility of board members for financial statements	legislative (directive existing legislation)
Convening a European Corporate Governance Forum to coordinate corporate governance efforts of Member States	non legislative (Commission initiative)

Table 5.2   Corporate Governance: Medium-Term Actions (2006-2008)

Description of action	*Preferred type of initiative*
Enhanced disclosure by institutional investors of their investment and voting policies	legislative (directive)
Choice for all listed companies between the two types (monistic/dualistic) of board structures	legislative (directive)
Enhancing the responsibilities of board members (special investigation right, wrongful trading rule, director's disqualification)	legislative (directive or directive amending existing legislation)
Examination of the consequences of an approach aiming at achieving a full shareholder democracy (one share / one vote), at least for listed companies	non legislative (study)

Apart from these actions which are described expressly as corporate governance measures, the European Commission's Action Plan has mentioned many other company law reform measures that concern corporate governance as well, though some only indirectly. These include capital maintenance, groups of companies and corporate pyramids, restructuring, the European Private Company, EU legal forms, and transparency of national legal forms.

External Corporate Governance and the European Union

The Controversial History of the 13th Directive on Takeovers of 21 April 2004 and the Different Philosophies as to External Corporate Governance

European law not only deals with internal corporate governance, but with external corporate governance as well. There is a large part of European statutory law that deals with banks, financial intermediaries, stock exchanges, and the capital market. The Financial Market Action Plan of 1999 was an impressive jump forward, and indeed was the model for the Company Law Action Plan itself. Though corporate governance – or more precisely, external corporate governance – was rarely mentioned in the relevant statutory laws and their preambles, it is clear that there was considerable disciplining impact on corporations and their governance. The 13th directive on takeovers was on the agenda of the Financial Market Action Plan from the very beginning, and here the nexus with external corporate governance was most clear and direct. Public takeover bids challenge the board of the target and its performance and give the shareholders the option of *exit*, especially if there is a provision for a mandatory bid to be made by the offerer if a certain control threshold, usually 30 percent or more, is reached. Traditional research has underlined the disciplinary function of takeover bids, especially – but not exclusively – of hostile bids. It is true that more recent empirical literature[33] has cast doubts on this function because both badly managed and well-managed companies with a bright future have been seen to be targets of public takeover bids. But it may be assumed that the threat of takeovers may have as much effect as actual takeovers on boards and that the takeover threat, though not inducing the board to maximise shareholder utility, may at least put a floor under board performance.[34]

The history of the 13th directive is long. The first proposal of the European Commission goes back to 1985. Already at that time, the British model prevailed because of the United Kingdom's and the City of London's long experience with public takeovers. The first report on takeover regulation for the Commission, the Pennington Report, had already been written in the 1970s by a company law expert from the United Kingdom. After several draft directives and a long period of discussion and quarrel, the European Council finally agreed on 19 June 2000 to a Common Position. What happened afterwards, when the German Chancellor Schröder withdrew unilaterally from this agreement under the influence of the Volkswagen corporation, is as thrilling as an international political detective story.[35] The end of it is well known. The European Parliament voted down the draft directive on 4 July 2001 with 273–273 votes. Still in the same month, the European Commission declared that it would present a new proposal. This was not only for face-keeping,

---

33 Franks and Mayer (1996); Franks, Mayer and Renneboog (2001).
34 Davies (2002), p.212.
35 Hopt (2003b), p.529.

but because the Commission rightly held takeover regulation to be a cornerstone of the European internal market and of external corporate governance. During the conciliation process, Commissioner Bolkestein and the European Parliament agreed that a group of international experts should explore how to proceed. Accordingly, in September 2001 the above-mentioned High Level Group of Company Law Experts was mandated. It presented its report on 10 January 2002[36] and the European Commission followed most of its recommendations in its new draft directive of 2 October 2002.[37]

One of the key controversial issues of the new draft was the antifrustration rule, which was shaped according to the British model. The idea of this rule is that it is not for the board of the target to decide whether a takeover bid should be successful or not; instead, the decision on engaging in frustrating action against a hostile bid should be up to the shareholders. Against this principle, it is argued by some that allowing the board to frustrate a takeover bid can be justified as a means of taking into consideration shareholder interests (the so-called collective action problem) and interests of other stakeholders in the company (i.e., the creditors of the company and, most prominently among them, the employees). This view was rightly rejected because of the unsolvable conflict of interests with which the managers are faced in a takeover situation, i.e., saving their own positions while pretending, or sometimes even being convinced, to act in the best interest of the company, its shareholders, and/or its employees. Instead, shareholders should be able to decide themselves, and stakeholders should be protected by specific rules on information, deliberation, and procedures of lay-off.

It is true that the board of American companies generally has broad discretion to put up defensive devices under the business judgement rule, which sometimes amounts to the so-called just-say-no rule. Yet the broad discretion of US companies to put up defensive mechanisms operates in a general legal and capital market environment which differs widely from the European environment. The US environment includes pressures on American boards to enhance shareholder value; the pressures from non-executive directors on the board, from investment banks and advisers, and in particular from institutional investors; the scrutiny of the media; the threat of a later proxy fight; and last but not least derivative actions and liability suits. Furthermore, takeover activity in the U.S. is intensive and European companies benefit to a very large extent from that activity. The current anti-takeover rules in the U.S. are contested even over there by an important body of both economic and legal literature arguing that the ultimate decision on takeover bids should not be by the board alone without involvement of the shareholders.[38] The view that the American rule would work very differently in Europe is shared by experienced businessmen such as former Mannesmann CEO Klaus Esser, who lost the spectacular takeover battle against hostile Vodafone, and the Chief Financial Officer of Allianz, Paul Achleitner.

---

36 High Level Group of Company Law Experts (2002a).
37 European Commission (2002).
38 For example, Bebchuk (2002).

The new draft proposal of the Commission of 2002 was also the object of long and bitter controversy. Germany did not want to change its takeover statute which it had just introduced in 2001 and which permitted the management board of the target to engage in defensive actions with the consent of the supervisory board. France and Sweden wanted to keep their double or multiple voting rights by any means. The Swedish Wallenberg family toured the capitals of Europe in order to find support for the Swedish position. The Parliament was not satisfied by the draft proposal because it did not really procure a level playing field in Europe and insisted on doing away with the double and multiple voting right by the breakthrough mechanism. Commissioner Bolkestein did not want to change the key provisions of the 2002 proposal and thought of letting the draft die for good rather than agreeing to a considerably watered-down version. In this context, it must be remembered that the Commission alone has the right to present a draft directive. So until the very end it was open whether there would be a European takeover directive at all.

The Content of the 13th Directive on Takeovers of 21 April 2004 and the Future of External Corporate Governance in the European Union

A compromise solution was finally found and accepted on 22 December 2003. The compromise consisted of the option model.[39] This route had first been proposed by the Portuguese delegation to the Council and was then taken up during the Italian Council Presidency. The final version of the directive of 21 April 2004 is a mere framework directive which leaves many details to the member states for regulation, thereby respecting the principle of subsidiarity. This is also in line with what many economists prefer, namely more competition of legislators. The directive relates to takeover bids for the securities of companies governed by the laws of member states, where all or some of those securities are admitted to trading on a regulated market. The three most controversial topics were the competence of the home or host state supervisory agencies in the case of takeover bids, the mandatory bid, and the prohibition of frustrating actions by the board of the target.

The first issue was solved by dividing the competences of supervision between the host state and the home state (Chapter 4). The details are highly complicated. Here it suffices to say that as a matter of principle, supervision takes places where the target has its registered office if its securities are admitted to trading in that member state. In specific other cases, matters relating to the bid price and the bid procedure are to be dealt with in the host state, while matters relating to the workforce of the target, to company law, to the percentage of voting rights which confers control, and matters concerning frustrating measures are reserved for the home state. The member states' fear of losing the last word in cases of transnational takeovers obviously prevailed.

The mandatory bid is the primary means of protecting the minority shareholders of the target in the case of takeovers. Once the bidder directly or indirectly acquires control of the target, it must offer minority shareholders the option to buy them out at an equitable price (Chapter 5). The threshold of control is not fixed in the directive itself, but most European member states have chosen a threshold of 30

---

39 European Parliament and Council (2004).

percent of the voting rights. The mandatory bid protects the minority shareholders by an early *exit* option if they fear the risk of future negative changes in the target by the new controlling shareholder. This protection is needed even in countries like Germany where there is a full-fledged group-of-companies law, since the latter comes in too late, i.e., only when a group has already come into existence, and the legal proceedings under this law can take many years. The directive also gives guidance on what constitutes an equitable price.

The most controversial issue was the prohibition of frustrating action. This is sometimes also called the neutrality principle, even though the board of the target must not really remain neutral since it has the right and the duty to report to the shareholders how it evaluates the bid, and it may very well advise the shareholders not to accept it. The board is also free to look for a white knight, an action which is in the interest of the shareholders because there is more competition as to the bid and the bid price. As to the prohibition of frustrating action, the directive offers a complicated opt-out compromise. As a matter of principle, the directive provides for the British solution, i.e., the board of the target (whether a one-tier board or a two-tier board) must leave the decision on the bid to the shareholders (Chapter 9). This is in line with the draft of the Commission and the recommendations of the High Level Group. Accordingly, frustrating actions must be permitted by the shareholders in a general assembly to be called at short notice. Furthermore, the bidder who has obtained 75 percent of the voting rights must have the opportunity to really get control of the company. Under the so-called breakthrough rule, no restrictions on the transfer of securities or on voting rights nor any extraordinary rights of shareholders concerning the appointment or removal of board members shall apply in such a case (Chapter 11). Similarly, multiple-vote securities shall carry only one vote each at the general assembly. By including the multiple-vote securities, the Parliament went even further than the Commission, which had shied away from the recommendation of the High Level Group and had proposed in the draft directive not to touch the multiple-vote rights.

So far so good. Yet all this came at a political price. The member states felt that the lack of a really level playing field – both within the EU and in relation to non-EU countries, in particular the USA – was unacceptable. The final directive provides for a double- or even triple-option regime (Chapter 12). First, member states may opt out of the rules on neutrality and breakthrough. This means that the member states can keep their protective regimes. It is expected that most of the member states will make use of this opt-out member state right. France has already done this and Germany is about to follow. Yet in such a case, the second option comes in. The member states are required by the directive to give an opt-in right to their national corporations. Large companies that are multinational players and need to tap the international capital markets may fear the reactions of large institutional investors and possible impacts on their share price if they engage in frustrating actions and keep foreign bidders away. Accordingly, the general assembly of the corporation may decide by a qualified majority (as needed for the amendment of the chapters of association) to opt for the neutrality principle and/or the breakthrough rule. This decision is revocable. The third option is again a member state option. The member state may exempt those corporations that have opted in from the regime they have chosen if they become the subject of a bid by a bidder who does not apply the neutrality principle and/or the breakthrough rule. The legal and political difficulty of this third option is whether it applies to non-EU bidders, such as an American corporation that is not covered by Chapters 9 and 11. Some member states including France are definitely of this opinion in order to get a level playing field between their own companies and those in the USA. Under the German draft law, the issue is not specifically dealt with, but a sentence in the official motives leads in the same direction.

Reactions to the 13th directive in the member states were somewhat mixed. The predominant reaction was satisfaction that we finally had a European takeover regulation which was essential for the internal market, shareholders, and external corporate governance. On the other side, the Commission, the European Parliament and the 'Europeans' in academia, practice, and industry were disappointed by the loose and watered-down regime of the 13th directive, in particular the opt-out possibility. There is still a slight chance that the European Court of Justice will intervene under the principles of its golden share cases. Yet this would require a considerable amount of courage, since up to now this case law has affected only trans-border restrictions by member state laws and rules and not restrictions by corporations under a fully private law regime.[40] It remains to be seen how the Court will decide the pending Volkswagen Statute case, and whether it will dare to tackle the problem.

References

Barca, F. and Becht, M., eds., (2001), *The Control of Corporate Europe* (Oxford).

Baums, T., ed., (2001); *Bericht der Regierungskommission Corporate Governance*, (Cologne).

Bebchuk, L. (2002), 'The Case Against Board Veto in Corporate Takeovers', *University of Chicago Law Review* 69: 3, 973.

Berglöf, E. (1997), 'Reforming Corporate Governance: Redirecting the European Agenda', *Economic Policy*, 12:24, 91 No. 93; London, (1997).

Davies, P. (2001), Struktur der Unternehmensführung in Großbritannien und Deutschland: Konvergenz oder fortbestehende Divergenz?, Beitrag zum Symposium 'Corporate Governance: European Perspectives', 60. Geburtstag Klaus J, Hopt, *Zeitschrift für Unternehmens – und Gesellschaftsrecht* (ZGR), 268-293.

Davies, P., (2002); *Introduction to Company Law* (Oxford).

Eisenberg, M. (1994), *Principles of Corporate Governance: Analysis and Recommendations*, American Law Institute, St Paul, Minn.

European Commission (2002), Brussels, 2.10.2002. Proposal for a Directive of the European Parliament and of the Council on Takeover Bids (Brussels), COM (2002) 534 final.

European Commission (2003), Communication from the Commission to the Council and the European Parliament, Modernising Company Law and Enhancing

---

40 See the comprehensive study by Grundmann and Möslein (2003) who encourage the Court to go ahead.

Corporate Governance in the European Union: A Plan to Move Forward (Brussels), COM (2003) 284 final.

European Commission, (2004a), Commission Recommendation of 14 December 2004 fostering an appropriate regime for the remuneration of directors of listed companies, Official Journal of the European Union L 385/55, 29.12.2004.

European Commission (2004b), Proposal for a Directive of the European Parliament and of the Council amending Council Directive 77/91/EEC, as regards the formation of public limited liability companies and the maintenance and alteration of their capital, Brussels, 29.10.2004, COM(2004) 730 final.

European Commission, (2005), Commission Recommendation of 15 February 2005 on the role of non-executive or supervisory directors of listed companies and on the committees of the (supervisory) board, Official Journal of the European Union L 52/51, 25.2.2005.

European Commission (2006), Proposal for a Directive of the European Parliament and of the Council on the exercise of voting rights by shareholders of companies having their registered office in a Member State and whose shares are admitted to trading on a regulated market and amending Directive 2004/109/EC, Brussels, 5.1.2006, COM(2005) 685 final.

European Parliament and Council (2004), Directive 2004/25/EC of 21 April 2004 on takeover bids, *Official Journal of the European Union* L 142/12, 30.4.2004.

European Parliament and Council (2005), Directive 2005/56/EG of 26 October 2005 on cross-border mergers of limited liability companies, Official Journal of the European Union L 310/1, 25.11.2005.

Franks, J. and Mayer, C. (1996), 'Hostile Takeovers and the Correction of Managerial Failure', *Journal of Financial Economics*, 40:1, 163.

Franks, J., Mayer, C. and Renneboog, L. (2001), 'Who Disciplines Management in Poorly Performing Companies?', *Journal of Financial Intermediation*, 10:3/4, 209.

Gillan, S.L. (2006), 'Recent Developments in Corporate Governance: an Overview', *Journal of Corporate Finance*, 12:3, 381–402.

Grundmann, S. and Möslein, F. (2003), 'Die goldene Aktie: Staatskontrollrechte in Europarecht und wirtschaftspolitischer Bewertung', *Zeitschrift für Unternehmens- und Gesellschaftsrecht* (ZGR), 317-366.

High Level Group of Company Law Experts (2002a), *Report on Issues Related to Takeover Bids*, Brussels: European Commission 10 January 2002.

High Level Group of Company Law Experts (2002b), *A Modern Regulatory Framework for Company Law in Europe*, Brussels: European Commission 4 November 2002.

Hommelhoff, P., Hopt, K.J. and von Werder, A., eds., (2003), *Handbuch Corporate Governance* (Stuttgart).

Hopt, K.J. (1999), Industriebeteiligungen und Depotstimmrecht der Großbanken als Problem der Corporate Governance, in *Shareholder Value und die Kriterien des Unternehmenserfolgs* ed Koslowski, P. (Heidelberg), 111-122.

Hopt, K.J. (2000), Corporate Governance: Aufsichtsrat oder Markt? – Überlegungen zu einem internationalen und interdisziplinären Thema –', in *Max Hachenburg, Dritte Gedächtnisvorlesung 1998* eds Hommelhoff, P. *et al.* (Heidelberg) 9–47.

Hopt, K.J. (2001), Corporate Governance: Experiences and Questions from Germany, in *The Internationalisation of Companies and Company Laws* eds Neville, M. and Engsig Sørensen, K., Copenhagen: DJOF, p.107−122.

Hopt, K.J. (2002), 'Grundsatz − und Praxisprobleme nach dem Wertpapiererwerbs − und Übernahmegesetz' *Zeitschrift für das gesamte Handelsrecht und Wirtschaftsrecht (ZHR)* 166: 375–432.

Hopt, K.J. (2003a), 'Modern Company and Capital Market Problems: Improving European Corporate Governance After Enron', *Journal of Corporate Law Studies* 3: 221-268.

Hopt, K.J. (2003b), La Treizième Directive sur les OPA-OPE et le Droit Allemand, *Aspects Actuels du Droit des Affaires, Mélanges en l'Honneur de Yves Guyon* (Paris) 529-541.

Hopt, K.J. (2003c), 'Die rechtlichen Rahmenbedingungen der Corporate Governance', in Hommelhoff *et al.*, eds. (2003) 29-50.

Hopt, K.J. (2005), 'European Company Law and Corporate Governance: Where Does the Action Plan of the European Commission Lead?', in Hopt *et al.*, eds. (2005) 119-142.

Hopt, K.J. and Wymeersch, E., eds. (1997), *Comparative Corporate Governance: Essays and Materials*, New York: Berlin.

Hopt, K.J. and Wymeersch, E., eds., (2003), *Capital Markets and Company Law* (Oxford).

Hopt, K.J., Kanda, H., Roe, M., Wymeersch, E. and Prigge, S., eds., (1998), *Comparative Corporate Governance: The State of the Art and Emerging Research* (Oxford).

Hopt, K.J., Wymeersch, E., Kanda, H. and Baum, H., eds., (2005), *Corporate Governance in Context − Corporations, States, and Markets in Europe, Japan, and the US* (Oxford).

Hopt, K.J. (2003c), 'Corporate Governance in Germany', in Hopt and Wymeersch (eds.) (2003), 289-326.

Hopt, K. J. (2006); 'Comparative Company Law', in Reimann, M. and Zimmermann, R. (eds.), *The Oxford Handbook of Comparative Law* (Oxford), 1161-1191.

Lutter, M. (2001), 'Vergleichende Corporate Governance, Beitrag zum Symposium 'Corporate Governance - European Perspectives,' 60. Geburtstag Klaus J. Hopt', *Zeitschrift für Unternehmens- und Gesellschaftsrecht (ZGR)*, 224-237.

Smith, A. (1789), *An Inquiry into the Nature and Causes of the Wealth of Nations*, 5th Edition (London).

von Werder, A. (2003a), 'Ökonomische Grundfragen der Corporate Governance', in Hommelhoff *et al.* eds (2003) 3–27.

von Werder, A. (2003b), 'Modernisierung der Mitbestimmung', in Berlin Center of Corporate Governance, Diskussionspapier, Berlin 26 November 2003.

Weil, G. and Manges, (2002), *Comparative Study of Corporate Governance Codes Relevant to the European Union and Its Member States 2002, Final Report*, January 2002.

Zimmer, D. (1999), Besprechung von K J Hopt/E. Wymeersch (Hrsg.), Comparative Corporate Governance: Essays and Materials, Berlin/New York 1997, *Zeitschrift für Europäisches Privatrecht*, 395–399.

Chapter 6

Transparency and Integrity: Contrary Concepts?

Frits Schipper

Introduction

Today, Corporate Governance arouses a world-wide interest, a development that can also be interpreted as an aspect of globalisation. Of course, there may be local differences in the way companies are being managed and in the way matters are structured by Law. The Anglo-Saxon one-tier system and the Dutch two-tier structure, with its distinction between the board and the executives, are examples of such a diversity. Also Germany knows a dual system of governance. Discussions of Corporate Governance often concentrate on the legal rules. We should realise, however, that the system created by these rules concerns only the formal aspects of this governance. Besides, there is always the substantial side of it, which comes, among other things, to expression in the values involved. During the last 10 years it has become rather common to focus on the content of Corporate Governance in terms of business ethics. All this notwithstanding, it is important to notice that both, form and substance, co-constitute Corporate Governance in a normative sense.

Daily practice may be distinct from the indicated normative meaning to different degrees, some of which imply a trespassing of particular limits of tolerance. If the latter indeed occurs, then the situation, dependent on the societal implications of what went wrong, creates a scandal or a crisis. In case of a crisis, this often leads to new rules of governance in order to restore societal trust, lost by the events. The new rules can focus on legal measures or on self-regulation, or being a mixture of both.

Although there is a tendency to uniformity, local differences may continue to exist, for example, due to the role of self-regulation. In the Netherlands, an example of self-regulation is the report of the *Tabaksblat Committee* (Tabaksblat Committee 2003).[1] The report deals with the governance of public companies, and, in the Dutch context, the Committee wants to connect with the 'best the Western world has to offer'. In trying to do so, the focus lies on transparency and integrity. The German Corporate Governance Kodex (May 2003), however, speaks explicitly only of transparency. Although this does not mean automatically that in Germany integrity is considered as being irrelevant, it can be seen as an illustration of local variation. Notwithstanding this variation, it is justifiable to say that the concepts of integrity and transparency are present in all cases where, at least in the Western world, the

---

1   This committee is named after its chairman Morris Tabaksblat, a former CEO of Unilever.

governance of companies and other organisations is at issue[2]; both concepts are indeed relevant for governance at all. This does not exclude local differences. The choice of subject matters which one wants to make transparent like wage systems, market relations, stakeholder interests or whatever, often depends on local influences.

The report of the *Tabaksblat Committee* unhappily lumps the concepts of transparency and integrity together without further analysis. I say 'unhappily', as I feel that both concepts have differences which deserve further attention. It is striking, for example, that audit firms like KPMG, in their advertisements following the publication of the report, underline the role to be played by transparency, whereas the reactions of company board members show more attention for integrity. I think that these distinctive reactions are not merely accidental. Audit firms are indeed expected to use an outside perspective (and we will see that transparency is narrowly related to this), whereas business activities require freedom of action, a liberty which the particular entrepreneur should explore and use in a responsible way. And this, at least, requires personal integrity.

The contrast just mentioned indicates that transparency and integrity cannot be treated simply as lying on the same conceptual level; perhaps both even have contrary connotations. Answering the question of how such matters are to be considered calls for further analysis and argumentation, and that is exactly what I am intending to do in this chapter. First of all, I will take a closer look at the concepts of transparency and integrity, respectively. Next, their relationship will be analysed, and I will end my argument by evaluating the results in connection with (Corporate) Governance.

Transparency

The concept of transparency is being used in connection with various domains of reality, such as material things, art, science and society. Besides, language also contains terms like 'open' or 'openness,' used, among others, for characterising and judging persons as well as organisations and often considered as synonyms for 'transparency'. Whether the latter can indeed be justified is questionable. Therefore, I would like to start by making some comments on the meaning of 'open' and 'openness'. Afterwards, I will concentrate on the concept of transparency.

Transparency and Openness

We call people 'open' when they are, in a positive way, sensitive to what is going on in the world and in themselves (feelings, concerns), not approaching matters only in terms of their preoccupations and prejudices.[3] It is, therefore, also possible to speak of a person as having 'world-openness' and 'self-openness', both expressions indicating a beneficial relationship. A second aspect of open people consists in the

---

2   *Transparency International* and the *Center for Public Integrity* are both institutes involved in the discussion.

3   The hermeneutic philosopher Gadamer distinguishes between two kinds of prejudices, i.e. those necessary for hermeneutic understanding and those who hinder such understanding.

fact that they tend to speak of themselves just by their own initiative. The latter, however, has some limitations. Putting everything on the table is considered quite soon 'not to be done' or, in some cases, even as pathological. We can also say that organisations are 'open', meaning that they have, metaphorically speaking, a willing ear for important (unique) situations – externally as well as internally. If so, then this (self −) openness limits the role of bureaucracy and also whistle blowers do not have to make their tune urgently heard in the outside world. Besides, 'open' organisations normally make public what they intend to do without heightening or downplaying matters at issue. Therefore, 'openness' is a normative, relational category, and the initiative to be receptive and communicative lies on the side of the open entity (person, organisation) involved. As we will *see below*, this does not coincide with transparency.

The use of the concept of 'transparency' does not have the same connotations everywhere. As far as material things are concerned, they are said to be transparent when light is going through them without noticeable loss of intensity. This quality gives them a visual 'non-presence,' often made use of in a sensible way. In some situations, however, the non-presence is (partly) undone for reasons of security (e.g., putting stickers on glass doors to prevent people and birds from colliding with them). Music, however, is considered as 'transparent' when all voices are clearly audible, and when melodies, rhythm and compositional structure are evident; the idealised limit being the complete presence of all this. Considered in this way, romantic music will not be an example of transparency. In the plastic and visual arts a sort of tension of presence and non-presence is often created, due to an aesthetic and skilful utilisation of the (in-)transparency of materials. Also, the concept of 'transparency' is being used in connection with organisations. This is the case, for example, when people speak of 'transparent' structures of decision or wage systems, viz. systems which are clear and manifest in their operations.

In all the indicated situations – and that is different from openness – 'transparency' is a non-normative quality of something, attributed to it while considering subject matters from an outside position. Of course, there is also the possibility of trying to 'transperise' things which, initially, do not have this property. However, initiatives to actualise it do not lie on the side of the entity at issue, but are taken by (one of the) other parties involved. Compared to what was said above about openness, this is indeed much different.

The Ideal of Transparency

As argued so far, transparency is to be seen as a possible *attribute* of different kinds of entities. However, this is not the whole story, because transparency can also be linked to epistemic, societal, moral or aesthetic *ideals*. An example of an epistemic ideal is involved by particular characteristics sometimes related to science, taken in a perfect sense. Striving for this perfection requires that theories consist of coherent systems of clearly defined concepts and ditto statements, without hidden knowledge claims. Especially during the twentieth century, this idea has been propagated, requiring that concepts and statements grasped more or less intuitively had to be reconstructed rationally, because of lack of clarity and ambiguities involved – a procedure often identified with the application of formal logic. Moreover, it was also supposed that – all knowledge claims being fulfilled – the realities which the involved theories had to 'meet,' became manifest and understandable for the human mind (almost) automatically. In line with this positive outcome, one can also hear people speak of 'transparent mental maps,' indicating systems of concepts not hindering our apprehension of things, realities, at issue. It is of course possible to question the realist epistemology implied by all this. However, what will remain, at least, is the transparency of concepts and knowledge claims, i.e. the complete presence of meaning and absence of hidden presuppositions, as a valuable epistemic aim.

As far as society is concerned, it is worth mentioning that the Enlightenment is widely known for connecting transparency with its ideal of rationality. Doing so, the Enlightenment preferred a society without dark areas and hidden agendas, without rationally unjustified traditions, privileges and other unclear structures and institutions. Rousseau was a philosopher who embraced this ideal, too. In the twentieth century, Jean Starobinsky took special notice of this kernel of Rousseau's thought: once upon a time, he remarked, the world, including one's own consciousness, was transparent everywhere, and it would be crucial to rediscover this happy reality. Hence, there is a '*Paradise Lost*' (Starobinsky, 1971, p.19; my translation) and a task lying ahead: 'to realise the ideal of transparency' (op.cit.: 39; my translation). Another twentieth century author, Gianni Vattimo (1992) talked about the 'ideal of self-transparency,'[4] which is, according to him, in opposition to the practice of 'fabulising reality'. All this can be taken in a general sense, having a potentially wide range of application. In connection with organisations, it is, for example, possible to concretise 'self-transparency' by relating it to the practice of internal auditing (see Section 2.3).[5]

The Commandment of Transparency

Transparency in the sense of *presence*, does not go along very well with ambiguity and complexity, especially when the latter implies difficulties in reaching an undistorted overview of matters at issue.[6] In situations characterised by ambiguity and lack of overview, there is pressure on transparency, and the making of judgements and evaluations becomes all the more puzzling. Science as well as society knows such situations, and people try to cope with them in different ways. In quantum mechanics, for example, there was this difficult problem of unclear wave/pchapter dualism, which induced the introduction of the principle of complementarity. Organisational

---

4   Whether the ideal of self-transparency is realisable at all, is a (though not simple) question which Rousseau could be confronted with. I will not discuss this, however. I do not know whether he uses the term, but it is possible to relate Habermas' concept of communicative rationality to this ideal.

5   As we have seen that transparency points to qualities to be discerned from an external position, some extra clarification is needed here. Doing so, we can say that 'internal' means the audit to be exercised by some *members* of the organisation having a relative 'outside' position in matters of governance.

6   This is also manifest in the philosophy of Merleau-Ponty with its interest in ambiguity.

and societal complexity and ambiguity are sometimes coped with by strategies of demarcation and hierarchisation. An example is organisational culture, considered as a management tool, used in order to influence the behaviour of personnel. Doing so depends on the introduction of a hierarchy of determiners, considering culture as an overarching, high level, one. If successful, then the complexity of decisive factors is reduced, and the possibility of getting an overview is increased. An example of using a strategy of demarcation is the introduction of so-called 'Chinese walls' in banking companies, in order to prevent the leaking of share price sensitive information from one part of the bank to another. Moreover, the widespread practice of auditing is also directed at attaining transparency.

As far as organisations are concerned, the aforementioned means of raising transparency all have a double aim. First (and metaphorically speaking), doing away with dark and unclearly woven organisational networks, in which the light – making clear sight and effective decisions possible – is absorbed. Second, making available unscattered and distinct streams of trustful information. Of course, it cannot be excluded that, in reaction to the implementation of transparency strategies, things will be kept in the dark or made ambiguous – behind the scenes. Whatever this may be, the use of these strategies always aims at creating or restoring transparency. In connection with this, it is striking that, in light of the recent crisis of confidence due to financial manipulations in some firms, people often speak of the *Commandment of Transparency* (CT). Obeying this crucial order is then to be achieved using particular rules and strategies, such as the aforementioned construction of 'walls'. At the utmost, however, it will result in an imposed transparency. As such, this will be very unlikely the direct 'natural transparency' ('transparency naturelle,' Starobinsky, 1971, p.37) discussed by Rousseau. Moreover, in all this it is indifferent whether the effort is done by self-regulation or by the force of law.[7]

What is more, we should notice that using transparency strategies within organisational contexts always introduces new measures, new elements. Exactly this may raise complexity, thereby inducing new possibilities of confusion and ambiguity. That transparency raising procedures indeed add something, is also clear from the extra costs to be made in order to put them in effect. In Holland, for example, precisely this motivated an important part of the reactions to the Tabaksblat report: Among other things, intensification of audits, as advised by the report, really requires professional experts to spend more time doing so, and this will cost extra money to be paid by the companies.

As such, the practice of auditing matches CT. In reality, however, it will mainly concern the external one, because internal auditing is at the utmost only conditional, never sufficient, for obeying CT. It was already the introduction of external auditing,

---

7 One can react by saying that there never has been and never can be such a direct, natural, transparency – we might also say 'powerfree transparency'. I will not deal with this issue because this requires a far reaching philosophical analysis, in which both epistemological and ontological matters are to be involved as well as historical positions to be discussed. Examples of the latter are the philosophy of Kant (the unknown 'thing-in-itself', the conceptual constitution of experience), as well as Husserl's primacy of the Lifeworld and the view of modern, mathematised, natural science as a cloth of ideas hiding the Lifeworld.

which happened many years ago, that added new dimensions to reality. Today, stressing the importance of external auditing for reasons of transparency is not different. It also causes a shift in focus of CT, now concerning auditing itself. For example, the recent discussion – caused by the problems with Enron and Ahold – whether it is necessary to split the practice of auditing and consulting (which during time became more and more intertwined in audit companies) points to using strategies of demarcation in connection with these firms themselves.[8] David Flint, in his still relevant book *Philosophy and the Principles of Auditing*, has made it clear that all audits have an intuitive component:

> in every profession ... there is an element of art and inspiration. These qualities have an indispensable and invaluable part to play in identifying the uniquely relevant evidence which an auditor should look for in the final analytical and judgmental review in the process of formulating an audit opinion or report (Flint, 1988, p.115).

If Flint is right, and I believe he is, then this unavoidable situation limits the possibilities of attaining transparency, at least as far as one tries to secure it through auditing.

Transparency and Normativity

Summarising what has been said so far, we find that 'transparency' has a double meaning and denotes two possible kinds of indeed *value-neutral* properties of various entities. Moreover, despite its original value-neutrality it can be connected to certain ideals. Although, in the present context, the primacy lies with the epistemic ideal, it is also possible to appreciate the transparency of something from other normative perspectives, such as a moral or an aesthetic one. In addition to this, it is clear that things can be transparent without being of a high value. The reward system of a particular organisation, for example, can be completely known to outside observers, i.e., all aspects of it, including rules of giving shares to personnel, are fully clear, without being morally justifiable at all. Sir Adrian Gadbury has noticed that transparent decisions do not necessarily display a moral quality (Gadbury, 2002, p.20). Likewise, it is possible that a crystal vase has no aesthetic value, despite the transparency of its material.

In *Organization Studies* (10 (2), 2003), some chapters on business ethics, politics and organising have recently been published which are relevant for the issues discussed in this chapter. One of the authors, Martin Parker, in his contribution, criticises the usual disjunction of business ethics and politics, especially in connection with the notion of social justice. In his view, this separation ('demarcation' in my terminology) 'de-socialises action changing it into the exercise of transparent personal reason' (Parker, 2003, p.193). According to Parker, the problem of social justice will consequently be excluded from the discourse of business at all. Posed in this way, it is indeed a rather strong thesis, but it might be justifiable if

---

8   It is not impossible, that those involved experience such a split as dichotomising their professional life. How this should be assessed depends on the meaning given to the professional practice involved. This, however, is not a matter of personal taste, but a philosophical issue.

the emphasis lies completely on transparency. Another author contributing to the issue of *Organization Studies*, John Roberts, in connection with CT, remarks that contemporary society knows strong systems of accountability, which are nothing but 'systems of visibility'. According to him, these systems consist of concepts functioning as lenses through which companies and other organisations become visible. At the same time, a self-disciplining logic becomes effective, leading to a pre-occupation with an imposed transparency that also shapes organisational reality. According to Roberts, and that is worth noticing, the following side-effect is likely: becoming indifferent to everything not required by CT (Roberts, 2003).

Of course, looking for transparency and self-discipline is not in itself an irresponsible and insensitive act. However, if the side-effect considered by Roberts becomes real, then responsibility and sensitivity will be limited to exactly the things required by CT. If so, the more wider organisational responsibility and moral sensibility are put on pressure and, instead of these, only a specific, imposed, transparency will rule organisational practice. Herewith, situations, characterised by a mindless pseudo-transparency, by which things lying beyond are not being considered at all, might come into being. Also, openness (see above) will be in jeopardy, in particular in circumstances were it is most relevant.[9]

Integrity

Like transparency, integrity is a concept that is being used in different contexts. In the medical world, e.g., people talk about the 'integrity' of the human body or of organs. In the bio-industry, it is said that animals have a right to 'physical integrity'. In technical affairs, it is not uncommon to use expressions like the 'integrity' of materials such as metal, membranes (for example used for cleaning water), ship structures, and nano-level connections. Besides, in the world of information the 'integrity' of digital archives and messages is of much concern. In a completely different area, the philosopher Walter Benjamin, in his discussion of Baudelaire's dealing with shocks and Freud's theory of shock defense, referred to the 'integrity of a shock' (Benjamin, 1974, p.615). Also disciplines are being discussed in terms of integrity. See, for instance, Parker in his (already quoted) chapter on business ethics, in which he mentions that the 'bottom line' is threatening the 'integrity' of this discipline (Parker, 2003, p.189). In the philosophy of auditing there are common expressions such as 'the integrity of financial information', 'the integrity of the audit function', the 'integrity of internal control', and the 'capacity for integrity' of the auditors (Flint, 1988). With the latter examples we are approaching the issue of corporate governance, and, more generally speaking, the subject matter of the ethics of the economy, of business and of enterprises. Within this field, current discussions and analyses indeed concern and make use of the concept of 'integrity', both the integrity of personnel as well as of organisations. In general, taking notice of integrity is closely related to the renewed attention for virtue ethics, which took

---

9   See also Steinmann's idea of the 'sensitive organization' (Steinmann, 2002, p.17).

place during the last decennia. Virtues are connected to concrete people, and because of this the integrity of a person is a persistent subject matter.

Integrity as Wholeness

Now, an important question is whether the varied use of the term 'integrity' is supported by a common meaning or not. Another question is to what extent applying the concept of 'integrity' to everything human adds connotations which are particularly relevant for the topic of this chapter.

'Integrity' comes from the Latin 'integer' which means something like 'whole', 'complete', 'unbroken', 'in one piece'. All the examples given above exhibit this meaning. If people state that the integrity of the human body is to be respected, then they are saying exactly that taking care of its 'wholeness' is an important rule of human action. It is only on special occasions that one is allowed to deviate, in a relative sense, from this rule, on the condition that not intervening will put the integrity of the body in jeopardy. In other words, what at first sight might appear as doing harm, e.g. making an incision, is to be considered an act of healing, directed towards preserving this very integrity. Of course, there is also a grey zone. No doubt, examples falling within this zone can be found in common medicine as well as in corrective surgery. As far as human beings are concerned, caring for bodily integrity is indeed widely accepted as a fundamental rule. However, in the case of animals there is still a debate going on, and the agricultural sector has to define its own responsibilities here. The integrity of technical artefacts also includes the connotations given above. If, for example, an important technical part is failing or if there is a fatigue of material, then the 'wholeness' or 'un-brokenness' of the technical artefact no longer exists.

Whereas the integrity of the body is closely related to its intrinsic value, the wholeness of an artefact points to its 'functional value' or, as can also be said, to its 'technical reliability'. Due to this concern with values, wholeness or completeness is related to integrity at all. This obtains, too, in cases where the integrity of messages is at issue, as seen above. They should be received in the same condition as they were sent, meaning that nothing should be missing or being disturbed. This kind of completeness is also linked to integrity, because of its value for human communication. In the examples, 'integrity' always involves a highly valued property, condition or situation. Also, viewing the wholeness of a discipline in terms of integrity is connected with a value. For example, in Parker's judgement of the lost integrity of business ethics, mentioned earlier, the key factor lies in his estimation of social justice as an essential aspect of it (Parker, 2003). Evidently, the integrity involved cannot be separated from the one concerning people, including managers, who are supposed to uphold business ethics.

Integrity and Person

The application of the concept of integrity to particular persons also points to things like 'wholeness', 'completeness', and 'un-brokenness'. Compared to the earlier examples, however, the new element here is concrete human action, with its intentions and consequences. In connection with this, the dimension of time is also playing an important role.

A person has integrity: when being 'in one piece,' the things done are indeed what he or she said; when not acting from sheer obedience or following rules; when being faithful to him- or herself, not having a hidden agenda; when not saying or acting at a certain moment 'A', and at the next moment, without any specific cause, 'not-A'. Moreover, such a person does not make others face unpleasant surprises, carries out his actions with good intentions and results, is not focused on his own interests alone, but also has an eye for the reasonable rights of other people and creatures. Such a person is open (see above) and trustworthy. In a professional context all this counts, too. For example, it belongs to the integrity of a doctor to take action only if urged by his best medical knowledge. By contrast, if he intervenes against his own professional judgement, for instance out of financial reasons, then, being a doctor, he does not act out of integrity, not 'in one piece'.

What I have just said is linked to several issues which are important enough to elaborate on further. The first concerns an aspect of integrity related to being loyal to oneself in all one's actions. This aspect can be called 'self-integrity,' and actions involved are determined by a person's 'self-value'.[10] The second relates to 'professional integrity'. The physician, mentioned above, sins against his professional integrity. In this context, a 'good action' is one that realises the professional values involved. Teachers and plumbers, for example, are also supposed to have such an integrity. The third aspect relates to 'moral integrity', linked, above all, to the 'moral good' and involving 'moral values'. Now, a person of integrity is able to keep all three aspects in mind at the same time, and has the capability of responsibly managing the complexities involved. Of course, ambiguities will occur in concrete situations, for instance, in the sense of tensions arising between the different values. How to deal with them is also a matter of integrity. It will be clear, however, that doing so is not easy or based on following rules. Nevertheless, the person of integrity is being trusted for managing the intricacies coming up.

Responsibly dealing with the different aspects just mentioned can be considered as an exercise of 'judgmental rationality' (Schipper, 1996). Contrary to Leibniz' ideal of the universal calculus, this kind of rationality implies that calculable rules and prescriptions can only have a limited meaning. Wherever complex situations are present, responsible judgemental rationality, and therefore integrity, is needed. It is important to notice, however, that some situations are so challenging that they can have a negative influence on integrity.

Keeping an eye on sociology, it is not uncommon to use the expression of 'role integrity', while at the same time pointing to the variety of possible roles and loyalties a person can have, including conflicts between them. Strictly speaking, the concepts at issue go beyond professional integrity. On the other hand, however, they might be applied to a specific profession. This means that one can distinguish different roles and loyalties even within a particular professional practice. Solomon, defending an Aristotelian, virtue-ethical, perspective on business ethics, speaks of integrity as a kind of 'super-virtue', saying that it is 'the essential virtue to a decent life [...]

---

10 In the context of psychology such a person is said to have an 'integrated personality'.

"getting it all together"' Solomon (1993, p.174). The different aspects can also be considered as 'partial integrities'. It is indeed possible to pay attention to only one of them. In that case, negative effects will likely happen. If a person focuses only on professional integrity, then the hazard of, for example, self-alienation or professional fanaticism, like saying 'don't bother me with all this, I am just doing my job', is not unlikely.

Added to this, there is also a relevant epistemological theme. Another person's integrity cannot be proven objectively, i.e., by means of a valid, inter-subjective and clear method. Nevertheless, judgements of integrity concerning other people are being made and even communicated. Unavoidably, these kinds of judgements are always a matter of interpretation, in which narrativity plays an important role, too. At the same time, it cannot be excluded that somebody has a fair insight in his own character, although it is very unusual that a person attributes integrity to him- or herself publicly. Moreover, it is possible that this insight differs from the one others think they have. In situations where a person's integrity is openly doubted, he or she, and this is an experienced fact of life, reacts mostly as if stung by a hornet. This is closely tied to the fact that it is very difficult to defend oneself against such doubts on the basis of knowledge. As said above, there is no proven methodology; integrity is vulnerable indeed. Anticipating the analysis presented later, I already would like to comment on this, by saying that, in connection with integrity, epistemic transparency eventually fails. In a more metaphysical language: Every person has his or her own mystery, inaccessible from the outside. This does not mean, however, that when integrity is at stake, we all do our dues in isolation.

Integrity and Identity

It is time now to make a few comments on the relationship between integrity and identity. Earlier on, I have been using the metaphorical expression 'in one piece' in order to characterise integrity.[11] However, the discussion of the three aspects has made it clear that this expression is not to be interpreted monolithically. The latter also obtains with respect to another reference which is important for understanding integrity: identity.

Taken as a whole, a person's identity is a very complex matter. It involves aspects related to origin, life story, culture, educational development, expectations for the future, place in life, work, as well as current social bonds and values a person wants to live in accordance with. Therefore, identity can also embrace issues related to a profession or to the organisation one is working for.[12] Analogous to integrity, it is possible to refer to partial identities. Statements such as 'being a manager, I am

---

11 As far as people are concerned, the English language also has expressions like '... of character', 'four-square fellow'.

12 In current parlance it is not unusual to speak of professional identity as distinguished from a personal one. This corresponds to the notion of professional integrity. It is not my intention to condemn this, but it might be critically asked when the distinction changes into a dichotomy.

dedicated to the bottom line, … ', and 'as a scientist I never listen to my emotions …, are examples in which such partial identities are being expressed.

Identity and integrity have a twofold relationship. First, integrity presupposes an identity to which one can be faithful. Second, integrity constitutes an important aspect of a person's identity. The first element of this double relationship is only possible if identity meets some conditions. What I have in mind are things like: i) continuity, ii) coherence/integratedness and iii) authenticity. If continuity is lacking, then there is basically no 'self' to be faithful to.[13] Moreover, 'attitudes' like opportunism and hyper-flexibility are not in alignment with the supposed continuity. By 'coherence' or 'integratedness', I mean that the different aspects of identity mentioned above comply, influence and support each other. If somebody has a 'split identity' or acts like having one, then it is difficult to link this to full sense integrity. Perhaps one of the earlier noticed partial identities might be involved. For example, this is the case when things believed on Sunday are in opposition to what is actually done during the week (hypocrisy). Furthermore, authenticity is important. If a member of an organisation works in accordance with the rules, just following them without any kind of reasoned commitment, or by being a sycophant, then this might offer a sort of identity, but not one with which integrity can be related to. The least one can say, is that such a person is 'a-integer'.

Authenticity is a theme on which Charles Taylor, in his *The Ethics of Authenticity*, has said important things. In his view, authenticity, involving individual diversity, has moral relevance indeed. But he is right in asking the question of whether it can be considered as pure self-determination, focusing on self-fulfilment only. If so, authenticity loses all of its content and becomes a purely formal criterion, just like continuity and coherence. In this way, according to Taylor, authenticity becomes trivial and loses its value (Taylor, 1991, p.38, 39). His diagnosis is also relevant for the issue of integrity. If authenticity is made something trivial, then from the aspects of integrity mentioned nothing except 'self-integrity' remains. A person of integrity is then just faithful to its 'self,' whatever the content of this autonomously determined self may be. Taylor, and that is important, underlines that authenticity can be meaningful only on the conditions that vistas of value (community, particular traditions) come into play.

Integrity and Organisation

Nowadays, it is not unusual to speak of integrity in connection with enterprises and other organisations. In this context, is it worthwhile to approach the subject matter from different angles, depending on how companies and other organisations are being considered, for example, as:

- A) instruments for the attainment of particular aims
- B) social environments, as work communities, in which concrete persons fulfil a central role
- C) moral agents, as 'citizens' of the wider society.

---

13 Continuity does not imply immutability. Identities may develop over time.

All these different perspectives influence the image of integrity which comes into view. If the organisation is taken as an instrument (A), then integrity means the 'un-brokenness' and 'proper functioning' of this very instrument, with a focus on subject matters like structure, internal coordination, internal stability, etc. However (B) and (C) are more important for this argument.

In connection with (B), for example, special attention to the integrity of personnel is crucial. Issues like removing organisational obstacles and other incentives with negative impact on integrity, as well as potential positive measures, cultivating integrity, now become important. In addition to this, it is also relevant to have an insight i) into responsibilities and integrity risks, especially in connection with the complexities and ambiguities of work, and ii) into the real purpose of the organisation. Everything said thus far about the integrity of persons remains relevant, perhaps somewhat more complicated. Take, for example, scientists working in an industrial lab. Besides being faithful towards the aims of science, they are also expected to be loyal to the interests of the company, and in some situations keeping both allegiances is no easy task.

Perspective (B), however, excludes the possibility of considering and evaluating matters, influencing the integrity of personnel, itself in terms of integrity. Perspective (C) is different in this respect, because it creates the possibility of talking about organisations themselves in terms of integrity, without reducing this to the integrity of the people involved. This way of thinking is, of course, in need of philosophical legitimisation.[14] An aspect of such an effort refers, for instance, to the question of whether the notion of a *Legal Person* is nothing but a legal fiction (Solomon, 2000), useful for ruling property relationships, or whether this concept also has, in today's society, moral relevance. Discussing this falls outside the scope of this chapter, however. Yet, it is suitable to notice, beyond the level of persons, some problems of organisational integrity which may induce speaking of organisations as moral agents. An important issue that should be mentioned here is the often unclear contribution made by particular people to the *actual* performance of the organisation taken as a whole. Everyone may have acted with integrity within the realm of his or her competence, yet it is possible that the final result is not that positive at all. This is known in the literature as the 'many hands dilemma' (Wempe, 1998). In such cases it might be worthwhile to use the perspective of the organisation as a moral agent. If integrity has to be faced on an organisational level, then insight must be gained i) in the identity[15] of the organisation at issue, ii) in the quality – a multi-dimensional, normative concept[16] – of what is to be accomplished (products, services, etc.), and iii) in important value-laden relations,[17] applying to the organisation as a whole.

14 This will also require a reflection on the use of the concept of identity in connection with organisations.

15 This identity refers to social-philosophical questions concerning principal differences between organisations (hospitals, companies, schools, universities), and (moral values) involved.

16 I cannot discuss this matter here.

17 The term 'stakeholder relation' is used quite often. However, 'relation' has more meanings. It is noteworthy that besides functional and causal relationships, there are others which involve one or more values (Schipper, 1996).

Organisational integrity, therefore, requires a responsible exercise of what I have called elsewhere 'relational rationality' (Schipper, 1996).

Nowadays, advocating a kind of 'integrity management' is quite common. In so far as this implies making an inventory of hazards of integrity, creating a real opportunity for personnel in order to deal with them responsibly, and management not only paying lip-service to the subject matter of integrity, this might have positive effects. Also, efforts of bringing the organisational self-image in accordance with that of a moral actor might be important. However, if 'integrity management' is considered in such a way that integrity is reduced to just being one of the many tools for controlling people, as a means to reach whatever goals chosen by the management, then integrity itself comes under pressure.

The Relationship between Integrity and Transparency

In the introduction, I suggested that transparency and integrity have something contrary about them. As far as the governance of companies and other organisations is concerned, it is important, however, to have a clearer understanding of their relationship. I will now pay attention to this issue, the following sub-themes being important: i) the opposition of integrity and transparency, and, ii) integrity as a presupposition of transparency.

Contrary Concepts?

Above, it was said that the question of whether a person has integrity could not be answered by an objective, validated, inter-subjective and clear research method. In other words: integrity is lacking epistemic transparency. This does not exclude the possibility of somebody *revealing* himself (despite the covertness of his inner life), making himself known over time in concrete actions involving particular situations. It is here that 'integrity' comes in as a concept crucial for characterising and judging what is revealed in the indicated way. Saying that a person has 'integrity' is pointing to an, indeed fallible, particular kind of *knowledge* of the 'other,' which can eventually be grasped only *receptively*, involving a kind of empathy.[18] Transparency is different, however. As I have said earlier, it is often connected to an epistemic ideal related to the *Commandment of Transparency* (CT). As such, it enables one to focus on what can described as *knowledge on demand*. Looking at things from an epistemological perspective therefore makes it clear that 'integrity' and 'transparency' function as contrary concepts.

In some contributions to the discussion, transparency is considered as being an integrity supporting virtue (Musschenga, 2002). In the light of what has been said so far, such a view cannot simply be endorsed *per se*. The reason is that transparency is an epistemic or an ontic characteristic rather than a moral quality. It can be imagined that under some circumstances, consenting to 'obeying', CT is defensible from an

---

18 Analogously, all this applies to organisations, too. A clarification of this analogy would require an answer to the question of what 'empathy' might mean with respect to organisations.

integrity point of view, whereas in others it might be not. As we have seen earlier, openness is different, however. It concerns normative-relational matters, involving sensitiveness to oneself and to the world, which is intimately related to integrity. As has been argued, transparency often functions in connection with an epistemic ideal, but this does not guarantee that moral values are being realised at the same time. In this sense, transparency is value-neutral. Hence, looked upon from a value perspective, transparency and integrity are not to be considered as contrary but are situated on different conceptual levels.

Mr Timmer, the former CEO of the NV. Philips, in his commentary on the report of the *Committee Tabaksblat*, has been defending the thesis that demands for transparency are in conflict with the 'privacy' needed for all entrepreneurial activities. Unfortunately, he does not explain his reasons for saying so, but one can imagine that this privacy is necessary because of warranting the creativity and competitive positions without which enterprises cannot function at all in a market economy. Companies indeed need, putting it in metaphorical language, a 'private space' of possibilities for action. Now, good governance requires this space to be 'coloured' by integrity. If complete transparency would exist, then the whole idea of integrity would have no relevance any more. Another issue worth mentioning is the hazard (discussed in section 2.4.) of becoming indifferent to everything not required by CT. Preoccupation with imposed transparency will probably bring the latter on the 'throne' of organisational governance, putting wider responsibility and moral sensibility of social entities under pressure. Hence, transparency strategies, such as hierarchisation and demarcation are not simply harmless in this sense. Indeed, over-emphasising transparency might put the wholeness of persons and organisations, i.e. their integrity, in jeopardy.

Integrity as Presupposition

In so far as it concerns companies and other organisations, the ideal of transparency manifests itself in the form of a commandment (CT). In accordance with CT, several kinds of measures can be taken in order to realise this ideal. However, new ambiguities may come into being as side effects of their implementation. A major problem is the confidence one must have in these measures and in their adequate application. From the focus of transparency, this would imply the need of a kind of meta-transparency, and so forth; a process, which eventually constitutes a *regressus ad infinitum*. In the background of this potentially unhappy situation there exists a general philosophical problem, i.e., the 'fact' that, without exception, rules can never control their own application (the 'rule problem'). In practical situations, the indicated *regressus* seldom becomes manifest in its full sense, while at a certain moment people are usually confident enough that further measures are not needed. An analogous complication is involved when it is intended to intensify the external audit as a means for raising transparency. Putting such an intention into practise introduces something unforeseeably new, thereby shifting the problem to another area. It is here that David Flint's correct remark that audits depend on elements of art and inspiration (Flint, 1988, p.115) is relevant again. Both, art and inspiration, are not paradigms of transparency indeed. Of course, people can try to cope with them by using protocols and other kinds of general, 'objective' rules. However, because of the rule problem, this can only be successful to a certain extent.

In concrete situations three parties are always present: 1) the organisation, the transparency of which is at issue, ii) the people responsible, in one way or another, for giving judgements of transparency, and iii) those who are in need of or have an interest in these judgements. All of them are being confronted with the problems mentioned above. Measures of transparency always have their organisational counterpart, and the rule problem will, unavoidably, manifest itself. In their work, auditors have to deal with this situation, and we have seen that they also have their own *quaestio transparensis*. Finally, those parties who are in need of transparency judgements therefore have to cope with a double-sided difficulty. In this situation, the risk of being confronted here with a sort of 'pseudo-transparency' is present all the time. Only on the condition that one can rely upon the integrity of all parties involved is it possible to deal with the potentially paralysing effect of this hazard. This implies that integrity is more fundamental than transparency. Even more, it is a presupposition of all transparency rules and judgements. Consequently, in so far as this is the case, both concepts are not contrary at all.

Concluding Remarks

From what has been said above, we can conclude that integrity and transparency have a varied relationship. The issue mentioned in the introduction has, therefore, been clarified. However, the way one should 'manage' or 'govern' this relationship *in concreto* has not been decided yet. Although this really is an important subject matter, it falls outside the scope of this chapter to discuss concrete situations, involving particular organisations and their stakeholders. Moreover, it would also have been a bit presumptuous to do so without co-operating with people active in the field. That is why I will now confine myself to a few general remarks.

The existence of transparency risks I have been referring to can strongly induce the view that in valuing integrity, it might be better to forget about the *Commandment of Transparency* completely. This might also motivate raising the issue of whether transparency is indeed of interest at all. Is it not better to forget about it anyway and drop all references to transparency related matters? Does integrity not suffice? These would then indeed be relevant questions to ask. However, answering them with an unconditional 'yes' would, in my view, be an overreaction and indeed a bridge too far.

In order to find a more suitable answer, one should realise that transparency is required in all cases where matters are at issue which, from a wider social perspective and in a particular period of time, are important to be accessible to independent, external judgement and evaluation. Nowadays one might think of global issues with local interests, such as the environment, safety, origin of products and labour circumstances. Also, financial matters, such as the giving of loans and moving of capital, relations between public and private organisations,[19] and the idea of 'market transparency', put forward by the former chairman of the Dutch Economic Council, Herman Wijffels, should be mentioned here (Wijffels, 2002). The latter has to be pursued when the 'receptive' knowledge, related to integrity, does not suffice in order to deal responsibly with market parties and the 'goods' they offer. One should realise that, besides transparency risks, there are also, generally speaking, hazards of integrity. In situations of strong temptation or high pressure it is seductive to give in, following only partial interests without others knowing it, thereby trifling with integrity and forgetting about the 'wholeness' of persons and the organisation involved. When acting under such conditions, it does make sense to demand a higher degree of transparency, thereby reducing hazards of integrity.

However, what has just been said is in no way detrimental to the fact that realising transparency always presupposes the presence of integrity. Besides, both concepts being in opposition in an epistemic sense and also different from a value perspective, does not exclude considering them as complementary. Taken together, this implies a varied relationship, which will become even more complex if openness is taken into account, too. How to handle this complexity in governing companies and other organisations can never be a matter of applying simple recipes. On the risk of simplification, it can only be said that the following maxim should be kept in mind: Openness if possible, transparency when needed, but integrity should always be. Keeping the three of them in a proper balance is indeed the continuous task of all involved by (corporate) governance.

References

Benjamin, W. (1974), *Gesammelte Schriften I.2*, Frankfurt a. M.: Suhrkamp Verlag.

Tabaksblat Committee (2003) *De Nederlandse Corporate Governance Code*, www. nivra.nl/download/code_corporate_governance.pdf.

Deutscher Corporate Governance Kodex. Regierungskommission DCGK Mai 2003. www.corporate-governance-code.de/index.html.

Flint, D. (1988), *Philosophy and Principles of Auditing. An Introduction*, London: Macmillan.

Gadbury, Sir A. (2002), *Business Dilemmas: Ethical Decision-Making in Business*, Chr. Megone e.a. (eds.) (2002), Case Histories in Business Ethics (London: Routledge).

Musschenga, B. (2002), Integriteit: een conceptuele verkenning, in *Integriteit in bedrijf, organisatie en openbaar bestuur* eds Jeurissen, R. J. M. and Musschenga, A. W., Assen: van Gorcum.

Parker, M. (2003), Introduction, Politics and Organizing, *Organization Studies*, 10, No. 2, 2003, 187–205.

---

19 The actual relations are very important. The citizens and other parties concerned should be able to have the justified conviction that, the state being involved in all kinds of relations, the public interest (problems of defining it notwithstanding) is still safe, avoiding favouritism or even the appearance of it.

Roberts, J. (2003), The Manufacture of Corporate Social Responsibility, *Organization Studies*, 10, No. 2, 2003, 249–267.

Schipper, F. (1996), Rationality and the Philosophy of Organization, *Organization*, 3, No. 2, 1996, 267–290.

Solomon, R.C. (1993), *Ethics and Excellence, Cooperation and Integrity in Business*, Oxford: Oxford University Press.

—— (2000), Historicism, Communitarianism and Commerce, An Aristotelian Approach to Business Ethics', in *Contemporary Economic Ethics and Business Ethics* ed Koslowski, P., Heidelberg: Springer-Verlag.

Starobinsky, J. (1971), *Jean-Jacques Rousseau: la transparence et l'obstacle*, Paris: Galimard.

Steinmann, H., (2002), 'Corporate Ethics. A German View', BRC Working Papers (Kowloon: Hongkong Baptist University Press).

Taylor, Ch. (1991), *The Ethics of Authenticity*, Cambridge (Mass): Harvard University Press.

Vattimo, G. (1992), *The Transparant Society*, Cambridge: Polity Press.

Wempe, J. (1998), *Market and Morality*, Delft: Eburon.

Wijffels, H. (2002), *Globalisering: uitdagingen voor de 21e eeuw*, Globalisation. Congresspecial Business Week. Rotterdam 2002, 30-31.

Chapter 7

Tangible Ethics: Commitments in Business Organisations

Eberhard Schnebel and Margo A. Bienert

Introduction

The rediscovery of ethics and ethical values as part of an active design of organisations and organisational structures is a continuing process. Among others, March and Simon (1958) opened the economic theory of organisations for cultural and symbolic aspects. Feldman and March (1981) emphasised the symbolic and signalling use of information in organisations, and, last but not least, Carruthers and Espeland (1991) focused on the rational aspects of business: Economy contains more than the adjustment of numbers. There is an understanding of the importance of ethics in business and organisations. But beyond the integration of ethics into economic theory of rationality, we realise that bureaucratic functions rise to occupy topics that had been in a classic sense subject to business ethics: More and more are we *organising* social aspects that had just been 'social' in earlier stages.

Yet there is no clear objective of the role ethics obtains in organisational settings, as we will show in some small cases. We emphasise the importance of clear ethics-related communication processes in organisations. We explain the use of communication theories inside organisational processes to clarify communication about such an abstract topic as ethics. Finally, we point out how, from our overview, a management of ethical ideas and cultural values must be designed in business enterprises according to economic ideas and according to the insights of new institutional theory.

On the basis of these practical insights, we will discuss in the following sections how ethics is the prerequisite for conducting any business and what advantages may be realised if a clear set of ethics is followed. We will discuss by means of six practical examples how ethical values can be discovered and developed in institutions with respect to economic theories. In the cases of ethics-based, values-added management of Boeing (US), HVB Group (Germany), SAP (Germany), Siemens (Germany), mmO$_2$ (UK) and GE (US), we explain the mechanisms of ethics in management to strengthen organisational success. All descriptions have the same focus: the fit of organisational commitment (perceived as commitment of its management and of established structures), understood in relation to its basic, communicated values. Business ethics needs to reflect the foundation of these manifest social structures.

Ethics as Intrinsic Function in Conduct Social Settings

Advancement and Morals in Social Life

Ethics, in the sense of an accepted set of rules, is a prerequisite for any social communication and therefore for economic transactions. As part of a normative framework, ethics represents social relationships in addition to institutionalised regulations like contracts, formal rules, etc. Parts of these social rules are covered by legal stipulations (Figure 7.1). However, these can hardly ever be fully comprehensive or up-to-date. They are made in specific situations and do not cover the more intentional area of social relationship. Plus, laws and regulations are usually the reflection and outcome of a clear and sanctionable set of morals that is understood as commonly given by the society that institutes and follows them.

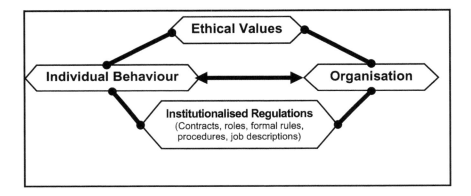

Figure 7.1   Institutionalised regulations and ethical values shape the actions inside organisation as normative framework

However, a liberal, capitalist-orientated economy can function only if the participants and the responsible players follow a certain set of ethics. This 'value canon' means, for example, that bills are to be paid, contracts are to be kept, employees, shareholders, competitors, suppliers and customers are treated according to existing contracts and the law. Only if a large majority of players in an economy adhere to these principles, can this economy function properly. These principles thus constitute the foundation of the economy.

According to Weber (1922) and Schumpeter (1976), the commercial and industrial society has been cast in an economic mould: its foundations, beams and beacons are all made of economic material. Prizes and penalties are measured and communicated in pecuniary terms. Even social phenomena like trust and credibility find equivalences in the way pecuniary reporting is done (Carruthers and Espeland, 1991). Within this frame, this social arrangement is – or in any case was – singularly effective (Schumpeter, 1976, p.73). It created a schema of motives that is unsurpassed in simplicity and force. The promise of wealth is strong enough to attract a large majority of people in a society, and success comes to be equated with business success (Schumpeter, 1976).

Schumpeter goes on to say that if however there were a way of measuring either this ability in general or the personal achievement that goes into any particular success, the premiums actually paid out are not proportional to either. Spectacular prizes much greater than these would have been necessary to call forth the particular effort of a small minority of winners, thus releasing a much more effective stimulus than would a more equal and more 'just' distribution do. A large majority of businessmen would on the other hand receive a very modest compensation, or nothing or even less than nothing, and yet would do their utmost because they have the big prizes before their eyes and overrate their chances of doing equally well.

In recent years, we have seen a dramatic increase in the willingness of managers to submit to unethical or illegal – or both – behaviour in order to belong to the small minority of overly compensated 'winners', in the sense of financial payments. In this respect, we can say that the value or measurement system of capitalism has already outlived itself, since pecuniary advantages can be achieved not only by efforts and efficiency, but also by bending the rules according to one's need in order to beat other competitors in the markets.

Taking this development into consideration, we are already on the road described by Schumpeter, according to which capitalism, by its success, will reinforce rationalism and will steer it in a certain direction: Rationality comes to be understood as thinking of yourself first, seeking only individual self-interest without consideration of social circumstances and foundations. This seems to be happening already. The next step would then be that the spread of rationality in such a sense undermines traditional values and institutions, i.e. undermines the legitimacy of capitalism itself. This is where the relevance of business ethics is clear. If a society is watching itself and detects the phenomena of its values and institutions being undermined, how can it react to ensure the basis of its system of social organisation can survive? Is there an intrinsic principle of the social economy that regenerates its own foundation?

Thus, we have a role of business ethics on a macro-economic level. In this sense, its role would be to show what dangers the loss of traditional values may bring. Its role would also be to develop theoretical approaches and practically applicable means of how to avoid, stop or slow this process. That is how to show the relevant players in the current social system that ethics is, indeed, a pure and inherent necessity. Apart from this, the role of business ethics would also be to show the advantages of ethical behaviour in the existing social system, which is the next point in this chapter. This would bring ethics from this macro-economic perspective to the level of micro-economics, i.e. of organisations and institutions.

Ethics as Prerequisite of Economic Communication

The interrelationship between these two principles – the establishment of self interest as rational principle and the unobtrusive function of traditional values – will be the challenge of business ethicists: They are asked to find out how social mechanisms are represented in economic and therefore organisational rationality or not, and also to learn how individual rationality is guided by social structures and values-based mechanisms.

One of the first philosophers who mentioned the complex and hidden relationships between self interest and social welfare was Mandeville. In his 'Fable of the Bees', he explored the benefits of pure self interest for the social life: 'The worst of all the multitude did something for the common good' (Mandeville, 1714, Part G). But at the same time, he revealed the problems of the absence of self-interest as rational principle of a society under the control of virtue and ethics: 'Fraud, luxury and pride must live; whilst we the benefits receive' (Mandeville, 1714). At the end, Mandeville advocates both the care for a social network of self interest as well as the virtuous care for traditional values and institutions. He named the dangers of pure self-interest and the need of strict social functions: 'so Vice is beneficial found, when it's by justice lopt, and bound.'

In particular, it must be demonstrated that ethical behaviour will prove to be advantageous. A reinterpretation of the widely taught Adam Smith has led a majority of businessmen and executives not to think so. Smith 'invented' the 'law' of the market. Thanks to the 'invisible hand' of the market, he believed that by self-interest, which drives men, 'private ... passions ...' are led into the direction 'which is most acceptable to the interest of the whole society.' Thus, competition will regulate 'self-interested profiteers'. But Smith also considered the need of the basic structure that links the self-interest efforts of complex social relationships as 'invisible hand' (Smith, 1759, p.322).

Generations of students have been taught to believe that man is essentially an acquisitive creature, the profit motive being as old as man himself, at least related to man's rationality for practical use. But it is not. It is only as old as 'modern man' (Heilbronner, 1975), a man who is able to set his own goals inside a social setting – but delimited from it – and also able to choose his own actions to reach his goals. There is, in fact, no evidence, that self-interest maximisation provides the best approximation to actual human behaviour (Letiche, in Sen, 1992), especially if we consider social aspects and social rationality as equally essential to explain human behaviour.

For all the new twentieth century developments, society still believes in the 'laws of the markets', following Adam Smiths explanations of the interrelationship between economic rationality inside social reality (Smith, 1776). What Smith meant was one thing, what proponents make him out to mean is another. He was made into the 'guru' (Sen, 1992) of self-interest as capitalist protagonists have known very well how to interpret Smith's work to mean 'leave the market alone' and, more importantly in this context, 'self-interest is good' – but only if you know the substantial contents of the invisible hand.

The Economic View of Moral Gains

But ethical behaviour is not only a synonym for the reintegration of social aspects into profit-maximising rationality. It can be reintegrated itself in terms of economic heuristics. From a neo-institutional economics point of view, two theories will be used here to explain ethical behaviour in terms of economic advantages. Both theories combine the advantages of a self-interest-based heuristics with the power of social constraints. They explain the combination of individual economic rationality and social prerequisite as organisational rationality and reintegrate ethical behaviour into the economic theory of action.

The transaction cost theory judges the efficiency of business transactions by production and transaction costs (Williamson, 1979, p.22). *Ex ante* transaction costs are, e.g., costs of information, negotiation and contracting. *Ex post* transaction costs are, e.g., costs of controlling and risk minimisation. Business partners that adhere to a clear set of ethics are able to minimise some of the costs (e.g., costs of negotiation and information) or even abolish others (e.g., costs of controlling and risk minimisation). An example is the 'handshake', if both business partners know this to be a binding finalisation of an agreement. There are no contracts (and therefore no fees or expenditures) to draft, set up and sign, and no costs arise to monitor their fulfilment. The more certain the business or transaction partners can be of each others' values and behaviour, the lower the transaction costs.

The focus of the principal-agent theory (Alchian and Demsetz, 1972) is on advantages and disadvantages that arise in transactions between the principal (owner or ordering party) and the agent (manager or contractor). Information is asymmetrically distributed, and as both the principal and agent will always try to maximise their individual self-interest, there arises a problem: the agent may or will use his better information to the disadvantage of the principal. There are four types of agency relationships: hidden characteristics, hidden intention, hidden action – which will lead to *moral hazard* (Trumpp, 1995) – and hidden information which can also lead to *moral hazard*. The risk of an agency problem or moral hazard is all the higher, the higher the uncertainty about the motives, or the bigger the alternatives and preferences of the agent. The more both principal and agent believe in the same values and adhere to the same fundamental ethical convictions, the smaller the uncertainty and the moral hazard will be. Ethical behaviour in the sense that both, the agent as well as the principal, want to create a win-win situation for both partners would mean that the problem of a conflict of two different individual maximisers of self-interest would not even exist. Thus, no moral hazard would exist. Were it not for the heuristics of the isolated '*Homo* oeconomicus', this problem would not exist to be discussed. But as every man is part of social settings and part of a community, *Homo oeconomicus* as a heuristic idea has spread to explain individual actions as rational actions.

Both the transaction cost theory and the principal-agent theory support the thesis that an organisation needs a fitting ethical basis. They explain in economic terms the need and the duty to care for the integration and maintenance of shared social values. In the following, we will explain the systematic aspects of a common understanding of these general social values and their problems, by defining them precisely.

Public Welfare and Organisational Values?

Organisations may reduce their frictions if they establish communication about their founding social values. This requires the transparent agreement on some ethical basics of an organisation as its own area of communication. It requires ongoing commitments to a general 'morality' that guides all actions internal and external. But often the focus of a moral fundament of an organisation is not yet discussed. Especially in multicultural settings there must be a general idea of the 'good', but the difficulties with 'good' start with the near impossibility to define it. From an historical point of view, different understandings of 'good' are offered. Plato believed that in the end we can at best find the 'idea of the good', Aristotle thought the good to be the 'collective well-being'. The theologian Schleiermacher, in the tradition of Hegel, pronounced the good as the world-public-welfare. The Christian view thought that to be good was to aspire to be as similar in actions and motives as Christ, respectively God. George Edward Moore finally showed the difficulties of defining what is good. Instead of a general idea of public welfare he developed a context orientated utilitarian ethics by which the morality of action is measured quantitatively at the production of 'good' utilities. This explanation refers consequently on cultural conditions as a framework of judgements shaping ethical orientation of actions. And it enables one to trace different tasks without renunciation of its comparability (Moore, 1903).

Utilitarianism realised that on the one hand, individual ideas of public welfare are not comparable and cannot be related to each other, but on the other hand, they still need to be communicated. In their entirety, they constitute the focus of a social group. Social value, in all its meanings, is therefore the value of its individual participants (Schumpeter, 1908). Hayek summarised the phenomenon of the impossibility to predict social results in terms of individual intention as 'expanded order' (Hayek, 1988). Only by systematic consideration of non-intentional results of intentional actions in economic models of communication can the emergence of public welfare be understood (Meyer, 2003). These circumstances result in a different concept of public welfare. Its power can only be communicated in adequately abstract media of communication.

The transformation of this concept of public welfare into the world of organisational goals is essential to understand how economic rationality and social communication fit into organisations. Their setting is almost parallel to that of social communities. Inside an organisation, the rational arguments and the efforts of actors are focused on their personal imagination of what they associate individually with the functioning of the organisation. However, contrary to social communities, the goals of an organisation are defined (more or less). For example, the main goal of the defence industry is to build powerful weapons. The main goal of a manufacturer of telecommunication equipment is to profitably build electric equipment. But beyond that, there is no shared agreement, visible in many examples of organisational discussions on how to develop and transform organisations. All members of the organisation have their own ideas and see their respective necessities. And this is their individual concept of organisational welfare. This will be strengthened by the continuing effects of 'multiculturalisation'. The main effects are that more and more very different understandings, varying cultural influences and individual meanings collide inside the organisations. Companies as organisations cannot rely on 'higher authorities' when defining what they take to be good. In order to ensure that the members of an organisation or company understand and – at least partly – share those values a company intends to stand for, a company needs to work on the development and definition of these values – they need to communicate and adjust permanently the understanding of their intrinsic 'organisational welfare'. There are different approaches to develop values and communication about ethics: top down and bottom up approaches, guided *versus* free-flow processes.

Communication of Social Values in Organisations

Value Communication and Value Consensus in Organisations

Values shape organisational processes as part of organisational communication. Values can be fixed and thus become a part of the code of the organisation. Or values can be more of a medium to communicate an autonomous ethical communication reflecting comprehensive social demands that create an ethical framework for organisations. In this case, the question arises whether values are to create a minimal consensus or rather give an impulse.

Consensus organisations need frequently repeated processes of discourse to create a shared understanding of their symbols and signals and of the values they contain. Impulse organisations communicate required commitments by articulating ethical values. These commitments in turn are the initial positions and framework for new impulses. These organisational commitments only work if there are corresponding individual commitments of the individuals. The two aspects of ethical communication are related to the ideas of consensus and impulse: the creation of consensus in various repeating discourse processes for meeting reasonable approval, and the communication of impulses as a framework for communication with the goal of commitment of all participants. The main challenge for both types is to judge the rationality of organisational goal-orientation and within this context the ethical dimension of communication processes (Figure 7.2).

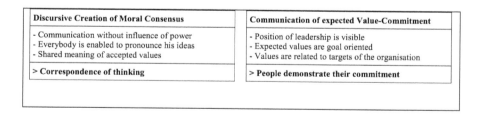

Discursive Creation of Moral Consensus	Communication of expected Value-Commitment
- Communication without influence of power - Everybody is enabled to pronounce his ideas - Shared meaning of accepted values	- Position of leadership is visible - Expected values are goal oriented - Values are related to targets of the organisation
> Correspondence of thinking	**> People demonstrate their commitment**

Figure 7.2   Two approaches to value-communication

'Consensus' can be understood as the correspondence of thinking of several individuals: two or more individuals come to a shared meaning (implicit and explicit) of thinking in several steps of communication. This leads to three questions: How is the consensus-orientated communication process designed? Is it possible to link meanings of individuals so closely that an 'identity of ideas' can emerge? Is there a basic difference in individual interpretations of ideas, so that we will have to speak about consensus in gradual steps?

These questions can be discussed from a Habermasian perspective. Habermas transferred the question of normativity from a content-orientated position to formal aspects of normativity (due to the impossibility of metaphysical or ontological value patterns). He transformed normative aspects of values into formal design of the communication process. He postulated the normative character of the ethical discourse requiring a process of frankness and many repetitions (Habermas, 1981, 1993a). Consensus of meaning between individuals in these terms is related to frank discursive communication processes. Only the structure and practice of discourse decide on the normative validity of the results. Habermasian discourse principles are designed to create an understanding of values in consensus of all participants under specific restrictions. Again: Not the resulting consensual values are normative, but the structure of the discourse itself. The restrictions are as following:

- Correspondence of thinking between two subjects
- shared view of meaning of values
- homogeneous understandings of consciousness
- 'understandability' of individual values
- communication process without influence of power
- equal chances of participation for all participants
- frequent repetition of discursive processes.

Niklas Luhmann criticised this position of a discursive creation of ethical consensus. In particular, Luhmann criticised the possibility of a linked meaning without differences. Even in the case of organisational reasons, he denied the fiction of a temporally unlimited process and the illusion of frequently repeated discourses in society and organisations. Moreover, he criticised the impossibility of two subjects getting to a point of full understanding of each other, particularly of implicit understandings of values. There are no objective criteria to assess whether one has the right understanding of the values and words of someone else. There is an impossibility of evaluating homogeneous understandings. Luhmann set the stage to talk about communication processes in the area of moral communication (Luhmann, 1995) and not about substantial values.

As a consequence, values, norms and rules are visible only in communication acts (Luhmann, 1992; *sic*: Parsons, 1951, 1968; Spencer Brown, 1972). The act of value-communication is now the relevant act itself (rather than values as content). This act is only visible as commitment between single actors, as communicated agreement on an expected behaviour, permanently observed and noticed in all variations, whether complied with or broken. In a 'market of communication', ethical values and entrepreneurial ideas compete with others to create an organisation. They succeed in commitments, where some ideas are superior (Luhmann, 1992, 1993). Commitment is the main criterion for evaluating communication processes.

Values Based Organisations: Social Commitments

Entrepreneurial ideas in a market economy draw their opportunities and therefore their strength from unknown actions and reactions. Events almost 'not expected' create new opportunities in new situations. New business ideas grow out of opportunities with outstanding success only in 'unregulated territory'. Opportunistic behaviour – in other situations the reason for conflicts – is the impetus for innovations and the essential engine for social success (Williamson, 1979, 1985).

So there is a fundamental need for the avoidance of consensus to achieve entrepreneurial character, success and innovative power. To be above-average, competitors need innovative actions and events, which are not ruled by social or organisational consensus. It requires being conscious of the organisational goals and of communicating them to employees, investors, customers and strategic partners. These stakeholders are interested not in consensus-orientated rules, but in differentiating the organisation from competitors. Social commitments are the pragmatic approval of concerned individuals to back up organisational ideas. Organisations depend on entrepreneurial success. They need structures for value-communication to protect the space of individual characters and even to avoid consensus in the society or market community on aspects of their organisational competitive advantage.

The agreement on market rules is a commitment of market participants to respect these market rules. It is the result of an ongoing social process of communication. In the same sense, rules of interpersonal behaviour are the result of an ongoing cultural process of moral communication. But next to them are areas where individuals refuse to obey these rules. In addition to rules, the market economy needs this inhomogeneous behaviour to create sensitivity and creativity. Rules therefore must be implicit, incomplete and open for different interpretation. And in the same regard, they structure social communication as a foundation of entrepreneurial success. In market economies, we assume a second principle besides the heuristics of economic rationality that structures social interaction in terms of flexible morality and ethical values. This second principle enables all participants to live their own moral imaginations and at the same time to participate in a shared process of communication about general ideas of morality.

It is the same with organisations: Commitments to organisational rules create the social framework for organisational participants to act inside organisational rules. The mere existence of rules for interpersonal behaviour is a result of organisational culture. Even the rule itself has to be incoherent and open for different interpretation in order to be the origin of corporate success. Within this understanding, a market economy needs a defined 'space' in which one can create one's own successful values, where instinct and creativity have the same right as deviate behaviour. These values then compete with other persons' ones.

The result will be a framework of rules of conduct and ethical values in a market economy scrutinised in its validity through permanent communication and therefore changing continuously. Still, this framework will guarantee both, fairness against others and freedom to do new businesses in new ways (in its interplay between consent and personal freedom).

The ethical judgement of values and behaviour in this sense changes the subject of economic theories. In the centre of a heuristics of economic rationality is a communicative framework that enables individuals to exercise their own responsibilities. This responsibility is relevant in decisions for values, which compete with other values and may prove to be superior. The social framework is the realm of values, the soft-law, and the rules of the game. Beyond these rules, there is space to develop one's own specifications of values. The ethical evaluation of this framework is to judge how it ensures the chances of individuals to compete with their values in solving problems and challenges.

Practical Requirements for Values-Based Communication

How can members or leaders of organisations navigate and control ethical communication in organisations? Conventional theories about the functions and mechanisms of giving impetus in organisations recommend setting clear substantial tasks and financial goals to incentivise top performance. These elements initiate behaviour in traditional ways of maximising individual profits. They are related to conventional economic intentions to structure organisational duties. As a stage to communicate a certain orientation in understandable ways, they have to enable the organisation to reach its goals.

But additional mechanisms are necessary to give impetus for communication of soft areas of management and co-operation and to avoid frictions and conflicts. Such mechanisms include 'soft facts' of moral communication for integrating moral values and structuring the area of emotions and behaviour as expression of social relationships. Communication about social values is communication to create open space for innovative impulses. Value-communication increases orientation and transparency in complex social settings and improves the effectiveness of normative rules and advice. The explicit communication of moral values clarifies the meaning of organisational handicaps with additional explicit impulses. As a tool of corporate governance and controlling, it relates to the following aspects:

- Definition of organisational goals to determine the use of the organisation
- Deriving measurements, incentives, instructions
- Making implicit aspects a subject of management
- Analysis of intrinsic goals of the stakeholders
- Pronouncing expected responsibility
- Creating a communication orientated 'soft-law' of behaviour

The particular communication of visions and emotions requires mechanisms in organisations which go beyond the classic tools of management. All members of the organisation need to relate their efforts to the rules of organisational visions and ideas. They need a chance to understand the goals of their organisation. Mechanisms are necessary that adjust the behaviour of the participants to the goals of the organisation, especially if the incentives in organisational structures are not totally compatible with the goals that should be achieved (Wolff, 1999). Discreet communication of visions and emotions needs processes of value-communication to harmonise social commitment and to enhance transparency of soft-law: Both, hard facts and soft advice need to be understandable.

These commitment processes have to be adjusted against goals and objectives as well as entrepreneurial visions and 'emotions' of an organisation. Participants should be enabled to evaluate independently whether they want to adapt themselves to the values and goals of the organisation or not. If they do not have this chance, they assume their own ideas about organisational fits or misfits and react in ways organisations cannot recapture (Söllner, 2000).

Tangible Social Values: Individual Commitments and Organisational Commitments

Moral communication improves efficiency in organisational communication processes. It enables and permanently modifies core agreements on substantial basics. It complements traditional communication of goals and targets which create frictions, as they are not clearly understandable to all participants in all details. Commitments to social values create an area of understanding between actors, in which non-explicit messages become clearer. These social commitments are a transparent measurement of acceptance of values within the company (or team), so that individuals and their colleagues can build a social group. These values are thus not obligatory for other social groups, but necessary for the cooperation within the group one belongs to (Luhmann, 1992, 1995). The character of social values an organisation or a society uses in its communication processes is not important for the functioning of this communication. What is important is that the symbolised values are credible and widely accepted, so that commitments may permanently emerge between the actors. The communication process is in principle based on agreement on the most fitting values to achieve organisational goals and to communicate, together with these values, the implicit aspects of leadership as credible commitments. This relates to the fact that organisations are always coined by participative structures and therefore have strategic impact on several participating groups and individuals. They have a high notion of the freedom of members to participate in autonomous decision-taking and creativity (Collier and Esteban, 1998).

The communication of social values is a prerequisite for differentiating between individual commitments to these social values and organisational commitments provided by rules, formal assumptions and other regulations. The mixture of hierarchical and participative aspects of organisations sheds light on individual behaviour as well as on intrinsic aspects of the organisation. It makes them explicit in both kinds of commitments. Individual commitments in this sense are purely personal relationships between individuals. Organisational commitments come about by an organisation facing individuals through contracts, job descriptions, formal assumptions and other institutionalised regulations. Organisational commitments can overrule individual commitment, whereas individual commitments are able to undermine organisational rules. This relationship structures internal communication effectively in terms of a 'core line' for constructive integration of individuals. It helps to control value dilemmas and therefore depends on transparent organisational commitments. Individual commitments are subject to this permanent process of communication in an organisation. They are related to the pragmatic goals of an organisation and simultaneously to their cultural surroundings. Processes of organisational communication create, change and influence the relations of social and organisational commitments to social values.

In the following cases, we therefore focus mainly on organisational commitments for explaining various factors of the communication process. We cluster three managerial approaches of establishing organisational commitments: integrity, leadership and management. Each one is a link between otherwise contrary principles of management.

- *Integrity-based* management *versus compliance-based* management (L. S. Paine, 1994) is chosen to react to legal demands. The organisational commitments here are to demonstrate the adequacy of the entire organisational structure for successful actions and at the same time to expand these structures due to new legal requirements.
- *Managerial* approach *versus communication-orientated* approach of leadership is a step towards the active integration of ethics into an organisation. The organisational commitments here are to understand ethics as a key facilitator of organisational communication. Social values therefore have to be a core element of leadership either to be managed or let go. The leading idea is to establish organisational commitments built on a basic structure of social values to integrate otherwise disparate imaginations of social values.
- Management of *strategic ethical impetus versus* management of *social equivalent* is the most advanced course to work with ethics in a strategic way. The organisational commitments here are to expect fully committed members with regard to social values. The goal of this approach is to design and influence the style of personal integration for organisational commitments and to elaborate organisational commitments.

A consistent concept to manage cultural values faces challenges emerging in an inhomogeneous set of social values. Inhomogeneous values can be taken as given especially in internationally operating companies with cross-cultural settings, but in the same systematic approach, they are a matter of fact in more single-cultural or local organisations. A balance of individual commitments and social values in terms of organisational commitments and the 'space' that is needed for organisational and entrepreneurial innovation is hard to establish. Yet this balance is crucial for the success of a company – and is an integral part of an organisation's value.

Discover and Develop Values: The Need of Tangible Ethics

In the following, we describe several corporate proposals where companies design communication processes of social values. We therefore consider practical cases of international operating companies. Each example shows unique facts of organisational communication empowering or dismissing personal engagement with ethical values. The case studies are grouped into three categories and follow the main direction of its three methods: Integrity, leadership and management.

In the field of 'integrity', we have grouped companies with the leading goal of safeguarding legal integrity as a basic behaviour in its management of ethical communication. The consequences of this adjustment for other areas of strategic management are less important. The main issue is to be up to the legal standards in various legislations. Boeing and HVB Group can be seen as companies dealing mainly with the legal issues of integrity. The differences between the ethical management of the two companies are described as integrity-orientated *versus* compliance-orientated (L.S. Paine, 1994, 2003). But both companies abstain from designing management systems and influence of leadership styles of the managers.

The field of 'leadership' includes all efforts of companies to shape the general orientation of business behaviour in spite of their strictly legally orientated methods (Driscoll and Hoffman, 1999). In these companies, the communication of ethical values takes an important role inside the organisational communication and leadership tasks. But there is still a shortcoming due to using this communication as part of specific strategic orientation. No links are established between strategic organisational structures and the companies' communication of social values. The two companies SAP and Siemens are exemplary in showing how management takes steps to set impulses for leadership with guided communication of values without influencing strategic operations directly.

Finally, the area of 'management' is reserved for companies who use the communication on social values to shape the organisational design and the changes of the company directly. Legal aspects are considered but are integrated only in a subordinate role. It is more important to manage the company with impulses based on social values. All employees and managers have to be adjusted to 'shared' values and to a common belief in the company and its way of doing business. The companies General Electric (GE) and mmO_2 try to channel the strategic behaviour of all participants with strategic social impulses. They are examples of how to manage organisations with focused values (GE) or social respectively organisational ideals (mmO_2).

In order to develop comparable descriptions of the companies and their managerial methods and also to describe simultaneously their significant differences, we recapitulate the central ideas of all companies after a short general description guided by three central questions:

a) What is the company's integrative approach inside the structure of organisational communication? What are the main organisational commitments?
b) What are the instruments to safeguard sufficient communication on social values? What are the organisational arrangements to suggest its commitments?
c) Are there fundamental ideas behind the organisational implementation of a transparent management of social values? What are the basic values behind organisational commitments?

Boeing: Legalistic Compliance- and Values-Management-System

The Boeing Corp. has established a traditional way of dealing with values-based issues in organisational ethics. The initial point for Boeing is the need to act as a member of the defence industry in accordance with strict regulative requirements.

Boeing defined the kinds of behaviour that they considered dangerous and harmful to the company. Priority is related to legal issues (US law) and regulative requirements (Security Exchange Commission, Department of Defence, Defence Industry Initiative) as a quoted stock corporation which makes a large part of its turnover and profit from public orders in the defence area. Boeing's work is traditionally closely intertwined with public-sector administrative bodies. Boeing had to be careful to avert penalties and exclusion from public orders on the grounds of unfair trading. Day-to-day work and decisions are related to public decisions, and many managers came from a background of public administration before joining Boeing. Because of close relations and high dependence on public orders they had to establish corporate values, fixed basic rules and a training programme.

The Boeing ethics programme is a response to the federal government programme against waste, fraud and abuse. They established a management guideline ('business conduct guideline') connected to an ethical management controlling system and a commitment to strict consequences for misbehaviour. In relation to these themes, Boeing built up a protective value-management system comprising:

- ethical business conducts,
- proper marketing practices,
- offering business courtesies,
- acceptance of business courtesies,
- conflicts of interest,
- proper relationship with suppliers,
- dealing with former US Government employees.

The dilemma of Boeing is transparent in two situations, where the organisational commitment to compliance got damaged: the first damage was a case of bribery, where the top management of Boeing bribed top managers of the Pentagon to get a big lucrative order in the defence area. The second hit on integrity was a personal failure of the CEO by breaking a corporate rule. He established an affair with a responsible person who had to be led by him. The point here is not to describe precisely all aspects of these situations but to point out the consequences for organisational commitment. If there is no strong link between ethical rules and organisational core aspects, credibility gets damaged. The general ideas are summarised in the following three aspects:

a) Together with its instruments for the communication of ethical values, Boeing establishes a mainly formal organisational process that should be able to safeguard ethical behaviour in business operations. This ethical behaviour is related to all requirements of public authorities for organisational processes. The missing links to the general business operations and to the top-management commitment take into account the assumed need for business-as-usual.

b) As managerial instruments, Boeing establishes everything the public authorities require: Codes of Conduct, detailed work instructions, comprehensive training and backup, a supervisory process to check compliance with the rules.

c) The aim is to establish instruments that make the management legally invulnerable, that has to work in grey areas of a worldwide defence and weapons industry and in the air and space industry. The exclusive focus of all the management efforts is to fulfil all administrative regulations of the US defence industry.

HVB Group: Integrity as Factor of Quality

The goal of HVB Group as one of the biggest European Banks with large exposures in Eastern European countries is to manage several risks related to economic transactions and to safeguard the legality of financial standards due to internationally accepted rules. Therefore, the focus of its management of business ethics is more the creation of a general sensibility of its employees on all levels of management than just the compliance with formal rules. Employees or managers should have the power and the knowledge to judge independently how to behave in critical or ambiguous situations. For this reason, HVB established, in two major steps, first a general values-based leadership system with several management tools (Schnebel and Bornmüller, 2003a), and adjusted in a second step an integrity management system based on these values (Schnebel and Bornmüller, 2003b). The core of the second step was the worldwide establishment of a general Code of Conduct valid in all affiliated companies and subsidiaries (Hypovereinsbank AG, 2001, 2002, 2003).

The aim of HVB is to keep the general banking business unchanged while adding several new areas of organisational commitments to the contemporary ones. The general goal is to commit HVB to the same style of financial service business they already had decades before. For this reason, the establishment of *new* ethical commitments of the organisation – while acknowledging its previous one – eventually led to making no organisational changes at all. Integrity management in HVB is an add-on without disruption of previous business practices. The following three general aspects guided the HVB efforts:

a) HVB establishes the development of 'integrity' as the core feature of its business and therefore tries to improve its own image as business partner, always dealing with integrity and without unpleasant and disagreeable surprises. This integrity is more than the formal control of the conduct of the members of HVB – it aims at the intrinsic 'business consciousness' of each individual for the ethical aspects in day-to-day business.

b) Apart from legal requirements, like compliance management, insider trading or money laundering, HVB developed two managerial instruments as core for further integrity management: the general 'Values of HVB Group' with direct consequences for leadership, and the 'Code of Conduct' as a general guideline. Both instruments bridge the gap between the corporate social values and the concrete guidelines.

c) The focus of all these efforts is both to motivate all employees on all levels to foster legal behaviour and to refrain from supporting methods of business dubious in a legal and ethical sense. In particular, all employees should be guided by a shared consciousness related to organisational cooperation. There is a general awareness to continue doing financial business in the previous style, improved by only minor changes.

SAP: Facultative Ethical Values

SAP has established no explicit corporate values, but nevertheless has a unique organisational culture which requires efficiency and which is orientated on achievement. They care for social communication about values for a very peculiar reason: SAP has a very ambiguous style of teamwork, where the teams are set up almost independently from hierarchical restrictions. For this reason, ethical values are social values of the personnel, by which managers will either attract other team members or fail. The importance of this values-based effect is stressed by the fact that all managers have no fixed number of employees, but, for each project they run, have to win team members to cooperate with effectively. SAP supports its basic organisational structure by offering and encouraging team values, in which managers and employees often change team members in a self-organising way. The cooperation of the teams is mainly orientated on customer projects. Corresponding to this, employees are able to select those projects and those managers with the most fitting values. Employees have to feel good in the teams, if they are free to leave the teams. SAP therefore has no binding set of core values structuring individual behaviour, but instead offers key rules for cooperation. Beyond these rules, all managers and employees have to find their own rules of cooperation inside their teams. Often team leaders fail to communicate their individual core values of cooperation in ways sufficient to allow their team members to accept them. This internal market for projects and leadership values creates an atmosphere of change and continuing adjustment of values inside organisational structures. In this way, SAP creates an internal job market that guarantees the changing of and adapting to values in organisational structures. A self-organising process of communication on issues of social values evolves, but only if the communication actually happens. Often no communication is set up and the process of value communication is lacking, but SAP has no instruments to intervene here. The employees as well as the managers are very discontented and focused only on short-term tasks (SAP AG, 1998), but that may be in reference to the very short term focuses of the software industry.

The key rules set by SAP are:

- *Quality*: Solve quality-related problems!
- *Development process*: Optimise the use of information technology throughout your enterprise!
- *Cooperation and communication*: Work together constructively to find the best possible solution!
- *One big team*: We do not think much of hierarchical structures and bureaucratic procedures.
- *Long-term partnership with customers and colleagues*

Viewed from a positive angle, SAP really established a self-guiding, self-referenced process of internal communication to adjust individual and organisational commitment. Management happens; there is no need to empower managerial instruments. The organisational commitment is only related to cooperation in respect of SAP's goals and not in respect of general social values. The efforts to care for corporate social responsibility issues in the last years (SAP AG, 2005) is more owed to aspects of 'fashion' than to the core business strategy. The general ideas are summarised in the following three items:

a) The aim of SAP's values-based concept of communication (if it really is a concept) is their employees' and managers' independent analysis of the moral foundation of their cooperation. Therefore, every SAP member has its free space of communication, which, besides the respective special issues, requires a communication on ethical and social commitments. SAP relates team building processes to this open space of communication.

b) The tool to stimulate this communication is the pressure of adaptation that applies to managers as well as to employees. Everybody in a team has to agree on the team values provided by the manager. The need for successful results in time, under pressure of scarce organisational resources, is the main instrument to enforce independent communication on social values within both the teams and the entire company.

c) The set-up of mechanisms of moral self regulation ideally leads to the development of a momentum of its own of social systems within the organisational dynamics. These social systems structure the cooperation inside SAP in a *quasi*-unstructured manner. To survive in the fast changing environment of software business is the primary goal behind these efforts, and therefore, SAP establishes only an organisational surrounding providing a platform for the individuals' self-realisation.

Siemens: Intrinsic Cultural Values as Leadership Competence

What prompted Siemens to establish a value management process was the need to integrate cultural and individual peculiarities into corporate communication processes (Hütter, 2002). More than optimising the fundamental corporate structure, the value management process at Siemens is driven to optimise cultural soft-facts of communication (Schnebel, 2002) (Figure 7.3). Siemens took calculated measures to avoid complications with ethical behaviour in the international context and to integrate people with different ideas into the 'SIEMENS Family'. As a side effect, value management should improve the success of the company's businesses. Management of intrinsic values of the managerial and organisational approach requires highly developed informal structures.

These informal structures are part of the Siemens tradition:

1. Focus on financial results with strict financial control.
2. Strategic and technical management without consideration of values.
3. Realisation of strategic orders without support of ethical values.
4. Clear managerial focus on technical and economic contexts.
5. Focus on individual personal development.
6. Top-management is recruited from complete Siemens careers.

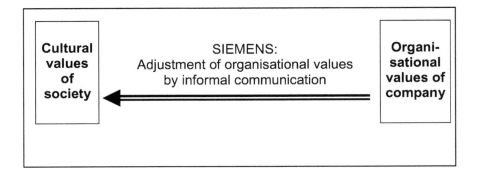

Figure 7.3. Value adjustment as organisational function

The term 'SIEMENS Family' stands for written rules and a fixed set of social values that, due to their complexity, could not be captured by basic rules or guidelines. But the complexity and vagueness of the 'Family' value-idea often lead to problems for new managers who join the company. They are often not able to clearly face the requirements of the Siemens value set and are drawn back on their own social intelligence. To characterise these effects, the Siemens values system can be summarised in the following three aspects:

a) The integrative proposal of Siemens is focused mainly on the company's employees and leaders to establish a shared organisational consciousness ('SIEMENS Family'). This shared consciousness is a tool to strengthen the organisational fellowship and the mode of cooperation. The proposal outlines many cultural elements of the Siemens culture explicitly. The aim is to create a realm of belonging together and of homogeneous leadership all over Siemens.

b) Due to this challenge, Siemens developed a guideline of leadership based on a company's worldwide opinion poll among its managers. This guideline contains the internal core values of cooperation. The respective values are integrated in regular personnel human resource development and a system of evaluation (balanced scorecard).

c) Siemens establishes an internal social relationship management in all areas and branches of the company. The orientation on core values facilitates the integration of all employees related into the explicit and implicit self-image of the company. The need for a community based on shared social values that are undisputable is the basic driving force behind the organisational commitment of Siemens.

mmO_2: Management of Social Commitments

The mobile telecommunication company mmO_2 had to solve various major problems simultaneously after its takeover of ViagIntercom. The company deals with an exchangeable product in a saturated market. The market itself differentiates itself only by pricing and therefore by effects of scale. In Germany, mmO_2 had been the smallest of four operators of telecom services and was continuously threatened by takeover attempts of its competitors. The way mmO_2 has taken to defeat this threat is to establish a brand identity, linking customer and employees in the same way and to the same ideas (mmO_2 2003). The general strategic ideas are summarised in the following three aspects:

a) Communication of social issues at mmO_2 is communication of corporate strategy. Its aim is to emphasise the functional peculiarities of mmO_2 as part of a well functioning social environment in opposition to its competitors. Employees and customers shall be proud of the services and the products of mmO_2.

b) For this reason, mmO_2 established a companywide guideline based on social values that particularly highlight the social relationships of mmO_2 and its services. In addition, mmO_2 developed its own social responsibility management to promote external social activities with links to the company.

c) The managerial intention of mmO_2 is to portray the company as socially responsible with ethical products adapted to the consciousness of customers and employees: 'to be the essential mobile brand by enriching people's life whatever they are doing, wherever they are'.

GE: Management of Strategic Setting

GE is a company who explicitly established the management and controlling of individual behaviour as one strategic element of its core management processes. With its stringent expectation of ethical values and morality penetrating all organisational areas and with its adjusted leadership instruments guaranteeing the communication, change and adaptation of the corporate values, the top-management tries to influence and control the strategic development of the company (Welch, 1998, 1999; Schnebel, 2002). The general managerial ideas are summarised in the following three aspects:

a) GE wants to establish a tight culture of leadership where a few values-based impulses of the top-management can navigate the organisation. Everyone who wants to succeed inside the organisation has to obey these values.

b) For this reason, GE communicates explicit 'corporate values' that symbolise the implicit expectations of the company with regard to the behaviour of its employees. At the same time, GE, in a strict top-down way, makes sure that all managers live up to the organisational values. This creates a basic commitment of all managers to the organisation.

c) The basic intention of this method is to make the core principles of an organisation – which are always very hidden and implicit – more visible, so the share of explicit parts reaches a higher level. The aim is to change a general intrinsic means of organisational culture into an explicit and recognisable one.

Conclusion

Social values are a substantial element of organisational life. As shown above, they are a core element of all social relationships. Even under the assumption that economic rationality guides all individual behaviour, there is quite a number of non-rational presuppositions of social cooperation. As we described in the practical examples, these non-rational presuppositions can be integrated into several levels of organisations: very formal and reactive ones, or progressive and content-related ones. Irrespective of this, social values always play the same role. They structure fundamentally all social communication in organisations, and the main course management can take is to establish individual or organisational commitments. In organisational examples, they define the general course of an organisation in relation to its funding values.

The examples of corporate practice therefore exhibit different types of establishing organisational commitments in relation to their basic social values in organisations. They are not judged individually. The possibly most fitting one of the six examples has to be judged separately with respect to the general strategy of the organisation. Further research can point to profit-maximising effects of fitting strategies in the combination of a social values and a strategic approach. We could only figure out possible tensions between organisational commitments and the founding social values.

One of the relevant facts most frequently observed is the relation between these organisational commitments and strategic fits or misfits. If we change the subject for our social observations from pure social values to commitments to these values, we get clearer insights into organisational problems: we get transparency. Our new thesis now is that the fit between transparent strategic topics can relate to transparent values-based commitments and *vice versa*. If there is a misfit in these relations, the commitments are lacking.

References and Further Readings

Alchian, A.A. and Demsetz, H. (1972), Production, Information Costs and Economic Organisation, *American Economic Review*, **62**, 777–795.

Anderson, R. (2003), Ethics Ain' t Rocket Science, *Seattle Weekly*, **6**. August, 2006.

Baecker, D. (1999), *Organisation als System*, (Frankfurt a. M.).

Bienert, M.A. (2002), *Organisation und Netzwerk – Organisationsgestaltung durch*

Annäherung an Charakteristika der idealtypischen Organisationsform Netzwerke, (Wiesbaden).

Boeing Corp (1995a), *Ethical Business Conduct Policy and Procedures*, Seattle: Boeing Corp.

Boeing Corp (1995b), *Business Conduct Guidelines*, Seattle: Boeing Corp.

Brittan, S. (1995), *Capitalism with a Human Face*, Aldershot: Edward Elgar.

Carruthers, B.G. and Espeland, W.N. (1991), Accounting for Rationality: Double Entry Bookkeeping and the Rhetoric of Economic Rationality, *American Journal of Sociology*, **97**, No. 1, 31–69.

Collier, J. and Esteban, R. (1998), Theorising the Ethical Organisation, *Business Ethics Quarterly*, **8**, No. 4, 621–654.

Driscoll, D.-M., Hoffman, W. Michael (1999), *Ethics Matters – How to Implement Values-Driven Management*, (Waltham (Massachusetts)).

Feldman, M.S. and March, J.G. (1981), Information in Organizations as Signal and Symbol, *Administrative Science Quarterly*, **26**, 171–186.

Gereke, U. (1998), *Soziale Ordnung in der modernen Gesellschaft: Ökonomik – Systemtheorie – Ethik*, (Tübingen).

Habermas, J. (1984), *Vorstudien und Ergänzungen zu einer Theorie des kommunikativen Handelns*, (Frankfurt a. M.).

Habermas, J. (1993a), Der Normative Gehalt der Sprache, in , *Der philosophische Diskurs der Moderne*, (Frankfurt a. M.).

Habermas, J. (1993b), Anerkennungskämpfe im demokratischen Rechtsstaat, in *Multikulturalismus und die Politik der Anerkennung* ed Taylor, C., (Frankfurt a. M.), pp. 187–196.

Habermas, J., (1981), *Theorie des kommunikativen Handelns*, (Frankfurt a. M.).

Hayek, F.A. (1945), The Use of Knowledge in Society, *American Economic Review*, **35**, No. 4, 519–530.

Hayek, F.A. (1988), *The Fatal Conceit – Errors of Socialism*, (London).

Heilbronner, R.L. (1975), *An Inquiry into The Human Prospect*, (London).

Hütter, G. (2002), Corporate Ethics and Social Responsibility: Principles and Practice at Siemens AG, in *Moral Leadership in Action* ed Weltzien Hoivik, H. V., (Cheltenham), pp. 205–221.

Hypovereinsbank, A.G. (2001), *Code of Conduct*, München: Hypovereinsbank.

Hypovereinsbank, A.G. (2002), *Sustainability Report 2002*, München: Hypovereinsbank.

Hypovereinsbank, A.G. (2003), Annual Report 2002, München: Hypovereinsbank.

Kluckhohn Clyde (1951), Values and Value-Orientations in the Theory of Action: an Exploration in Definition and Classification, in *Toward a General Theory of Action* eds Parsons, T. and Shils, E. A., Cambridge: Harvard University Press, pp. 388–433.

Kreps, D.M. (1997), Intrinsic Motivation and Extrinsic Incentives, *American Economic Review*, **87**, No. 2, 359–364.

Luhmann, N. (1989), Ethik als Reflexionstheorie der Moral, in , *Gesellschaftsstruktur und Semantik. Studien zur Wissenssoziologie der modernen Gesellschaft, Band 3*, (Frankfurt a. M.).

Luhmann, N. (1992), *Gibt es in unserer Gesellschaft noch unverzichtbare Normen?*, (Heidelberg).

Luhmann, N. (1993), Wirtschaftsethik – als Ethik?, in *Wirtschaftsethik und Theorie der Gesellschaft* ed Wieland, J., (Frankfurt a. M.), pp. 134–147.

Luhmann, N. (1995), Intersubjektivität oder Kommunikation: Unterschiedliche Ausgangspunkte soziologischer Theoriebildung, in , *Soziologische Aufklärung, Band 6*, (Opladen), pp. 169–188.

Luhmann, N. (2000), *Organisation und Entscheidung*, (Opladen).

Mandeville, B. (1714), *The Fable of the Bees – or, Private Vices, Public Benefits*, (London).

March, J.G. and Simon, H.A. (1958), *Organizations*, New York: Wiley.

McIntosh, M. *et al.* (1998), *Corporate Citizenship: Successful Strategies for Responsible Companies*, (London).

Meyer, M. (2003), F. A, Von Hayek und die heuristische Dimension ökonomischer Modelle, in *F. A. Hayeks konstitutioneller Liberalismus* eds Pies, I. and Leschke, M., (Tübingen).

mmO₂ plc, (2003); Corporate Responsibility Report, (2003), (London: mmO2 plc).

Moore, G.E. (1903), *Principia Ethica*, (Cambridge).

Paine, L. S. (1994), Managing for Organizational Integrity, *Harvard Business Review*, **3–4**, 106–117.

Paine, L. S. (2003), *Values Shift: Why Companies Must Merge Social and Financial Imperatives to Achieve Superior Performance*, McGraw-Hill (Boston).

Parsons, T. (1968), On the Concept of Value-Commitments, *Sociological Inquiry*, **38**, 135–160.

Parsons, T. and Smelser, N.J. (1957), (1956), *Economy and Society, A Study in the Integration of Economic and Social Theory*, London: Routledge and Kegan Paul.

Picot, A., Dietl, H. and Franck, E. (1997), *Organisation: eine Ökonomische Perspektive*, (Stuttgart).

SAP AG, (1998), Annual Report 1998, (Wiesloch-Waldorf: SAP AG).

SAP AG, (2005), Annual Report 2005, (Wiesloch-Waldorf: SAP AG).

Schnebel, E. (1997), *Management – Werte – Organisation. Ethische Aufgaben im Management der Industrie*, Wiesbaden: Westdeutscher Verlag.

Schnebel, E. (2000), Values in Decision-Making Processes: Systematic Structures of J Habermas and N. Luhmann for the Appreciation of Leadership, *Journal of Business Ethics*, **27**, 97–88. [DOI: 10.1023/A%3A1006465030955]

Schnebel, E. (2002), Cultural Differences of Values-Driven Management – the Value-Management Programmes of the General Electric Company and Siemens, in *Moral Leadership in Action* ed Heidi von Weltzien, H., (Cheltenham), pp. 222–243.

Schnebel, E. and Bienert, M. (2004), Implementing Ethics, *Journal of Business Ethics*, **53**, 203–211.

Schnebel, E. and Bornmüller, A. (2003a), Code of Conduct als Instrument Des Wertemanagement in Banken, in *Ethik in der Bankenpraxis, pp* ed Wagner, A.

Schnebel, E. and Bornmüller, A. (2003b), Vertrauensoffensive statt Kulturkampf – Kommunikation und Integration als strategische Faktoren im Fusionsmanagement, in Peter Knauth and Artur Wollerteds ; *Human Resource Management – Neue*

Formen betrieblicher Arbeitsorganisation und Mitarbeiterführung, (Köln), pp. 1–47.

Schumpeter, J.A. (1908), On the Concept of Social Value, *Quarterly Journal of Economics*, **23**, 213–232. [DOI: 10.2307/1882798]

Schumpeter, J.A. (1951), *On Entrepreneurs, Innovations, Business Cycles, and the Evolution of Capitalism*, (Oxford).

Schumpeter, J.A. (1976), *Capitalism, Socialism, Democracy*, (London).

Sen, A.K. (1992), *Inequality Reexamined*, (Oxford).

Slater, R. (1999), *Jack Welch and the GE-Way*, McGraw-Hill, (Boston).

Smelser, N.J. (1963), *Theory of Collective Behaviour*, New York: Free Press.

Smith, A. (1759), *Theory of Moral Sentiments*, (Edinburgh).

Smith, A. (1776), *An An Inquiry Into the Nature and Causes of the Wealth of Nations,*, (Edinburgh).

Söllner, A. (2000), *Die schmutzigen Hände – Individuelles Verhalten in Fällen von institutionellen Misfits*, Tübingen: Mohr Siebeck.

Spencer Brown, G. (1972), *Laws of Form*, New York: Julian.

Trumpp, A., (1995), *Kooperation und asymmetrische Information, eine Verbindung von Prinzipal-Agenten Theorie und Transaktionskostenansatz*, (Neuried).

Weber, M. (1972), (1922), *Wirtschaft und Gesellschaft. 5, Auflage*, Tübingen: Mohr.

Welch, J. (1998), Three Roads to Growth, *Executive Speech Reprints*, Fairfield, Connecticut: General Electric Company.

Welch, J. (1999), GE and the Internet, *Executive Speech Reprints*, Fairfield, Connecticut: General Electric Company.

Williamson, O.E. (1979), *The Economic Institution of Capitalism*, (New York).

Williamson, O.E. (1985), Transaction Cost Economics: The Governance of Contractual Relations, *Journal of Law and Economics*, **12**, No. 2, 233–261.

Wolff, B. (1999), *Anreizkompatible Reorganisation von Unternehmen*, (Frankfurt a. M.).

PART III

GLOBAL JUSTICE

Chapter 8

A Theory of Global Justice Focussing on Absolute Poverty

Elke Mack

Absolute Poverty is undoubtedly a key question for global justice, because no other moral deficit withholds fundamental human rights from so many people, a number of approximately 1.1 billion absolute poor in 2005 (Chen and Ravallion, 2004). Each year we count 18 million deaths because of poverty related reasons, among them 11 million children (WHO, 2005). There is no singular key to a just reduction of worldwide poverty, but for the first time in history, there is a chance to eradicate absolute poverty worldwide (Sachs, 2005, pp.353–374) within a medium-term period.

Since John Rawls published his last great systematic book on 'The Law of Peoples' in 1999, there is a new debate on how to establish global justice, not only among Anglo-Saxon philosophers, but also among development economists, ethicists and Christian theologians in Europe. I will try to handle the problem from the view of an interdisciplinary approach of ethics, which has a Christian hermeneutic comprehension of human beings.

A multidimensional set of means for a specific worldwide poverty reduction are necessary, among which three means seem to be the key issues: Markets, aid (out of solidarity) and institutions are the main instruments that are discussed within a global business ethics and development economics. So far no way alone has been sufficient, because there is no single key to the poverty problem.

Answering the questions in what intensity, in what relation and under which condition the means for justice can be set, is the main purpose of this chapter. It is also an ethical challenge for a Christian social ethics which has the scientific aim to argue for just institutions out of a tradition of humanity. This theological background will build the hermeneutic reference to a universal normative argumentation of secular ethics and socioeconomic evidence, which is also important for ethical argumentation in the first place, in order to receive universal acceptance of norms and institutions.

Thesis 1: Markets should have a Heuristic Preference according to the Principle of Subsidiarity

Global research on poverty discovered a connection between economic poverty and a non-participation in global markets (as in North Korea, e.g.). Apart from civil wars, juridical anarchy and political corruption, the main problem of the least developed countries of the world is their economic inactivity and their ineffective agriculture. *Vice versa* we can also draw the conclusion – relying on empirical evidence from the last decade – that the greatest progress in overcoming economic poverty has been made by interaction of the poor in global markets because of their production of manufactured goods.

If we ask the question whether this empirical evidence can also be proved by ethical reflection, we should consider the following: If markets are a way of self-sufficiency and if they are combined with the chance of growth-promotion or of individual prosperity, they are also an expression of free interaction and a chance to promote one's own living condition. Participating in them successfully offers self-determination and autonomy.[1] As far as markets help to contribute to freedom, income and independence of human beings, they are object to the ethical principle of subsidiarity. According to this principle, there has to be a first rank for the smaller unit in front of the bigger unit: Whenever the smaller unit can manage something out of its own, it may not be withdrawn from it.[2] This is valid for states, communities, groups and even single persons. Complementary is the duty of solidarity for the bigger unit, then and in so far as the smaller unit cannot care for itself. This prevents Christian ethics from claiming a responsibility too extensive or encroaching. With the help of the principle of subsidiarity, we can claim a step-by-step responsibility. The extension of this responsibility is fixed by the possibility and might that a single person, entity or state has. This principle highlights the social responsibility and gives criteria of demarcation and non-interference. It is a fundamental democratic and federal principle that has been taken up by the European Union in order to argue for federalism, and it also can serve business ethics in arguing for the self-organisation of free people in society, markets, religion and science.

Under the condition that the causal connection between the reduction of poverty and the engagement in market activity is correct, economic efficiency in markets should have a heuristic preference (not an absolute). Interferences in markets should only be undertaken if autonomous measures of helping themselves do not succeed, or if market failure or market control takes place. This means to respect the autonomy of the subsystem of economy. Benedikt XVI. argues in a similar way: 'A moral philosophy or theology that wants to leap over the expertise of economic science is not moral science, but moralism, which is the contrary'. (Ratzinger, 1986, p.58.)

Referring to global poverty, this would mean that a Christian social ethics would argue for a heuristic preference for self-organisation of states, communities, groups and also single persons. The right to autonomy and self-organisation refers to cultural,

---

1   We can vividly see this in Bangladesh, where poor women have the chance to participate in markets with the help of the Grameen-Bank, so that they can invest in their own business.

2   This principle has its origin in the papal Encyclica Quadragesimo *Anno* 1931 (Nr. 79). 'Subsidiarity (…) entails a corresponding series of negative implications that require the State to refrain from anything that would de facto restrict the existential space of the smaller essential cells of society. Their initiative, freedom and responsibility must not be supplanted.' Pontifical Council for Justice and Peace (2004), Compendium of the Social Doctrine of the Church (Città del Vaticano) Nr. 186, 105.

social, political as well as economic action and can therefore not exclude markets as the main instrument of economic interaction. In this respect, the instrument of the market has to be approved, because it can be understood as interaction of households and their members as well as interactions of firms.

Nevertheless, there is one big restriction that has to be taken into account. Markets are only an expression of successful self-determination if they are built into fair frameworks, so the competition in markets is complete. Then, markets build up justice of performance and exchange, so that performance can lead to freedom from poverty and to an increase of welfare for every person participating in them. Under these circumstances, markets are strong powers for development. In times of ongoing globalisation, there is in total six times as much foreign direct investment as governmental development aid. Due to the global perspective, there are great incentives for work-intensive production of goods in developing countries, in view of great cost advantages compared to the high-cost situation in industrial countries. The growth rates of developing and especially transforming countries can be two-digit as we saw lately, which could not be reached in industrial countries.

We can see the superiority of markets proved in human history. Europe was severely poor at the turn of the 18th to the nineteenth century shortly before the industrialisation took place. With the engineering progress of the industrialisation, specialisation and division of labour took place that could not be surpassed by any power other than free markets with their efficient processes of optimal allocation. When the power of markets was no sooner socially fertile, social security systems, social law and progressive tax systems were established to allow transfers to the poor.

Regional markets of poor developing countries are in a situation comparable to Europe in the middle of the industrialisation. They are even in a better starting position, because there would be sufficient technological know-how and global capital to let them live up to prosperity. Countries on the threshold like Taiwan, South Korea or China have shown how successful the transfer from a development country to an infant industrial country can be. Through a worldwide division of labour, the use of advantages of specialisation, the diffusion of new technologies, foreign direct investment in developing countries and the chances of export of manufactured products as well as intensive competition have great effects of prosperity that could never be financed by government development aid. I disagree with ethical objections that argue for the possibility of giving up the special culture and way of life of the poor: Hunger has to be appeased first to save lives. Philosophically, I would argue for this with the help of a hierarchy of fundamental goods in favour of the individual in question. Besides, economic interactions can be undertaken in a culture-specific way and with respect to the regional particularities without a colonisation of living conditions. National governments in developing countries have the power of decision through national law and jurisdiction.

The thesis: 'We cannot achieve poverty reduction against the process of globalisation, but only with it', has been proved several times by scientific research. This makes it necessary to simultaneously consider the implementation of norms, when justifying norms and reasoning in their favour. In order to do this, duties and rights should be institutionalised in accordance with economic incentives on a global level. This is one aspect of a global theory of justice: to formulate associations of norms in a way that they can be pursued in accordance with economic interests. The economic strategy to promote pro-poor growth, which the World Bank has taken up in its general policy and which is in accordance with global economic processes, seems to be the right approach for development economics.

According to the principle of subsidiarity, a global theory of justice can be founded that puts a limit to social justice, but makes justice a condition of exchange and performance. This limit has also been set because the ideal of equality cannot be egalitaristic, but utmost egalitarian combined with an understanding of individual freedom that allows cultural, social and also economic differences. This means that in the light of a Christian Ethics as well as in the name of a Rawlsian theory of justice, we are not allowed to reach for a worldwide equalisation of living conditions, especially not up to the highest level of consumption. Nevertheless, this limitation of ethical duties has to be correlated with a strict justification of economic and social differences, which I will argue for later.

In general, markets should only have a heuristic, not an absolute priority as an instrument of poverty reduction. They are not the exclusive instrument of poverty reduction, because although we can observe the phenomenon of global competition, we can also observe market failure and power in markets, which are not the result of competition. The exclusion of poor countries, almost two-thirds of the developing countries, is a problem that cannot be solved alone within markets. Also, markets can honour performance and efficiency, but nothing more. Justice traditionally has always been more complex than justice of performance. Therefore, we have to consider other means of poverty reduction and dimensions of justice.

Thesis 2: Aid Requires a Socio-Scientific Orientation in Favour of the Poor

There is a debate whether 'Trade instead of Aid', 'Aid instead of Trade' or 'Trade and Aid' are appropriate means of global justice. Scientifically, only the last can be valid. In Kantian ethics of human rights and in theories of justice, duties of emergency as well as a global principle of aid are discussed, which are required by the peoples and by a global society.

In the tradition of Catholic social ethics, in which a liberal market model has never been promoted and in which complete material equality or equal justice of ends was also never pleaded for in the official statements, the duty of solidarity found its place in order to guarantee social rights or rights of freedom (Pesch 1924, pp.408–455). Pure *caritas* is seen as a first step towards institutionalised social structures and rights within social systems (Ketteler, 1911), where *caritas* is not seen as superfluous or insufficient in certain situations. Since then, solidarity has become a core concept of Christian social ethics. It has been developed from the concept of French solidarism, which used to be an ontological term, into a rational principle of solidarity, which is still in use, and finally into an ethical statement of argument, in which solidarity functions as 'regulative leading idea'.

Since the end of the twentieth century, the concept of solidarity has been discussed again (Bayertz, 1998). Solidarity is placed between owed duties of right and meritorious duties of virtues. Solidarity reaches out beyond the morals of justice into the realm of love and caring (Höffe, 1999, p.414). Next to theories of the good life, which are influenced by certain life styles, and next to formal theories of justice, solidarity is a third source of social integration (Habermas, 1997, p.278). Habermas talks about the social integrative power of solidarity and argues for the concept of solidarity to be taken up in a broader public and in the constitutional procedure of democratic decisions. Today, in addition to the matter-of-fact ethics of justice, there comes along a philosophy of mutual caring (Honneth, 2000, p.170).

This fairly new discussion corresponds to a social realistic tradition of Christian social ethics. As a linking principle, the principle of solidarity claims to be more than a philosophical principle of justice, because, as a social principle, it refers to the social in its original meaning, namely the social interactions that are stabilised by structures, orders and systems. Thus, solidarity does not only refer to the rules of action, but also to the human beings, the subjects of rules. Solidarity is a rule, relevant for action, which rises the claim for interpersonal responsibility especially for those who have the opportunity to help others, who are poor, weak and in need. Christian social ethics still makes the principle of solidarity a central moment of its argumentation (Anzenbacher, 1998, p.198). This is in accordance with Karl Homann's thesis that solidarity – even in modern societies – has to remain a core aim of all interactions (Homann, 1998, p.30).

This becomes relevant in our context, because global markets did not really succeed yet in diminishing absolute poverty at its roots. One can conclude that besides markets, which are not free from solidarity, but in which solidarity emerges from competition through growth and the rise of prosperity, we do need another, additional form of solidarity, namely intentional solidarity. In markets, solidarity comes up as a non-intentional result of intentional actions under suitable ramifications (Habisch and Homann, 1994, pp.113–137). Intentional solidarity goes beyond economic investments, undertaken because of market incentives. This form of solidarity still has to take into account the socio-scientific conditions of implementations, if it is to make a contribution to just regulations and if it is not to show counterproductive effects. Therefore, we have to distinguish between two forms of solidarity: the owed solidarity and the optional solidarity.

The Level of Owed Solidarity as an Element of the Ethics of Rights

Within most philosophical and theological traditions, especially since Immanuel Kant founded an ethics of rights, aid to survive is not an act of optional responsibility, but a duty of securing negative rights of freedom, which are owed to every human being. Kant tried to solve the problem by distinguishing between the laws of nations and the laws of world's citizens. He talked about the necessity to complement the right of humans by a public right that could be secured by the right of a world citizenship (Kant 1992, orig. 1795, 357 und 1991, orig. 1797, § 62).

Similarly, the principle of solidarity in a Christian tradition is no act of charity, but a principle of the ethics of rights ('Rechtsprinzip'), which makes social cooperation a duty. Its specific aim is to establish the human rights status of the person for all others. Therefore, global aid for the fight against poverty is theologically required and ethically binding. Yet the duty of solidarity can only refer to the extent of its being necessary for a fundamental supply of goods and rights in order to preserve the dignity of human beings. Thus, an imperative of right can be derived, namely justice of distribution in terms of *a basic maintenance of the poor*. A justice of distribution in this sense does not aim at adjusting the conditions of living for all, but is a target of supply with fundamental necessities in terms of fundamental goods. Therefore, this level can only be reached on a global level through institutions and by law, which has not happened yet.

Still, the need of investment to eradicate poverty is not yet fulfilled by a supply of fundamental goods, because the poor need to claim the first step of development (Sachs, 2005, p.75). It has already been stated that global deregulation of markets and profit-orientated investment did not suffice, in many developing countries, to close the gap of poverty and to break the circle of poverty. The capital which is necessary to lead the poor out of their quandary is more than fundamental aid for surviving. Not only are *ad hoc* stabilisations of crisis necessary, but also a development-orientated financing in order to supply an initial provision for the poor in developing countries, so that they are able to claim the lowest level of development and can therefore participate in local, national and global processes of economic exchange.

As a fundamental condition of possibility for an independent life of the poor, this form of solidarity is necessary in terms of development economics as well as social ethics. Therefore, a second imperative can be derived, the justice of participation. This will be primarily focused on financing the initial provision of the poor in developing countries in order to let them participate in global interactions. Ethically, this argument can be derived from a qualitative concept of fundamental goods. This concept cannot be determined by economic needs alone, but has to include human rights as rights of freedom, fundamental needs in the sense of a transcendental exchange between human beings (Höffe), fundamental functioning and capabilities (Sen) and psychological conditions of self-respect (Rawls).

Therefore, a global duty of solidarity may not only refer to an economic maintenance of the poor, but also to their capacities in regional social and cultural as well as economic interactions – especially in regional markets. Therefore, the ability of self-organisation has to be more than subsistence, if we think in the category of a global justice of participation. Suitable means to reach participation are not only financial transfers, but primarily aid to invest in local infrastructure and social systems (education and health systems), economic and juridical assistance for democratic institutions, humanitarian action for peace and also providing credit for local units and persons, especially women and families (Mack, 2005, pp.79–100). Finally, many partial markets have to come into being by aid out of solidarity, because this would mean too much an effort to invest for private capital or would just be to uninteresting for it. Simple optimising of rural production, for instance, could save the poor of a region, but it probably would not bring enough return on investment to a private investor.

In this context, there is a debate between Pogge and Rawls whether a liberal principle of aid or a multifunctional egalitarian principle should be argued for in terms of a global security for fundamental goods. I would argue for a third variant in between, because as a Christian ethicist, I have to judge the justice of a global order depending on its consequences for all human persons, especially the poorest among them. A subsidiary principle of solidarity has to offer justice of distribution in terms of fundamental goods for everyone, and justice of participation in terms of an autonomous self-determination and interaction of the poor, but no egalitarian justice of ends. We can argue for the condition of the possibility to lead an autonomous life in dignity for every human being by the help of a world society, and this can be achieved by acting out the two concepts of justice, I have presented.

The Level of Voluntary Charity as an Element of an Ethics of Care

We should distinguish this level of solidarity for two reasons: First, an overwhelming responsibility and solidarity without borders may not be laid on everybody as a claim, but is an act of voluntary solidarity and social love. Other than the ethics of rights in a Kantian sense, we also need an ethics of virtues or an ethics of charity, argued for in theology. Second, it has been proved by development economics that an excess of charity will push away the poor in their own ability of autonomy and subsistence in regional markets. The problem is discussed by the keyword of 'deadly aid', in which awful disincentives come up together with well-meaning charity. This has often happened in the context of aid given in natural products, and it happens regularly when industrial countries deliver their superfluous rural products, which are heavily subsidised, onto the world markets. Homely goods in development countries cannot be deposited to real prices on local markets, which finally can lead to a descent of agriculture in these countries.

One can avoid these counterproductive consequences of charity if solidarity is taken up with the motto 'help you to help yourself', which also has to conform with the rules of the market. In this case, the principle of subsidiarity again is helpful, which requires the engagement of the bigger unit only if the smaller unit is not able to help itself. Aid out of solidarity can unfold a positive effect, if the needy will hereafter be able to help him- or herself with fundamental goods. Charity should therefore be understood as 'aid to action' (also on markets). The Second Vatican Council gives us a good hint to this: 'You have to eradicate the causes at its roots, not only at its consequences. The aid should be organised in a way that the recipient should be able to gradually escape an outer dependence, in order to help oneself'. (Rahner und Vorgrimler (1984), Apostolicam Actuosam No. 8.)

I argue to respect the distinction between social justice and social love, which has been made in Catholic social teaching since 1931 (Quadragesimo anno, Nr. 88), especially in the context of global business ethics. Social love is the theological ground of motivation, but cannot be an indifferentiated criterion for aid. Therefore, *A Theory of Justice*, combined with knowledge of social sciences and economics, delivers a better ethical argumentation ('criteriology'). Also, material criteria like 'bona humana' (Messner), existential purposes (Kant) or constitutive conditions of human life (Nussbaum) and material concepts of development (Sen) can give orientation for solidarity, but they all do not yet deliver a strategy of operation in poverty reduction. Charity in the form of voluntary aid can be a sensible means of intermediate solidarity fitting in between market failures and global structural poverty policy, especially when it overrides the solidarity owed to the poor because of claims of justice.

Both forms of solidarity, the obligatory and the voluntary, have a positive function in terms of poverty reduction if they meet the motto 'help to help yourself', and if they do not hinder autonomy. Therefore, both should engage in developing powers of self-action. In the public debate, solidarity can be understood as 'aid to survive' as well as 'help to trade'. I would add that solidarity is best understood as 'help to action'. In order to stabilise this action of the poor, solidarity must not stay in a realm of arbitrariness, but needs global institutions and organisations, which can provide a political frame for global solidarity.

Thesis 3: Institutions Build the Ramifications to Liberation from Poverty

From the angle of socio-empirical research, the political prerequisites for wealth and the end of poverty are, besides functioning markets, freedom and the rule of law (Nuscheler, 2005, p.428). Researchers do not agree on democracy being necessary in order to reduce poverty, because there is a tremendous success in eastern Asia (a poverty reduction from 60% to 15%). So one better talks about good governance, which is on the way to the rule of law. Legal systems, which guarantee property rights (at least for a certain medium-term period) and at least a solid basis of social rights, are necessary conditions to reduce poverty. If poverty reduction is not to rely on chance, independent legal and social security systems have to be established within a social system. Development economists even prefer national institutions to global institutions, without challenging the necessity of a global order in favour of fair trade, political stability and security for freedom.

From the perspective of Christian social ethics, the Christian command of love has to be converted into a universal claim of justice, which has to be secured by institutions and organisations. Unlike the global theory of John Rawls, I would conclude from the point of view of a Christian ethics in accordance with egalitarian authors that global institutions cannot only have an assisting function. I disagree with the thesis that a global balance does not include any compensation or any justice of distribution. I want to argue for the counter-thesis that global institutions are necessary for the organisation of global solidarity and for ramifications of global markets. Modern societies are anonymous and cannot be governed by individual actions. Stable structural and organisational connections of global solidarity can only be built up by global institutions and organisations.

Voluntary help as well as governmental development assistance have to be complemented by a global system, which is enduring and stable. A quest like this can be argued for theologically, by means of a principle of subsidiary solidarity. This principle requires justice of distribution as well as participation, and equally considers the autonomy of the persons concerned. Even markets need institutional ramifications, which have to be equal for everyone and should not contain special rules in favour of one side (no barriers of trade). Only structural measures can offer reliable, enduring and affective means to reduce poverty, build the foundation of a global binding law of peoples, enforce sanctions on those who violate the rules and build a fundamental infrastructure for global interactions, within which development for all can take place.

A Christian approach will therefore neither share a realism of political science nor a pure strategic theory of economics, but argue that institutions of a global order always have to be determined by ethical criteria of justice. We can follow a thesis of Peter Koller, who says: 'The global order has to be construed in a way that the advantages of international exchange and cooperation have to be for all, especially for the economically less developed and poor nations' (Koller, 2005, p.113). In addition to that, I would like to mention that the advantages do not only have to be for nations, but for parts of societies and groups of people who live in absolute poverty within states. Here a co-responsibility of governments is needed that has to care for a structural balance of income and wealth.

In an ethical sense, we can establish two levels of poverty reduction, an economic and a political-social one, which should just be named shortly:

a) The following suggestions for the reorganisation and correction of world-wide economic institutions are made, which are all reasonable, but could not yet be implemented: in the economic field, the opening of markets is one of the most important ethical demands, because tariffs on trade, protectionism of all sorts and subsidies can only be justified in infant industries of developing countries for a limited time, but not in industrial countries. Besides, several suggestions have been made for an international economic policy (Klasen, 2005), a global pact for structural investments in developing countries (Sachs, 2005), a global dividend of resources (Pogge 2002), a global structural policy (Müller and Wallacher, 2005) or a global 'Ordnungspolitik' through global governance (Messner and Nuscheler, 1996).

b) Claims on a political level for global and good governance refer to a global legal order, a world domestic policy, a global social organisation (parallel to IWF, World Bank and WTO), a reform of the United Nations and its institutions (Höffe, Klasen, Nuscheler), a global federal world order with world courts, a world criminal law, a world social security for a basic standard of living (Höffe) with a limited restriction of national sovereignty (Pogge) and a federal world republic (Kant, Höffe). These are all suggestions which are discussed seriously. I want to refrain from an evaluation at this stage, but only want to bring two dimensions of justice into discussion, which should be fulfilled by all institutions.

First, global institutions have to fulfil the requirements of *justice of distribution and participation*. Generally, on the basis of our previous argumentation, international government organisations should be globally equal, compatible with economic processes, not interventional, but focusing on poverty by presenting ramifications of a political, legal and economic order of the world. Structural promotion of interdependences and prevention of exclusion through external and internal institutions seem to be the most important aims. In the debate on global differences of income, a global justice of participation leads to certain conditions of justice, which claim participation in property rights and productive income in societies. I therefore suggest a reformulation of a global difference principle, and I combine this with the condition of certain institutional possibilities of implementation which go beyond national borders and regional federations. I proclaim a moderate difference principle on a global level:

Social, political and economic differences have to be to the advantage of the poorest and have to be justified with regard to them, so that their chances will be increased, so that they receive access to fundamental goods as well as to real chances, and so that they can develop capabilities to participate in global processes of prosperity.

Second, all institutional initiatives are subject to the claim of political justice. Here we should take up ideas from the theory of justice and democracy. This means that within international organisations and within elements of a world order, at least hypothetical means of agreement of the persons concerned and a practical and representative participation of voting for all peoples proportionally to their populations should be guaranteed. Rawls demands a proportional right of participation between equal peoples, which he plans to reconstruct through a second original position: in an international process of decision on global norms, it would be necessary that all human beings are equally represented and that peoples are taken into account proportionally (Rawls, 2002, p.46). I would agree with this view, because the adequate participation of the poor is the condition of the possibility for their development even in the context of a global structure. This means to establish a dimension of consent building as a primary expression of political justice, which is also the condition of the possibility for further forms of justice like justice of participation of the poor in economic or social processes. In this way, global norms and structures deserve legitimacy from the poor and by the poor. By establishing a qualified principle of consent for fundamental questions of justice on a global scale (combined with qualified rules of majority for single political questions), global institutions and organisations would receive validity from the persons concerned and would therefore really be universally accepted as just rules. They could in this way deliver a global frame for a self-development out of poverty and act out a theological option for the poor through a pragmatic implementation of justice.

After having discussed the three main means of poverty reduction, I would like to add some hermeneutic reflections which constitute the foundation of a Christian ethics in view of the poor.

A Universal, Subsidiary Cosmopolitanism

In a Christian understanding of theological hermeneutics, global justice is founded on the universality of Christian love. The love to one's neighbours is extended to the community of a society and further extended to every human being. This means that humankind is not understood as a species, as a community of fate or as a contract of world citizens, but as a unity and as a family of humankind, for every human being is equally worthy and dignified. The universalism of modern normative ethics can be correlated with a Christian hermeneutics of Christian love for everyone, although the dignity of the human being was not combined with rights before the enlightenment.

In contrast to classical-liberal, neo-Aristotelian and communitarian approaches, a Christian ethics will hold the position that a global responsibility towards every suffering human being can ethically be claimed, because 'we are responsible for all people' (John Paul II. (1984), No. 38). A double standard between members of the own nation or family and between all others cannot be justified. Global justice can only be argued for if it does not make a difference, and if it is universally equal in its fundamental claims. This universality does not contradict a responsibility in regional and national autonomy. Global justice is meant for everyone, but in his or her individuality, culture, philosophy, faith and way of life. Global justice will therefore not be egalitarian, but an egalitarian subsidiary cosmopolitanism.

Conclusion

All three means of poverty reduction have to be used in a certain intensity and relation:

a) In the case of self-organisation, free markets and economically motivated investments are enough to deliver fundamental goods for former poor and will manage their participation in economic processes of prosperity. The claim to equality will back up in favour of freedom and self-determination of societies, peoples and individuals.
b) In all cases in which there is exclusion and poverty nevertheless, global justice reaches out not only for a guarantee of fundamental goods, but for an initial financing of self-organisation of the poor, which allows them to participate in economic, political, cultural and social processes of communication and exchange.
c) Global poverty reduction will need transnational structures of political justice, which can secure global justice in the form of legal institutions – as a world's legal, social and economic order – and in the form of legal organisations in solidarity with the poor.

A subsidiary and universal cosmopolitanism constitutes the hermeneutic background for a theory of global justice. Poverty therefore is a moral problem, in which humankind questions its own self-understanding as long as it exists.

References

Anzenbacher, A. (1998), *Christliche Sozialethik. Einführung und Prinzipien*, Schöningh, (Paderborn).
Bayertz, K. (1998), *Solidarität. Begriff und Problem*, Suhrkamp, (Frankfurt).
Chen, Sh. and Ravallion, M. (2004), *How Have the World's Poorest Fared since the Early 1980's? World Bank Policy Working Papers 3341*, World Bank (New York) (http://www.worldbank.org).
Habermas, J. (1997), *Die Einbeziehung des Anderen. Studien zur politischen Theorie*, Suhrkamp, (Frankfurt).

Habisch, A. and Homann, K. (1994), Der Ertrag der Kooperation, Institutionenethische Zugänge zur Nord-Süd-Problematik, in *Signale Der Solidarität. Wege Christlicher Nord-Süd-Ethik* eds Ulrich P. and Habisch, A., Schöningh, (Paderborn) pp.113–137.

Höffe, O. (1999), *Demokratie im Zeitalter der Globalisierung*, Beck, (München).

Homann, K. (1998), Normativität angesichts systemischer Sozial- und Denkstrukturen, in *Wirtschaftsethische Perspektiven IV. Methodische Grundsatzfragen, Unternehmensethik, Kooperations – und Verteilungsprobleme* ed Wulf, G., Duncker & Humblot, (Berlin), pp.17–51.

Honneth, A. (2000), *Das Andere der Gerechtigkeit. Ansätze zur praktischen Philosophie*, Suhrkamp, (Frankfurt).

Johannes, P. II., (1984), *Sollicitudo rei Socialis* (Rom), in Texte zur katholischen Soziallehre – Die sozialen Rundschreiben der Päpste und andere kirchliche Dokumente ed. Bundesverband der katholischen Arbeitnehmer-Bewegung – KAB, (Ketteler: Bornheim).

Kant, I. (1992, orig. 1788), *Zum ewigen Frieden. Ein philosophischer Entwurf.* [first published in *Kant's gesammelte Schriften 8 (Ak. Ausgabe)*, Berlin 1923, 341-386] (Meiner: Hamburg).

Kant, I. (1991, orig.1797) *Die Metaphysik der Sitten* [first published in *Kant's gesammelte Schriften 6 (Ak. Ausgabe)*, Berlin 1914, 203-493] (Suhrkamp: Frankfurt).

Ketteler, W.E.von (1911), *Wilhelm Emanuel Kettelers Schriften B.I-II*, W.E. von: Kösel, (München).

Klasen, S. (2005) *Armutsreduzierung im Zeitalter der Globalisierung*, in *Ibero America Institute for Econ. Research (IAI) Discussion Papers No 146* (Göttingen).

Koller, P. (2005), Soziale und globale Gerechtigkeit, eds. Neumaier, O. and Sedmak, C., (ontos: Heusenstamm), pp.89–120.

Mack, E. (2002), *Gerechtigkeit und gutes Leben. Christliche Ethik im politischen Diskurs*, Schöningh, (Paderborn).

Mack, E. (2005), *Familien in der Krise. Lösungsvorschläge Christlicher Sozialethik*, Utz, (München).

Messner, D. and Nuscheler, F. (1996), *Weltkonferenzen und Weltberichte. Ein Wegweiser durch die internationale Diskussion*, (Dietz: Bonn).

Müller, J. and Wallacher, J. (2005), Entwicklungsgerechte Weltwirtschaft. Perspektiven für eine sozial- und umweltverträgliche Globalisierung, (Kohlhammer: Stuttgart).

Nuscheler, F., (6/2005), *Entwicklungspolitik.* Lern- und Arbeitsbuch, Dietz (Bonn).

Pesch, H. (1924), *Lehrbuch der Nationalökonomie, Grundlegung*, Bd.1 (Herder: Freibug).

Pogge, Th. (2002), *World Poverty and Human Rights, Cosmopolitan responsibilities and reforms,* (Polity Press: Cambridge, MA).

Pontifical Council for Justice and Peace, (2004), *Compendium of the Social Doctrine of the Church* (Città del Vaticano).

Rahner, K. and Vorgrimler, H. (1984), *Kleines Konzilskompendium* (Herder: Freiburg) (Apostolicam Actuositatem No 8, Rom 1965).

Ratzinger, J. (1986), Marktwirtschaft und Ethik, in *Stimmen der Kirche zur Weltwirtschaft* ed Roos, L., (Köln), pp.50–58.

Rawls, J. (1999), *The Law of Peoples*, Harvard University Press, (New York).

Rawls, J. (2002), *Das Recht der Völker*, de Gruyter, (Berlin).

Sachs, J.D. (2005), *Das Ende der Armut. Ein ökonomisches Programm für eine gerechtere Welt*, Siedler, (München).

World Health Organization (2005), Health and the Millennium Development Goals, Geneva (23.8.2005). www.who.int/mdg/publications/MDG_Report_08_2005.pdf.

Chapter 9

Just Relations between North and South in International Financial Markets[1]

Bernhard Emunds

This chapter deals with the moral criteria for designing international financial markets. The most important issue is whether or in what sense international economic justice can be a legitimate criterion for evaluating the institutions enabling financial relations between private agents in industrial countries, on the one hand, and companies, financial institutions, and governments of developing countries, on the other hand. After an introduction to the object of the ethical reflection, criteria for evaluating international financial markets will be given. Whereas the goals of 'functionality' and 'political justice' are a common interest of all participating countries, international economic justice focuses on the extremely poor people's interest in surviving taking priority over the material interest of those whose survival is not endangered. Finally the question is analysed whether the goal of international economic justice suggests a certain profile of designing international financial markets.

Introduction to the Object of the Ethical Reflection

International Financial Markets

The term 'international financial markets' is defined here in a broad sense; it includes not only stock or currency exchanges, but, e.g., also the meeting of the offer of and the demand for bank credits, bank deposits or policies of insurance companies: on financial markets, money and claims for future payment (other than property or use of a material asset) are exchanged. Financial markets are called 'international financial markets' if a participant of the transaction is located in a country different from the one in which the transaction takes place, or if a foreign currency (or a monetary claim in a foreign currency) is exchanged. Parts of the international financial markets are the foreign exchange markets, the international derivative markets, the international markets for loans, the regular international securities markets, and the offshore markets, which are less regulated than the regular financial markets. Except for the foreign exchange markets and the offshore markets, the international financial markets are not institutions on their own, separated from the domestic market. In fact, the existing national financial markets 'became' international by their integration into the international capital flows. Almost all transactions of foreign currency, securities

---

1   Thanks to Judith Hahn for translating the bulk of this chapter. The author is responsible for any remaining errors.

and derivatives take place on the industrial, newly industrialising and transition countries' territory exclusively and between transaction partners of these countries.[2] The following ethical reflection refers to the investors' (especially institutional investors') regular financial transactions with securities issued by borrowers of the newly industrialising countries of Latin America and Asia as well as to transactions with these countries' currencies. Problems concerning offshore markets and the over-indebtedness of developing countries' governments are not taken into account.

In this chapter, all relations not remaining within national borders are called 'international'. Regarding their extension, there is a distinction between 'regional' and 'global'. International relations are called 'regional,' if they are restrained to a world's region (e.g. Western Europe, South-East Asia). 'Global' are relations not limited to a region. Regarding the actors involved, there is a distinction between 'inter-national' and 'transnational'. 'Inter-national' relations exist between societies (countries, nations, peoples, states) or between their governments. Cross-border relations between private agents are called 'transnational'.[3]

The widespread rhetoric of globalisation nurtures the misconception of the global economy as a ubiquitous close-meshed net of interactions incorporating all economic actors worldwide: according to this picture, on global markets, all suppliers of labour, commodities, services or financial assets compete against each other across all national and regional borders. This opinion not only ignores the white spots on the map of international economic integration already mentioned for the case of financial markets, but also underestimates the role of national economies and regional economic areas. The less spectacular opinion is more appropriate: Global markets cross-link the national economies and regional economic areas (e.g. the Common Market of the European Union). In comparison with the 1950s, 60s and 70s, this process of cross-linking has become considerably more dynamic. But it has not given rise to a global economy as a melting pot, in which the national economies have been dissolved. Besides the areas of regional economic integration, the national economies continue to be the most important level of economic analysis and reflections in economic ethics.

In general, international goods and financial markets are perceived as institutions of *transnational* co-operation between transaction partners: There is an interaction of direct participants of the market: companies, financial institutions, wealthy private participants and governments. Regarding this, an ethical reflection analyses

---

2   By the end of 2001, the stock of cross-border securities investments was estimated to be about 12 trillion US-$; only 5% of the claims were issued by borrowers from developing countries (*Economist* 2003, 6). Financial capital flowing from North to South was available "to just a handful of recipients" (ibid.). Because of the relation of a country's cross-border assets and liabilities to its gross domestic product, a survey by the IMF (Prasad *et al.* 2003, 72) classifies the following developing countries as "more financially integrated": Argentina, Brazil, Chile, Columbia, Mexico, Peru, Venezuela, as well as China, Hong Kong, India, Indonesia, South Korea, Malaysia, Pakistan, the Philippines, Singapore and Thailand, also Egypt, Israel, Morocco, South Africa and Turkey.

3   Cross-border economic relations between a private agent and a governmental institution, which acts only as a market participant among others, are called 'transnational,' too.

the efficiency, commutative justice and fairness of the economic transactions (*cf.* Boatright, 1999). Moreover, an international market can be seen as an institution of *inter-national* co-operations between societies: Not only does a single transaction have an impact on the participants directly involved, but the sum of transactions on the international market cumulatively influence the participating (and the non-participating) countries. The relevance of national governments as agents needs to be taken into account, too. They establish the conditions of market participation for their citizens and the legal regulations for all transactions taking place in their territory. This chapter particularly deals with the morally legitimate shaping of the *inter-national aspect of co-operation* in financial markets. Which regulation of the financial markets should financially integrated countries prefer over other profiles of regulation, because its cumulative effect is more positive for all participants, or because it serves the interest of a certain group whose claim takes ethical priority over other interests?

Effects of International Financial Markets on Development

The cumulative effect of international financial markets on the development of an integrated country is mainly due to its effects on the national financial system. Such a system consists of a multitude of economic institutions, above all the financial markets and financial institutions, the central bank and the financial supervisory authority.

International financial markets, *on the one hand*, can support or obstruct a country's financial system in fulfilling its functions for the national economy as a whole. For the purpose of this chapter, two of these functions are the key issues:

First, the financial institutions and securities markets provide those agents with more money who expect income in the future, but want to spend more money in the present than they own (deficit units).

- The money, which is additionally provided to the deficit units, can come from savers placed in the same national economy. The financial system enables the flow of money from these surplus units to the deficit units ('financial intermediation').
- Checking account and other deposits are liabilities of commercial banks, but are widely accepted as a medium of payment. Therefore, commercial banks are able to create the money they additionally supply to the deficit units ('money creation') by granting a loan to the deficit unit and extending the unit's account balance.
- The money provided additionally can also stem from foreign investors. Except in dollarised national economies, this money cannot be used in the capital importing country until it has been changed into local currency, i.e. the money that the central bank (domestic cash) and the country's commercial banks (domestic checking accounts) can create themselves.

Second, to enable growth, it is necessary that additional (and saved) money is provided mostly to economic units that will contribute to the growth by increasing the quantity or the quality of goods in the national economy. To have money at one's disposal permits one to acquire resources. So the function of the financial system discussed here is to contribute to an efficient allocation of resources.

- Commercial banks and securities markets cover the function of *selecting* the appropriate borrowers (i.e. deficit units with a high probability of repayment or with high expected profits).
- Furthermore, commercial banks and securities markets have to *control the use* of the provided money. The banks can, if required, influence the disposal of funds, e.g., by threatening to stop the lending. In securities markets, this control function is achieved by an increase in risk for the issuer of the security, so that it might be impossible in the future to place other securities (control of borrowers, especially corporate control).

On the other hand, international financial markets can massively interfere with a country's economic development. This happens when international investors trigger or intensify a national financial crisis. A financial crisis in many cases is a crisis of banks: bank deposits are mainly accepted as money because deposit customers are confident that they can always change their deposit one-to-one into cash money if required. If their confidence erodes and if many deposit customers demand their account balance being handed out as cash money ('bank run'), the commercial bank's capital is greatly reduced: to mobilise the cash money demanded, the bank is forced to sell its long-term assets quickly and generally crash-priced. If the affected bank collects its claims on other banks or if other banks arouse comparable suspicion, the run will be extended to these institutions.

But also a crash, i.e. a massive slump of many asset prices (in most cases: stock prices or real estate prices), is called a financial crisis. A crash often emerges from a loss of trust in the macroeconomic development at the end of a cyclical upturn. The agents prefer to protect themselves against possible financial difficulties by trying to exchange their long-term assets for money (and money-like assets). Because the slump does not change the payment obligations undertaken in the past, highly indebted holders of securities and real estates can become insolvent. That is why a slump of asset prices is particularly problematic for the economy as a whole, if the investors of the stock or real estate markets are highly indebted.

Banks and their credit customers are important investors on the stock markets. This is why bank crises and price drops on the stock or real estate markets occur at the same time. However, there have rarely been major financial crises in the industrial countries since the Second World War. This is due to the fact that these countries' central banks adequately function as a lender of last resort which effectively safeguards the domestic commercial banks: if the central bank credibly states that solid banks would at any time, and without limits, receive all the cash money they need to pay out their customers, there is no reason for depositors to doubt the possibility of a one-to-one exchange of their deposits into domestic cash.

In contrast, newly industrialising countries as well as other peripheral countries are, from time to time, afflicted by a massive financial crisis, which often goes hand in hand with a currency crisis, i.e. with a quick and intense devaluation of the domestic currency compared to the key currencies (i.e. US-$, Euro, Yen). The reason for this coincidence is that in the case of a financial crisis, foreign investors (and wealthy residents) do not want to hold the country's money, which is in danger of losing its value. In turbulent times, they want to hold money or financial assets of a crisis-proof currency. Immediately, they exchange the currency of the crisis-ridden peripheral country into Dollar, Euro or other industrial countries' stable currency and thus trigger exactly the currency crisis feared. The preference for big industrial countries' crisis-proof currencies is at the same time a key reason why the peripheral countries' financial systems are more crisis-prone than the industrial countries': the central bank of a peripheral country can assure solid commercial banks unlimited access only to the cash money of its own currency. This lender-of-last-resort-function is of reduced value, because the money requested in turbulent times is key currency money, accessed by the central bank only on a restricted scale (mainly its own international reserves).

Criteria for an Ethical Evaluation

Functioning

The ethical reflection on international financial markets asks, first of all, whether these markets fulfil their function, e.g., whether they enable cross-border monetary transactions or a management of currency risks to microeconomic agents, whether they make it easier for the integrated countries to achieve a trade surplus or to finance trade deficits by building up or reducing the net accounts of cross-border claims and debts. The decisive question is whether the international financial markets assist the integrated country's economic institutions in fulfilling their function for society as a whole.[4] It is assumed here that the function of the economic institutions (in conjunction with others, mainly governmental and municipal institutions) fulfils the material condition for society's reproduction, and that it does so in such a way that the chances of personal development and of satisfying social participation increase for many members of society. This means that a long-term, ecologically sustainable growth for the benefit of the vast majority (in the following shortly called 'growth target') is the decisive goal of economic institutions.

Moreover, the segments of the international financial markets and the standards of international banking are to be surveyed concerning *how well* they fulfil their functions. First, the institutional arrangements of international financial markets should be *efficient*, i.e., there is no other noted arrangement fulfilling the favoured level of function more cost-efficiently or increasing the level of function at equal cost. Second, the international financial markets should be *stable*, i.e., they should durably maintain their own capacity for fulfilling their function and it should be unlikely for them to cause a financial crisis in an integrated national economy or to intensify a financial crisis caused by other reasons.

---

4 Approaches to ethics in finance rooted in the Aristotelic tradition deal with this aspect in respect to the question, whether institutions correspond to their 'nature', *cf.* Nell-Breuning (1928); Koslowski (1997).

Political Justice in International Relations

Beyond functionality, a society expects their economic institutions to correspond to other ethical criteria (e.g., a just distribution): the way these institutions work is supposed to benefit – or at least not to affect too negatively – the achievement of other goals valued as ethically legitimate by the society's citizens. In the ethics of international financial markets, this leads to the assumption that regarding the moral legitimacy of an institutional arrangement of these markets, its positive effects on the growth target of the participating national economies are a necessary, but insufficient condition. In fact, the arrangement's side effects on the achievement of other targets of a morally legitimate international order have to be taken into account.

Considering justice, first of all, one has to analyse the influence of the international financial markets on the political realm of integrated societies as well as on the political system of inter-national relations. A list of elementary principles of justice for political relations between peoples can be obtained by acting on the assumption that peoples, in so far as they fulfil certain minimum standards (e.g. the prevention of the rights of freedom and political participation domestically, the renouncement of violence and aggressiveness externally), acknowledge each other as coequal members of the inter-national community (*cf.* Rawls, 1999). They will reciprocally acknowledge the right to independently organising themselves according to the citizens' ethical norms and values, and independently from the calculated influence of other peoples. The right to self-determination does not exclude that peoples co-operate on common issues. But in general, they will demand that the regulation of shared matters derive from an inter-national process of deliberation and decision, which allows all participating societies to bring in their interests (principle of participation).

The mentioned list of elementary rules for international political relations and the idea of nationally organised societies, standing behind it, is relevant for the international financial markets in a twofold way. *First*, transactions on the international market are part of the shared matters, structured by international regulations and defined in inter-national opinion-forming processes (despite of reservations of sovereignty in implementing them). These processes often do not fulfil the requirements even of a minimal principle of participation. This is noticeable in the structures of the institutions in which these processes take place, e.g., the Basel Committee on Banking Supervision, whose 'recommendations' the supervisory authorities of financially integrated industrial, transition and newly industrialising countries can hardly avoid, is formed only by representatives of 10 leading industrial countries. An ethical reflection of international financial markets has to find criteria of participative justice criticising the countries' unequal influence on shaping the structures of the international financial markets.

Second, the impact of the international financial markets on a society can be so strong that under certain circumstances the very idea of a society, dealing with its issues independently according to its citizens' norms and values, is challenged. Part of this problem of self-determination mainly inflicting peripheral countries is the danger of the integration into international financial markets massively restricting the economic and socio-political flexibility of democratically elected governments.

For if a transition or newly industrialising country has attracted quickly removable financial capital (mostly by cross-border selling domestic securities) on a big scale, the government runs the risk of becoming manipulable: If it takes a political path at variance with the international investors' interests and political ideas, it might trigger a financial and currency crisis with devastating results for its own economy. Therefore, the ethical reflection on international financial markets should include a criterion demanding the compatibility of the international financial markets with the societies' self-determination.

International Economic Justice

An institution is called a just institution if competing claims of different actors are restricted inside by universal rules acceptable on good grounds by all persons affected. If international markets are seen as *transnational* institutions, questions of justice are mainly questions of commutative justice: Are profits and costs or chances and risks of a certain transaction (or of a certain type of transaction) justly divided up between the actors directly involved? But concerning the *inter-national* aspect of an international market, the most important question of justice is whether the allocation of long-run positive and negative effects on the different participating countries and their groups of citizens, caused by a certain institutional arrangement of the market, can be valued as just.

International economic justice is mainly understood here from the target of universal sufficiency. This means that the influence the institutional arrangement of an international market has on the allocation of economic chances and risks on different groups of citizens in different countries is above all evaluated from the angle of the following question: How much does the arrangement contribute in the long run to providing a certain minimum standard of availability of goods ('sufficient means') for all people? One line of argumentation, which convincingly establishes a human right not to suffer from severe poverty, assumes that people are needy, vulnerable beings with a sense of pain, who form and follow their own interests, create own ideas of a good life, but are only able to realise them if three fundamental interests are met: First, if they are protected against violation of life and limb (interest of existence); second, if they are sufficiently provided with goods, so they neither have to live in existential need, nor their health suffers under a permanent lack of supply (interest of subsistence); third, if they get the chance to further develop their personal abilities and to participate as an equal in the life of their society (interest of personal development) (*cf.* Kersting, 2002, pp.128–137).

The following argument is based on two suppositions: First, at least each human being's right to existence and subsistence and therefore also to goods essential for his survival (prevention of extreme poverty) can be convincingly established. Second, there is a universal duty of support corresponding to this universal right. This duty in principle commits every human being to do everything that is possible and can reasonably be expected in order to overcome extreme poverty. But with the notion of a general duty, it is not yet clarified who in detail is obligated and to which action.[5] It is comprehensible after all, that – different from, e.g., the duty to help after a car accident – this general duty is not about the actions of a single person in support of another person or of a few other persons, but generally about the duty to contribute to the buildup and to the maintenance of institutions' capability to effectively help many (*cf.* Hinsch, 2003).

The crucial point in concretising these duties is the acknowledgement of the fact that extreme poverty – apart from individual careers by chance – can only be permanently overcome by a society's development. In other words, for permanently reducing extreme poverty, the society in which the poor are living has to achieve a lasting economic development. It has to launch a permanent, ecologically sustainable process of growth, above all benefiting the poor ('pro-poor growth;,' *cf.* Klasen, 2004). The process of growth becomes permanent, when connected to a positive political and socio-cultural development. The necessity for a society to develop itself implies, as well, that its political institutions shape the changes as much as possible according to values and ethical norms (including concepts of justice) accepted by the overwhelming majority of the citizens. What is necessary is the creation and permanent securing of a democratic constitution, a functioning administration, a reliable state always in accordance with the rule of law and a vibrant political publicity, but also the buildup of social networks and intermediate associations as well as the creative development of established values, norms and world views. Because overcoming poverty permanently is an integral part of a process of development carried out by the developing society itself, the primary responsibility for overcoming poverty lies with the members of the society poor people are living in.

This does not free the people in the industrial countries from the duty to help the extremely poor in the developing countries with appropriate institutional arrangements. They are obliged to give development aid as a help to self-help. In addition, it has to be taken into account that the positive development of many developing countries is complicated or obstructed by institutions on the global level (*cf.* Pogge 1999). One might think of the international financial institutions, above all IMF and World Bank, massively intervening in the economic and social policy of many developing countries' governments by imposing their conditionalities; this brings up a whole number of ethical problems which cannot be dealt with here. Not less significant indeed is that segments of global markets are shaped in such a way that they inhibit the development in countries of the South. The international legal order, for example, lacks an international insolvency law for states. This contributes to the enduring extreme external indebtedness of some developing countries massively inhibiting their economic development (*cf.* Dabrowski et al., 2003).

The policy of international financial institutions and the structures of international market institutions both influence the development processes of the South, but are mainly determined by the democratically elected and controlled governments of the North. This is why most notably the people in the industrial countries are obliged to stand up for a policy of international financial institutions and for a reform of

---

5   Concerning the problem of assignment of duty, *cf.* O'Neill (1999), Hinsch and Stepanians (2005) and Georg Marckmann's and Matthis Synofzik's chapter in this volume.

international markets institutions, so that both become development promoting (*cf.* Müller and Wallacher, 2005), i.e., so that both will positively influence the economic, political and socio-cultural development processes of the countries in the South. These obligations are an especially important part of their co-responsibility for permanently overcoming extreme poverty in the developing countries. Citizens who actively support such a one-world-policy of their government act in line with a duty of all human beings to support those who live in extreme poverty.

Because of the special urgency of the interest of the extremely poor, there is a priority of their interest of subsistence over the interests of other agents to enhance their chances of personal development and social participation. In respect to this priority, markets have to be designed in such a way that their cumulative results are as positive as possible for extremely poor people's chances of development. This criterion of priority can be concretised for international financial markets. Therefore, two suppositions have to be made. First, in comparison with the *status quo*, the poor people's chances of development in financially not integrated developing countries cannot be reduced by any institutional reform of the international financial markets which increases financial stability. Second, the different possibilities of institutional reform resulting in sufficient financial stability have nearly the same development effects on these poor people. If these conditions are given, the international economic justice demands a certain distribution of the profits and costs of the co-operation on the international financial markets between the participating countries: If the functionality and stability of the international financial markets is sufficiently ensured, the international financial markets should be shaped in such a way that in the long run the extremely poor people's chances of development in the newly industrialising countries (as well as in the poorest of all financially integrated countries) are maximised. In implementing this criterion, it has to be taken into account that net advantages – also for the poor in the newly industrialising countries – are only to be expected if the co-operation is carried on. That is why the participation in these markets has to be profitable as well for the private actors of the industrial countries in the future; their net advantages as a result of their co-operation have to be positive in comparison with a non-attendance ('condition of participation').

The aspect of international economic justice in the focus of our attention can be called the criterion of promoting development, according to which international markets should be shaped in such a way as to promote a pro-poor development of developing countries. Can this criterion be viewed as a criterion of international distributive justice? Of course, the answer depends on the definition of the concept of 'distributive justice'.[6] Here, this concept is used only if competing claims to limited non-public goods have to be restricted and if for each participant, in comparison with the *status quo*, having more of these goods means being better off. Concerning international *goods markets*, it seems to be possible in most cases to view the currency receipts of the exporting industries of a country as such a good. Thus, the division of these receipts between the trading countries in the long run, deeply influenced by the regulation of these markets, can be evaluated from the

---

6 In the German version of this chapter, a broader concept of 'distributive justice' was introduced and applied in the ethical reflection of international financial markets.

perspective of distributive justice (*cf.* Kapstein, 1999). But it is not appropriate to evaluate the institutional arrangements of the international *financial markets* from the perspective of distributive justice: for quite a lot of newly industrialising and transition countries, it is not a reasonable target to attract financial inflows as much as possible (or even only substantially more than today), because those countries, by importing net capital on a large scale, massively increase the risk for a financial and currency crisis in the future. This risk rises if a country imports more net capital than it needs to finance its current account deficit, and especially if it attracts more capital by selling securities, which international investors can quickly re-sell in the case of a change of mood in the market. Moreover, if a domestic financial system functions well – as shown above – foreign capital is not needed to finance the internal processes of growth. Therefore, it is not in the interest of most citizens in these countries to attract much more capital.

Perspectives for Reform

Instead of widely opening the floodgates of the newly industrialising countries for international financial flows, it is a key issue to arrange for the integration of these countries into the international financial markets in a morally legitimate – this includes: economically reasonable – way. A necessary step is that the governments of the developing countries increase the transparency of their macroeconomic data, accept the international standards of regulation and supervision of financial institutes (if necessary with modifications), but also implement instruments to control the amount and the maturity structure (less short term, more long term financial investments) of the capital import (*cf.* the Chilean example of high and non-interest bearing reserve requirements on foreign capital). Besides these steps of the newly industrialising countries' governments, bond clauses have to be mentioned which will facilitate a consensual rescheduling. Because bonds in large part are issued and traded at exchanges in the industrial countries, the governments and financial institutions of the North are in demand for introducing these clauses. All of these reforms aim at reducing the probability of a financial and currency crisis. The above-mentioned criterion of promoting development is not needed for establishing them; they rather derive from the common interests of all participants in stability on the international financial markets. Although a political implementation is still lacking to a large extent, there is a broad consensus in economics that such measures would be useful. Instead of ethically reflecting on these instruments,[7] the rest of this chapter focuses on the question whether the criterion of promoting development suggests a *specific* profile of regulation beyond this consensus of reform.

Inside a national economy, financial markets and financial institutions providing an efficient allocation of financial resources are a vital condition for a permanent process of growth. There are primarily two strategies for a growth-orientated promotion of national financial systems: a calculated buildup and extension of securities markets

---

7   For a short reflection of the instruments, *cf.* Emunds (2003), 350 *et seq.*; for an instructive overview of the economic discussion, *cf.* Frenkel and Menkhoff (2000), 21–50; 60–74.

or an *improvement and strengthening of the sector of domestic commercial banks*. For most newly industrialising countries, the prior aim of improving the development chances of the poor will lead to a preference of promoting the banking sector.[8] Because banks cover many people's demand for financing and saving possibilities better than highly developed securities markets (*cf.* Hellmann, Murdock and Stiglitz, 1997), the strategy of promoting banks suits a pro-poor growth better, i.e., a process of growth with an above-average increase of income for the poorest sections of population. It is almost only big companies that can finance themselves by issuing securities, and because of high volatility of prices, buying securities is no form of saving that can be recommended to large parts of the population in the newly industrialising countries. Domestic commercial banks, on the other hand, can be motivated by governmental subsidies to build branches for the credit and deposit business in the rural sector. This strategy, namely to build up a strong plural banking sector for the whole country, can in addition weave in the promotion of micro-finance institutions specialised in the financial needs of very small businesses and in the very restricted saving possibilities of non-wealthy private households.

According to this internal strategy of promoting banks, the integration of these countries into the international financial markets has to be organised in a way so that disturbances of the targeted continuous refining of the domestic banking sector will be as few and as unlikely as possible. In the overall, this can be obtained by means of those instruments which can already be justified as measures to improve the financial stability by reducing the probability of financial and currency crises in newly industrialising countries. But apart from these instruments, the protection of domestic commercial banks in these countries can be reinforced by including the often neglected international monetary order into the agenda of reforms.

Before the Asian economic crisis (1997/98), many newly industrialising countries pegged their rates of exchange, i.e., they tied their own currency, more or less permanently, to a key currency, especially to the US dollar. They wanted to achieve a planning reliability for domestic companies operating in international trade or borrowing abroad, and also for their business partners and capital suppliers. They tried to increase the probability of a continuous stability-orientated monetary policy, without renouncing the option for a devaluation of domestic currency if necessary. Before and at the beginning of the Asian economic crisis, the central banks of South-East Asia clung to the fixed rates of exchange too long. After the currency reserves were exhausted, the resulting devaluation was extremely strong.

Because of this insight into the role of the pegged exchange rates in the Asian economic crisis, many economists concerned with the question of the exchange rate regime recommend to the newly industrialising countries to choose one of the two

---

8   The qualifying formulation 'for most newly industrialising countries' is intended to make it clear that the assumed conflict of aims 'strong securities markets' *vs.* 'strong domestic commercial banks' is not given in all countries. In general, broad securities markets will in fact narrow the profit margin of domestic banks in lending to big corporations and thereby reduce their capacity to build a broad network of branches (*cf.* Hellmann, Murdock and Stiglitz 1997). But vital securities markets can also strengthen the domestic commercial banks by partially relieving them of the task of maturity transformation.

possible extreme 'solutions': Either they should completely liberalise their rates of exchange (except from smoothing short term fluctuations), or they should irrevocably fix their rates of exchange in terms of a key currency by abolishing their own central banks ('currency board'). In both cases, the newly industrialising countries have to carry nearly the whole burden of the international monetary order. Of course, in the first case the participants of the market would not furthermore speculate that the newly industrialising country eventually has to renounce on its exchange rate targets. This speculation often exaggerates the necessary devaluation of the country's currency and transforms it into a currency crisis. But also without such speculations, strong devaluations can be caused by international investors' mood change. These have major recessive consequences for the country, which derive from the insolvency of the corporations and financial institutions highly indebted in foreign currencies.[9] In the second case, the country abstains from the instruments of monetary policy enabling its central bank to slow down or increase the country's economic growth according to the specific situation of the domestic business cycle. Beyond this, the commercial banks are deprived of the protection achieved by the central bank functioning as a lender of last resort; for the domestic central bank was abolished without the engagement of the key currency's central bank to guarantee that, if needed, all deposits in the commercial banks of the newly industrialising country with the currency board can be exchanged at a certain rate into money of the key currency.

As an exemplary case that shows how the burdens of monetary policy can be shared in another way, Peter Bofinger's (1999, 2000) proposal for a monetary co-operation between the central bank of a key currency (especially the American Federal Reserve Bank or the European Central Bank) and the central bank of a newly industrialising country shall be cited here. In such a co-operation, the newly industrialising country's central bank has to determine the interest rate of the money market and the exchange rate (target) in such a way that the money invested for 1 year in the country's money market achieves exactly the same rate of return as the money which would be exchanged in the key currency, invested in the money market of the key currency's country for the whole period and exchanged back in the domestic currency by the end of the year (*cf.* interest rate parity). That way it can be excluded that a lot of financial capital temporarily pours into the newly industrialising country for achieving an exceptional high rate of return. If the newly industrialising country moreover credibly contracts a solid economic policy and an effective supervision of banking, the Federal Reserve Bank or the European Central Bank could guarantee to intervene and support the external value of the newly industrialising country's currency, if it is on the brink of an excessive devaluation. In this way, a currency crisis would be avoided. Above all, this arrangement would allow an effective protection of the developing country's commercial banks by a lender of last resort. The country's domestic banking sector would be relieved from a brake heavily straining the expansion of its credits and deposits business: As the co-

---

9   After a devaluation of domestic currency, debtors with obligations to be paid in foreign currencies have to obtain much more receipts in domestic currency than before to accomplish the fixed debt service in the foreign currency in the future.

operation of an industrial country's central bank credibly guarantees a floor for the external value of the newly industrialising country's currency, bank customers in this country now have an effective protection of their account balances by a powerful lender of last resort. As this protection is anticipated by the customers, it reduces considerably the probability of a bank run or a currency crisis.

Unlike the extreme 'solutions', Mr Bofinger's proposal suggests that the industrial countries, namely those consenting to participate in such a monetary cooperation, carry part of the burden of a stable international monetary order. In fact, for this co-operation, they have to cut back on their monetary sovereignty – even though only to a minor degree. For if the newly industrialising country's currency needs an intervention of the co-operating central bank in the North, the bulk of the additionally created liquidity would probably appear in the currency area of the industrial country. In fact, it should generally not be difficult for the co-operating Northern central bank to neutralise this liquidity; furthermore the advantage of higher stability of international financial markets must be taken into account. Nevertheless, it is quite possible that the citizens of the key currency's country (or region) attach greater importance to the small reduction of monetary sovereignty than to the advantage of more financial stability. If one further assumes that the realisation of Mr Bofinger's proposal would in fact have *great* advantages for the poor in the newly industrialising country, the demand to realise this model of monetary cooperation could be justified by the above-mentioned criteria of promoting development: While ensuring functionality and stability of the markets and meeting the 'condition of participation' regarding the private actors of the industrial countries, the international financial markets should be shaped in such a way that the expected advantages of the extremely poor in the newly industrialising countries were maximised.

References

Boatright, J. R. (1999), Ethics in finance, *Foundations of business ethics 1* (Malden/ Massachusetts-Oxford: Blackwell).

Bofinger, P. (1999), The Euro and the "New Bretton Woods", *The European Union Review* 4/1, 7-25.

(2000), Währungspolitik in "emerging market economies", in: Hengsbach, F., and Emunds, B., eds., *Finanzströme in Entwicklungsländer – in welcher Form zu wessen Vorteil? Frankfurter Arbeitspapiere zur gesellschaftsethischen und sozialwissenschaftlichen Forschung* 24 (Frankfurt am Main: Nell-Breuning-Institut), 108-116.

Economist, The (2003), A cruel sea of capital. A survey of global finance (3.5.2003).

Emunds, B. (2003), *The integration of developing countries into international financial markets. Remarks from the perspective of an economic ethics*, Business Ethics Quarterly 13, 337-359.

Frenkel, M., and Menkhoff, L. (2000), *Stabile Weltfinanzen? Die Debatte um eine neue internationale Finanzarchitektur*, (Berlin: Springer).

Hellmann, Th., Murdock, K., and Stiglitz, J.E. (1997), Financial Restraint. Toward a New Paradigm, in: Aoki, K., Kim, H.-K., and Okuno-Fujiwara, eds., *The Role of Government in East Asian Development* (Oxford: Clarendon), 163-207.

Hinsch, W. (2003), *Die Verschuldung ärmster Entwicklungsländer aus ethische Sicht*, in: Dabrowski, M. et al., eds., Die Diskussion um ein Insolvenzrecht für Staaten. Bewertung eines Lösungsvorschlages zur Überwindung der Internationalen Schuldenkrise, (Berlin: Duncker & Humblot), 17-44.

Hinsch, W., and Stepanians, M. (2005): *Severe Poverty as a Human Rights Violation – weak and strong*, in: Føllesdal, A., and Pogge, Th., eds., Real World Justice: Grounds, Principles, Human Rights, and Social Institutions (Dordrecht: Springer), 295-315.

Kapstein, E.B. (1999), Distributive justice and international trade, *Ethics & International Affairs* 13, 175-204.

Kersting, W. (2002), *Kritik der Gleichheit. Über die Grenzen der Gerechtigkeit und der Moral* (Weilerswist: Velbrück Wissenschaft).

Klasen, S. (2004), In search of the Holy Grail. How to achieve pro-poor growth?, in: Tungodden, B. et al. eds., *Toward pro-poor-policies. Aid, institutions, and globalisation* (Washington D.C.: World Bank), 63-94.

Koslowski, P. (1997), *Ethik der Banken und der Börse. Finanzinstitutionen, Finanzmärkte, Insider-Handel*, Beiträge zur Ordnungstheorie und Ordnungspolitik 154 (Tübingen: Mohr Siebeck).

Müller, J., and Wallacher, J. (2005), *Entwicklungsgerechte Weltwirtschaft. Perspektiven für eine sozial- und umweltverträgliche Globalisierung*, (Kon-Texte 7 Stuttgart: Kohlhammer).

Nell-Breuning, O. von (1928), *Grundzüge der Börsenmoral*. Studien zur katholischen Sozial- und Wirtschaftsethik 4 (Freiburg/Br.: Herder).

Pogge, Thomas (1999), Menschenrechte als moralische Ansprüche an globale Institutionen, in: Gosepath, St., and Lohmann, G., eds., *Philosophie der Menschenrechte*, 2nd edition (Frankfurt/Main: Suhrkamp), 378-400.

Prasad, E., Rogoff, K., Wei, Sh.-J., and Kose, M.A. (2003), *Effects of financial globalization on developing countries. Some empirical evidence* (Washington D.C.: International Monetary Fund).

Rawls, J. (1999) *The law of peoples. With: The idea of public reason revisited* (Cambridge/Mass.: Harvard University Press).

Chapter 10

Access to Essential Medicines: Global Justice beyond Equality

Georg Marckmann and Matthis Synofzik

Introduction

Millions of people in low-income countries have little or no access to safe and high quality medicines. They suffer and die from medical conditions that can be treated in other parts of the world. Effective drug treatment now exists for many infectious diseases that are among the leading causes of death in poor countries: About 10 million people die each year from acute respiratory disease, diarrhoea, tuberculosis or malaria. Most disastrous for the people in low-income countries is certainly the HIV/AIDS pandemic. Forty million people have been infected with HIV at the end of 2005, with the majority (25.8 million) living in sub-Saharan Africa. Out of the five million new HIV infections worldwide in 2005, more than 3 million occurred in this region. Although the national HIV prevalence rates in sub-Saharan countries recently showed a more variable pattern (e.g. declining rates in Kenya, Uganda, Zimbabwe, but rising in Mozambique and Swaziland) – making it inaccurate to speak of single 'sub-Saharan AIDS epidemic' – it remains by far the most affected region of the world.[1] While there is still no cure for HIV, antiretroviral drugs can significantly improve the course of the illness and increase life expectancy.[2] Some drugs have proven to reduce the mother-to-child transmission of HIV (Brocklehurst et al., 2002; Jackson et al., 2003). In sub-Saharan Africa, however, less than half a million people – i.e. only one in 50 persons with advanced disease – have access to effective antiretroviral drugs and basic medications against HIV-related disease.[3] As a consequence, about 11 million children have lost one or two of their parents due to AIDS and grow up in societies in which most of the adult authority figures are

---

1   *Joint United Nations Program on HIV/AIDS (2005): AIDS Epidemic Update* (2005), Geneva: UNAIDS; Available at: www.unaids.org (Accessed on 12 February 2006).

2   As mathematical models of HIV infections and fatality rates in Sub-Saharan Africa show, treatment measures lead to an impressive benefit especially if they are combined with preventive interventions (Salomon et al. 2005). With respect to the ethics of allocating scarce resources, it might be even more interesting that increased spending on prevention will not only reduce the number of new infections by half, but also result in net financial savings, as future costs for treatment and care are averted (Stover *et al.*, 2006).

3   World Health Organisation (2004) The world health report 2004: Changing History. Geneva: World Health Organization. Available at www.who.int/whr/2004/en (accessed February 12, 2006).

dead.[4] In 2005, more Africans died of AIDS than in any other year so far – about 2.4 million people.

Lack of access to essential medicines not only inflicts tremendous suffering on poor populations, but also keeps them in the poverty trap. Serious illness is one of the major reasons for declining economic productivity and stagnating development. Poverty is both cause and effect of the high burden of disease.[5] Hence, for people living in low-income countries it is virtually impossible to escape from this vicious circle of poverty and illness. Even if drugs are available in these countries, they are often unsafe, not distributed properly in a deficient health care system or not used appropriately (Pecoul et al., 1999; Henry et al., 2002; Quick, 2003). Other non-medical factors further aggravate this fatal situation: Many people are undernourished; they lack access to safe water and basic sanitations and have no adequate shelter.

There have been several initiatives to alleviate this disastrous situation. Among the first was the Model List of Essential Medicines launched by the WHO in 1977 to help countries to select, distribute and use essential drugs that satisfy priority health needs.[6] This list has since then been revised every 2 years and can be seen as a breakthrough in international public health that is even discussed as a model for health care planning in high-income countries (Hogerzeil, 2004). Another recent WHO activity was the '3 by 5' initiative, launched to provide 3 million people with HIV/AIDS in low- and middle-income countries with life-prolonging antiretroviral drugs by the end of 2005.[7] Some pharmaceutical companies have lowered prices for patent protected drugs or offered medications for free (Cochrane, 2000). Other organisations and private persons have donated funds to low-income countries (e.g. the Gates Foundation). Yet, these efforts have not been very successful so far: There is still a huge gap between the potential to save millions of lives with safe and cost-effective drugs and the sad reality of extremely high morbidity and mortality in most low-income countries of the world. There is little controversy on that this situation is morally unacceptable and that something should be done to improve access to essential drugs for these deprived populations. So, one might ask, is the lack of access to essential medicines really a genuinely *ethical* problem in the sense that we do not know what is morally right or wrong? The moral imperative seems to be as clear as it could be: We should ensure access to essential drugs for all people in the world!

However, while there is little disagreement *that* something should be done, there is considerable disagreement *what* should be done: What are the most effective strategies to change this obviously unacceptable situation? On the face of it, this

---

4   This fact is very impressively illustrated by the projected population structure in Botswana with and without the AIDS epidemic (Attaran, 2004).

5   For further analysis of the impact of improved access to essential drugs on reducing severe poverty see, e.g. Pogge (2005). For the effects of poverty on impairing access to essential drugs see, e.g. Attaran (2004).

6   For the latest version, the 'WHO's Thirteenth Model List of Essential Medicines', see: www.who.int/medicines/organization/publications/essentialmeds_committeereports/en/index.html.

7   World Health Organization, – The 3 by 5 Initiative. Available at: www.who.int/3by5/en (Accessed on 12 February 2006).

again does not seem to be a real *ethical* problem: Is it not rather a question of instrumental reasoning if we try to find the most effective means to achieve a – more or less – uncontroversial goal?

This first impression certainly has some plausibility: There are several different approaches that could contribute to alleviate the access problem: Some have suggested price reductions on behalf of the pharmaceutical industry. Following the concept of 'differential pricing', the companies should sell their drugs to low-income countries at prices near the marginal cost of production, while regaining the investment for research and development (R&D) through maintaining high profit margins in high-income countries.[8] Others have called for increased donor funding for the purchase of essential drugs. Bulk purchasing arrangements, as performed by the Delhi Society for Promotion of Rational Use of Drugs, have been proposed to achieve significantly lower prices on the market (Ahmad, 2002). Still others have suggested compulsory licensing of patent protected drugs to allow the production of cheaper generic equivalents (e.g. Schüklenk, 2002). And the WHO Commission on Macroeconomics and Health (2001) has favoured a voluntary arrangement by the pharmaceutical industry for pricing and licensing of production in low-income markets.[9] Which of these different approaches we favour certainly depends on instrumental judgements about which strategy will be most effective to improve access to essential drugs in low-income countries.

However, below the surface of these instrumental considerations there is a truly *ethical* issue that represents a major obstacle to straightforward solutions of the access problem: '*Who* should do *what* for *whom*?' (O'Neill, 2002, p.42). While there is wide agreement that we have *some* obligation towards people who lack access to essential medicines, there is considerable disagreement about *how* this obligation should be allocated: *Who* is obliged to help the people in low-income countries to get access to essential drugs? And *what* concrete actions do these obligations require? And *who* are the appropriate recipients of the required actions? In our opinion, this 'allocation of obligations' represents the biggest ethical challenge in improving access to essential drugs in low-income countries. What we need is an ethical justification of how we should allocate responsibilities among the different agents and agencies that could contribute to alleviate the access problem.

Why does this 'allocation of obligations' pose such a hard problem for ethical analysis? The reason is the *global* scale of the issue: Access to essential drugs is impeded by a web of causations that include local as well as global factors, involving many different agents and institutions (Pecoul et al., 1999; Quick, 2003; Attaran, 2004; Barton, 2004). How can we identify and ethically justify obligations to improve the

---

8   The World Trade Organization ministerial Conference in Doha and the joint Global Health Council/World Trade Organization/WHO workshop emphasised the need for differential pricing to minimise the adverse effects of patent protection; Available at: www.who.int/medicines/library/en/ (Accessed on 12 February 2006). A method to derive differential prices for essential drugs in countries of variable national wealth has been proposed by Lopert et al. (2002).

9   Report of the WHO Commission on Macroeconomics and Health 'Macroeconomics and Health: Investing in Health for Economic development' (2001), 86–103 (www.cmhealth.org).

access problem within this global web of causations? Do these obligations transcend national borders? To what extent are people in high-income countries responsible for the situation of people in low-income countries? There are two common strategies to ethically justify access to essential medicines: a distributive justice and a rights-based approach. In the following we would like to show that neither of the two approaches is able to give a sufficient justification for the allocation of responsibilities. Rather, one should start with a systematic account of *obligations*, because it makes more explicit what action is required by whom to improve access to essential drugs (O'Neill, 2002). This will narrow the gap between the rather abstract considerations of distributive justice and concrete action to improve access to essential drugs.

Distributive Justice Beyond Equality

Due to its global scale, the access problem presents a big challenge for traditional theories of distributive justice that usually focus on the distribution of goods within states or bounded societies.[10] During the last 10 years, several authors have tried to extend these theories of distributive justice to a global scale. It would be far beyond the scope of this paper to give a detailed account of the different approaches that have been proposed so far.[11] Therefore, we limit ourselves to some general considerations. Without doubt, there is enormous *inequality* between high-income and low-income countries in the world. Though constituting 44% of the world's population, the 2.7 billion people who – according to estimates of the World Bank – live below the poverty line of $2 per day account only for approximately 1.3% of the global social product. They would need an increase of just another 1% to escape the so defined poverty. The consumption of high-income countries (955 million citizens), by contrast, amounts to 81% of the global social product with an average *per capita* income that is almost 180 times greater than that of the poor (Pogge, 2005). As poverty is one of the main causes of ill health, these economic inequalities also contribute to large inequalities in health status. And the income gaps are greater today than 50 years ago and most likely will continue to grow. The large discrepancies in life expectancy between low-income and high-income countries – for example 26.5 years in Sierra Leone *vs.* 73.6 years in Japan[12] – are a clear indicator of these tremendous global inequalities. Theories of global distributive justice now have to show that these inequalities are morally unacceptable.

Drawing on the work of the political philosopher Charles R. Beitz, we distinguish *direct* from *indirect* reasons why social inequalities are objectionable (Beitz, 2001). *Direct* reasons are based on the assumption that distributional inequality is a morally bad thing in itself. These reasons are usually derived from an egalitarian account of distributive justice, which is probably the most common approach. *Indirect* or *derivative* reasons, by contrast, show that social inequality is a morally bad thing by reference to other values than equality. In our opinion, these derivative reasons

---

10 E.g. Rawls' "Theory of justice" (Rawls, 1971).

11 For a selection of recent papers see Pogge (2001).

12 Healthy life expectancy at birth (HALE), The World Health Report (2001) (http://www3.who.int/whosis).

provide a philosophically less ambiguous and practically more promising approach to global inequalities.

There are several derivative reasons why global inequality matters (Beitz, 2001). First of all, social inequality is usually associated with *material deprivation*: the worst off live in terrible conditions, suffering from severe poverty, hunger and ill health. Here, not inequality *per se* is morally compelling, but the concern with the tremendous suffering of the poor that could be relieved by a comparably small sacrifice of the rich. *Prima facie*, this constellation is a strong moral reason that calls for improving the living standard of disadvantaged populations. A second derivative reason is that large inequalities of resources significantly restrict a person's capacity to determine the course of her life (Daniels, 1985). By use of their political or economic power, the better off can exercise a considerable degree of *control* that limits the range of opportunities open to the worse off. Like the material deprivation, these restricted choices are reasons that apply both to domestic and global inequality because they refer to *basic human needs* that show little variability across different cultures and societies.[13] Any human being has the need for decent basic living conditions and a reasonable freedom of choice. We set aside for now the deeper philosophical question of exactly defining 'decent' living conditions and a 'reasonable' degree of freedom of choice. A third derivative reason that makes inequality unacceptable is *procedural unfairness*. Global inequality often is associated with asymmetric decision procedures that are dominated by the rich and sometimes even exclude the poor. One example is the UN Security Council that grants a veto to the five permanent members but not to representatives of those states that are the potential recipients of humanitarian interventions.[14] Again, it is not inequality *per se* that matters but the distorting impact on the process of decision making that puts the interests of the poor at a disadvantage.

Compared to the *direct* equality-based reasons, these *derivative* reasons have several advantages. They do not depend on some theoretical ideal of a global egalitarian distribution of goods which is deeply rooted in the Western culture of social democracy and which appears to be too abstract and formal to give concrete guidance on how we can improve the extreme deprivation of the people in low-income countries. In addition, egalitarian accounts of distributive justice are philosophically ambiguous: Just consider the 'equality of what?' debate that has preoccupied philosophers for decades. *Derivative* reasons, by contrast, focus on the concrete situation and living conditions of deprived populations. This can help to develop policy measures that directly address their most important needs by reducing poverty, by improving nutrition and access to essential medicines and by creating fair international decision procedures. Certainly, the resulting policy measures will reduce inequality in the world even if it is not their primary objective. We do not

---

13 Cf. the Neo-Aristotelian capabilities approach of Martha Nussbaum. She identifies a list of universal *human capabilities* that are all implicit in the idea of a life worthy of human dignity (Nussbaum, 2006, p. 76).

14 Another example are the international trade negotiations about intellectual property rights that resulted in the TRIPS agreement which will raise the cost of technology to poor countries.

argue that global inequality does not matter. Rather, we would like to draw attention to non-egalitarian considerations that are ethically at least as compelling and practically more useful in directing attention to concrete policy measures. However, these arguments still do not provide a sufficient answer to the question of *who* has the responsibility to finance and conduct these policy measures that will eventually reduce global inequality.

Rights to Health and Health Care

Before further pursuing this question, we would like to discuss briefly another line of ethical argument that is often used in the campaign for global access to essential medicines. These arguments are based on human rights, assuming that there is a right to health or a right to health care. The most prominent example certainly is the constitution of the WHO: 'The enjoyment of the highest attainable standard of health is one of the fundamental rights of every human being.'[15] While the right to health certainly has both some intuitive appeal and an important rhetorical function in the WHO's campaign for better global health, it is a philosophically highly problematic concept. In general, human rights create corresponding obligations for other people to respect these rights. For example, the right to life (Chapter 3, UN Declaration of Human Rights) requires other people to refrain from killing the bearer of this right to life. Or the right to freedom of movement and residence within the borders of each state (Chapter 13) requires other people to refrain from restricting the freedom of movement of the right-holder. Consequently, rights are only meaningful if there is someone who can fulfil the corresponding obligations. And this is not the case with the right for health: for many medical conditions, no effective treatment is available, so virtually nobody can fulfil the corresponding obligations. 'The main difficulty is that assuring a certain level of health for all is simply not within the domain of social control.' (Buchanan, 1984, p.55.) Hence, it is philosophically incoherent to claim that people have a universal right to health.[16]

A more promising candidate in this respect seems to be a *right to health care*. A right to health care, however, still raises difficult philosophical questions, especially regarding its justification and scope. For the issue 'access to essential medicines', some preliminary remarks will be sufficient. The most promising approach to justify a right to health care has been proposed by Norman Daniels who has extended Rawls' theory of justice to the sphere of health care (Daniels, 1985). According to Daniels, the function of health care is to restore or maintain normal species functioning. As an impairment of normal species functioning through disease and disability restricts an individual's opportunities, health care promotes equal opportunity by preventing and curing diseases. Hence, if people have a right to fair equality of opportunity – which has been established by Rawls' theory of justice – they also have a

---

15 Alike, the United Nations Secretary-General Kofi Annan refers to health as a human right: 'It is my aspiration that health will finally be seen not as a blessing to be wished for; but as a human right to be fought for.' (www.who.int/hhr/en/)

16 This is not to deny that we have strong beneficence-based obligations to help sick people.

(derivative) right to health care. It is certainly the strength of Daniels' approach to have demonstrated convincingly the moral importance of health care: Health care contributes to maintaining or restoring fair equality of opportunity. As this derivative right for health care is not based on a particular conception of the good, it must be considered a *universal* right that can provide an ethical justification for a global access to essential drugs.

What remains unclear, however, is the *scope* of this derivative right: do people have a right to any health care that is technically feasible no matter what the costs are? Or do they just have a right to a *decent minimum* of health care? Given the resource constraints we face, only the second interpretation seems to be feasible. But Daniels' approach does not tell us what constitutes a decent minimum or basic level of health care.[17] Alike, a rights-based approach does not specify the corresponding obligations: '*Who* ought to do *what* to protect and restore *whose* health?' Therefore, a rights-based approach does not bring us very far in solving the most controversial ethical issue in the access problem, the allocation of obligations. Onora O'Neill rightly has emphasised: 'If we want to establish intellectually robust norms for health policies it would be preferable to start from a systematic account of obligations rather than of rights.' (O'Neill, 2002, p.42.) We should focus on required actions rather than on entitlements to receive.[18]

Three Principles for the Allocation of Obligations

In the following section, we will try to outline how the ethical obligations to improve access to essential drugs should be allocated to different agents and institutions. Who bears *remedial responsibilities* concerning access to essential medicines? 'To be remedially responsible for a bad situation means to have a special obligation to put the bad situation right, in other words to be picked out, either individually or along with others, as having a responsibility towards the deprived or suffering party that is not shared equally among all agents.' (Miller, 2001, p.454.) Remedial responsibility falls on individual agents as well as on social institutions, with individual agents bearing responsibility for those social institutions they are able to restructure in order to improve access to essential drugs.

According to which principles shall we allocate remedial responsibilities? Three different approaches are frequently used in the debate: 'The first appeals to agents' responsibilities based on their *connectedness* with those suffering. The second allocates responsibilities to agents on the basis of their *contribution* to the current crisis. The third claims that remedial responsibilities ought to be allocated according to the *capacity* of different agents to discharge them.' (Barry et al, 2002, p.63) Interestingly, these principles are not only invoked to allocate responsibility but also to evade responsibility, because one has – allegedly – not contributed to the suffering or one has not the capacity to help. The further analysis of the three principles will

---

17 This argument has been developed in more detail by Ezekiel Emanuel (1991).

18 Or, as Thomas W. Pogge has put it: We need an *active* concept of justice that 'diverts some attention from those who experience justice and injustice to those who produce them'. (Pogge, 2002, p.75.)

show that they have different moral force with the connectedness resulting in the weakest and the contribution resulting in the strongest remedial obligations.

According to the principle of *connectedness*, the agents who are connected in some way to the deprived people bear a special responsibility to alleviate their suffering. The connection can be based on joint activities, shared institutions, membership in the same community or in the same state, for example. It is thereby possible to distinguish between different degrees of connectedness. While intuitively it seems to make sense that we have greater responsibility to care for those with whom we are related in some way, the criterion of connectedness has some disturbing consequences: As the rich tend to be closer connected to the rich and the poor closer to the poor, the criterion will systematically favour the rich. And there is another reason that makes this principle ethically less compelling: Why should we have less ethical obligation to help those in dire need just because we are not so closely connected? With respect to the moral importance of the suffering of the poor, the connectedness seems to be morally somewhat arbitrary and therefore conveys only limited moral binding force.

According to the second principle, people who have the *capacity to act* bear the responsibility to help those in dire need, irrespective of their connectedness or their causal contribution to the deprivation. Consequently, all those agents who have the required technology or resources also have an obligation to improve access to essential drugs. The capacity to act depends not only on the available resources but also on the opportunity costs that are caused by the remedial action. It is important that capacity to act refers both to the capacity of individual agents and to the capacity of several agents to act collectively. Action may be possible within the existing institutional framework, but sometimes it may be required to change the institutional framework itself to alleviate the situation.

According to the third criterion of *contribution*, agents are responsible for situations if they have been involved in causing those situations. This causal relationship is certainly the most compelling ethical reason: If someone has contributed to inflicting harm to someone else, he or she bears an especially strong remedial obligation. The principle of contribution is grounded in the ethical asymmetry between omission and commission: Obligations not to harm others (principle of nonmaleficence) seem to be ethically more stringent than the obligation to help them (principle of beneficence). Given the web of causations that impedes access to essential medicines in low-income countries, it is not surprising that there is much controversy about the causal contribution of different agents and institutions. The pharmaceutical industry, for example, argues that not the patents but rather the severe poverty is the main barrier to access, while NGOs like Médecins sans Frontières (MSF) emphasise the impeding role of patents (Goemaere et al., 2002; Goemaere et al., 2004).

Allocation of Obligations According to the Three Principles

These three principles can now be used to assign responsibility to different agents and institutions. It seems most plausible to apply the principles in combination and give each of them the appropriate weight. In this last section of the paper, we would like to sketch how remedial responsibility for improving access to essential drugs in low-income countries can be allocated according to these three principles.

We start with the much blamed pharmaceutical industry. Pharmaceutical companies certainly have the *capacity* – and hence the responsibility – to improve access to essential drugs by various means. Intuitively most appealing would be lowering prices for expensive drugs or offering medication for free, as already done by some pharmaceutical companies (Cochrane, 2000). However, while these measures certainly provide some immediate and direct relief, they are no sustainable long-term solution to the access problem. On the contrary, price reductions and drug donations are limited by time and quantity, mainly suitable for the few medicines that are highly effective with short treatment courses (e.g. antihelmintics, antibiotics). The experience of GlaxoSmithKline shows the limits of this approach: Although the company was the first to discount its HIV/AIDS medicines in low-income countries (Cochrane, 2000), NGO activists still considered the prices excessive, inviting other pharmaceutical companies to scorn the effort (Friedman, 2003).[19] This measure is, however, not only of limited utility, but also morally at least ambiguous (Schüklenk, 2002): It perpetuates the dependence of people in low-income countries on charitable action from organisations and companies in high-income countries.

Which other strategies could pharmaceutical companies use to comply with their remedial responsibility? It is commonly assumed that patents impede access to essential medicines in poor countries. Especially NGO activists claim that 'patents [are ....] a barrier in many places to accessing affordable medicines'.[20] Yet, most pharmaceutical companies do not seek patents in poverty-stricken countries very often, since little revenue is at stake (Attaran et al., 2001; Friedman, 2003). Only 17 out of 319 products on the World Health Organization's Model List of Essential Medicines are patentable, although not actually patented, so the overall patent incidence is only 1.4 per cent (Attaran, 2004). Most of these medicines are antiretroviral (ARV) drugs since HIV/AIDS is a rather recent disease. But even ARVs are patented only in a few African countries, and generally only a small subset of them (Attaran, 2001). Moreover, patented drugs are not necessarily more expensive than generics. Since nearly all of the patented essential medicines (except Cipro and Lariam) are already discounted in low-income countries, the brand-name products and their generic counterparts often have similar prices (Attaran, 2004). This also applies to ARVs: a recent study by the Hudson Institute using data collected by Médecins sans Frontières shows that patented ARVs are often provided at even lower prices than ARVs of generic manufacturers (Noehrenberg, 2004).

---

19   In addition, the initiative by GlaxoSmithKline seems to be hypocritical: While initiating drug discount programmes in some parts of Africa, its patent on the ARV drug 3TC in China blocks the availability of one of the most simple and affordable AIDS treatments available worldwide, the WHO recommended fixed-dose combination of d4T/3TC/NVP (Goemaere *et al.*, 2004).

20   Médecins Sans Frontières, Canadian HIV-AIDS Legal Network, Oxfam Canada, Interagency Coalition on AIDS and Development, Canadian Council for International Cooperation, Canadian Treatment Action Council. An open letter to all members of the parliament. 25 October 2001. Available at: www.msf.ca (accessed 12 February 2006). See also Goemaere *et al.* (2002, 2004).

Nevertheless, even a minor number of patents can be an obstacle to the development of a competitive market in which prices equal marginal costs of production. It can therefore also be a sufficient – yet sometimes overstated – reason to reform the rules of intellectual property rights. Two different options have been proposed: compulsory and voluntary licensing. Since the Doha 'Declaration on the TRIPS Agreement and Public Health' in 2001, compulsory licensing has received great emphasis as a nation's tool to override patent protection standards which before had been strengthened by the Trade-Related Aspects of Intellectual Property Rights (TRIPS) in 1995 (Barton, 2004; Sterckx, 2004). The Doha Declaration confirmed a nation's right to use the exceptions of TRIPS – such as compulsory licensing – to meet public health concerns stating that 'public health crises, including those related to HIV/AIDS, tuberculosis, malaria and other epidemics, can represent a national emergency'.[21] Compulsory licensing can be ethically justified, both by consequentialist (Schüklenk, 2002) and social contract arguments (Ashcroft, 2005); yet, the practical effect of compulsory licensing has been very limited so far (Attaran, 2003). Its utility seems to lie more in the argumentative power as a possible tool of litigation when negotiating with pharmaceutical companies.

Given the small number of essential medicines that are both patented and overpriced, it seems more effective to concentrate specifically on each of these drugs and find flexible solutions that evoke less conflict and acrimony than compulsory licensing.[22] One promising approach is the use of 'out-licensing' as a form of voluntary licensing: Brand-name companies voluntarily agree to license generic alternatives for their patented essential medicines in low-income countries, but retain their licenses in high-income countries, thus preserving their core pharmaceutical markets in rich countries (Friedman, 2003; Attaran, 2004). As only a few of the essential drugs are patented and the market is far less profitable in low-income countries, these out-licenses would only negligibly affect the companies' revenues.

According to the principle of *contribution*, we must ask: Who is causally responsible for the intellectual property framework? As the TRIPS rules have been set up by the World Trade Organization (WTO), it is the WTO and not the individual pharmaceutical firm operating within this framework that bears primary remedial responsibility in this respect. In fact, as emphasised by the Doha Declaration, the TRIPS agreement already permits compulsory licensing in situations of national emergencies. However, compulsory licensing has been effectively prevented by the intensive lobbying of the pharmaceutical industry. Hence, the pharmaceutical industry is causally connected to the access problem and therefore bears remedial responsibility, at least for refraining from this intensive lobbying. Also, the principle of *capacity to act* applies to this context. Within the framework of TRIPS, there are still many different ways for pharmaceutical companies to alleviate the access problem, e.g. by drug donations, out-licensing or supporting non-profit pharmaceutical

---

21 World Trade Organization, Declaration on the TRIPS Agreement and Public Health, 20 (November 2001); www.who.int/medicines/areas/policy/tripshealth.pdf (Accessed on 12 February 2006).

22 Accordingly, the WHO Commission on Microeconomics and Health favours voluntary licensing agreements as a primary tool for lowering prices of patented drugs.

companies (see above). In any case, the intellectual property rights play only a minor role in improving the access to essential medicines. It is therefore misleading and often counterproductive to primarily concentrate on the ethical aspects of patents and licensing. Instead of patents and patent laws, a variety of *de facto* barriers impede access to essential drugs, including *inter alia* the high cost of some medicines (e.g. ARVs), national regulatory requirements for medicines, tariffs and sales taxes, and insufficient international financial aids (Attaran, 2001).

Accordingly, also the low-income countries themselves bear responsibilities to improve the access problem. Inasmuch as not only national regulatory requirements and sales taxes, but also corruption and mismanagement inhibit access to and rational usage of essential medications, these countries or their governments respectively bear responsibility to improve these conditions (principle of *contribution*). In addition, they have the *capacity to act* by improving their health care delivery system and ensuring the effective distribution and rational use of essential drugs. One example is the DREAM (Drug Resource Enhancement against AIDS and Malnutrition) project in Mozambique, an innovative programme developed by the Ministry of Health in cooperation with the Community of Sant' Egidio. In this programme, patients get free access to highly active generic anti-retroviral drugs (HAART) and laboratory tests and also receive further support by a nutrition programme and health education. This project does not only show high compliance rates and a decrease in viral loads (Marazzi, 2006), but also an increased overall survival rate (Palombi, 2004; Wenderlein, 2004). Thus, drug programmes specifically tailored to African nations under the responsibility of their national Ministries of Health provide effective means to improve access to essential medicines. The sub-Saharan nations therefore bear the responsibility to establish appropriate regulatory regimes for the utilisation and distribution of these drugs.[23]

Based on the criteria of causal involvement and capacity to act, the *individuals* in low-income countries also bear a responsibility to alleviate the access problem. Their responsibility applies mainly to the field of primary prevention: in low- and high-income countries alike, individuals bear the responsibility to take care of their own health status by avoiding unhealthy life-styles and by engaging in prevention. For example, malnutrition and alcohol or nicotine abuse are wide-spread causes of preventable diseases which often require ongoing expensive treatment. Since sexual transmission is the predominant mode of HIV spread in sub-Saharan Africa (Schmid, 2004), safer sexual behaviour is a major factor in preventing HIV infections and thus for reducing the need for antiretroviral therapy. This in turn will improve – indirectly – the access problem. However, since prevention requires a comprehensive set of interventions backed by wide-scale treatment and political support (Stover et al., 2002; Stover et al., 2006), the reference to individual responsibility for health simultaneously points to new obligations on a national and transnational level.

And last but not least: What obligations do the citizens in high-income countries have to improve access to essential medicines in low-income countries? While they

---

23 Cf. the report of the WHO Commission on Microeconomics and Health "Macroeconomics and Health: Investing in Health for Economic development" (2001), 88-89 (www.cmhealth.org).

are not closely connected to these poor populations, they bear remedial responsibilities based on the principles of contribution and capacity to act. As citizens who live in rich democratic states, they sustain the global economic order that *contributes* to the severe poverty in many low-income countries, which is itself a major barrier to access to essential drugs. While being greatly concerned about the few cases of patented essential medicines in low-income countries, the WHO hardly criticises the enormous agricultural subsidies ($310 billion) of Asian, European, and North American governments, which prevent the agrarian populations of low-income countries from exporting their own products and accumulating wealth (Attaran, 2004). As pointed out sharply by the President of Uganda, Yoweri Museveni: 'If there were no agricultural subsidies ... [we] would earn enough money to buy all drugs we want.'[24] The failure of billions of patients to receive necessary therapies might therefore also be a consequence of economic policies by high-income countries.

But what is ethically even more compelling, is the *capacity to act*: People in affluent countries could prevent so much harm at so little cost to themselves that they have a rather strong obligation to increase financial support for low-income countries. According to estimates of the WHO Commission on Microeconomics and Health, 0.1 per cent of donor-country GNP – that is one penny out of every $10! – would be enough to reduce total deaths in low-income countries due to treatable or preventable diseases by around 8 million/year by 2015.[25] This increased financial assistance would not only improve access to essential drugs but would also stimulate economic development and reduce overall poverty. The people in high-income countries certainly should not miss this opportunity to break the vicious circle of poverty and ill health.

Limitations

The three principles connectedness, capacity to act and contribution provide plausible ethical arguments to allocate remedial responsibility. However, they do not contain sufficient content to address all details of complex, real-world decisions. They rather offer a general ethical framework that requires further interpretation for practical application. To determine the actual remedial obligations, we must specify and balance the different principles:[26] *How much* assistance does the capacity to act require from people in rich countries? Is 0.1% of GDP too much or too little assistance? What concrete measures should the pharmaceutical industry undertake to meet its remedial obligation? What *relative weight* shall we assign to the remedial obligations of different agents, e.g. the obligations of the pharmaceutical industry *vs.* the obligations of the WTO? The openness certainly restricts the problem-solving power of this principled approach: It 'does not offer a mechanical answer to questions of that kind, but it provides a way of thinking about them – highlighting

---

24   November 2003 Africans for Drug Patents' (Editorial), *Wall Street Journal*, 7.

25   Report of the WHO Commission on Macroeconomics and Health (2001), p. 92 and p. 103.

26   Most ethical approaches that are based on mid-level principles share this problem (e.g. Beauchamp and Childress., 2001, p. 15ff).

their complexity – that may in the end prove to be more illuminating.' (Miller, 2001, p.471.) That we cannot infer straightforward solutions from this ethical approach is certainly a weakness. Given the empirical complexity and moral diversity of our world, however, this openness can also be considered as a chance.

Concluding Remarks

While there is little controversy that something should be done to improve access to essential medicines in low-income countries, there is considerable disagreement about *what* should be done. On the one hand, this is certainly a question of instrumental reasoning: What are the best means to improve access to essential drugs? On the other hand, there is a genuine ethical issue that represents a major obstacle to a solution of the access problem: Who ought to do what for whom to improve access to essential medicines in low-income countries? We have argued that neither theories of distributive justice nor approaches based on a right to health (care) provide sufficient guidance in the allocation of remedial responsibilities. Rather, one should start with a systematic account of obligations that draws attention to required actions rather than to entitlements to receive. We have discussed three principles that can justify the allocation of obligations: connectedness, capacity to act and contribution, with an increasing strength of moral obligations from connectedness to capacity to act and finally to contribution. More exemplary than systematically, we finally gave an outline of how these principles could be applied to specify the obligations of different agents, agencies and institutions for improving access to essential drugs. However, there still remains a considerable degree of discretion in specifying and balancing these principles. These principles do not offer a simple algorithm to solve the access problem, but they provide a useful means to structure the ethical and political discourse on how to allocate remedial responsibility for improving access to essential medicines in low-income countries.

References

Ahmad, K. (2002), Access Denied to Essential Medicines in Developing World *Lancet Infectious Diseases*, **2**, 12, 711.

Ashcroft, R.E. (2005), Access to Essential Medicines: a Hobbesian Social Contract Approach, *Developing World BioEthics*, **5**, No. 2, 121–141.

Attaran, A. (2003), Assessing and Answering Paragraph 6 of the Doha Declaration on the TRIPS Agreement and Public Health: The Case for Greater Flexibility and a Non-Justiciabilty Solution, *Emory International Law Review*, **17**, No. 2, 743–780.

Attaran, A. *et al.* (2001), Do Patents for Antiretroviral Drugs Constrain Access to AIDS Treatment in Africa?, *Journal of the American Medical Association*, **286**, No. 15, 1886–1892.

Attaran, A. (2004), How Do Patents and Economic Policies Affect Access to Essential Medicines in Developing Countries?, *Health Affairs*, **23**, No. 3, 155–166. Barry, C. *et al.* (2002), Access to Medicines and the Rhetoric of Responsibilities, *Ethics and International Affairs*, **16**, No. 2, 57–70.

Barton, J.H. (2004), TRIPS and the Global Pharmaceutical Market, *Health Affairs*, **23**, No. 3, 146−154. [DOI: 10.1377/hlthaff.23.3.146]

Barry, C., Raworth, K. (2002), Access to Medicines and the Rhetoric of Responsibility, *Ethics & International Affairs*, **16**, No. 2, 57–70.

Beauchamp, T.L. and Childress, J. (2001), *Principles of Biomedical Ethics*, New York: Oxford University Press.

Beitz, C.R. (2001), Does Global Inequality Matter?, in *Global Justice* ed Pogge, T. W., Oxford: Blackwell Publishers, pp. 106−122.

Brocklehurst, P. *et al.* (2002), Antiretrovirals for Reducing the Risk of Mother-To-Child Transmission of HIV Infection, *Cochrane Database of Systematic Reviews*, **1**, CD003510.

Buchanan, A. (1984), The Right to a Decent Minimum of Health Care, *Philosophy and Public Affairs*, **13**, No. 1, 55−78.

Cochrane, J. (2000), Narrowing the Gap: Access to HIV Treatments in Developing Countries A Pharmaceutical Company's Perspective J Med, *Ethics*, **26**, No. 1, 47−50; Discussion 51−53.

Daniels, N. (1985), *Just Health Care*, Cambridge: Cambridge University Press.

Emanuel, E.J. (1991), *The Ends of Human Life: Medical Ethics in a Liberal Polity*, Cambridge, MA: Harvard University Press.

Friedman, M.A. *et al.* (2003), Out-licensing: a Practical Approach for Improvement of Access to Medicines in Poor Countries, *Lancet*, **361**, No. 9354, 341−344.

Goemaere, E. *et al.* (2002), Do Patents Prevent Access to Drugs for HIV in Developing Countries?, *Journal of the American Medical Association*, **287**, No. 7, 841−842; author reply 842-3.

Goemaere, E. *et al.* (2004), Patent Status Matters, *Health Affairs*, **23**, No. 5, 279−280; author reply 281.

Henry, D. *et al.* (2002), The Pharmaceutical Industry as a Medicines Provider, *Lancet*, **360**, No. 9345, 1590−1595.

Hogerzeil, H.V. (2004), The Concept of Essential Medicines: Lessons for Rich Countries, *British Medical Journal*, **329**, No. 7475, 1169−1172.

Jackson, J.B. *et al.* (2003), Intrapartum and Neonatal Single-Dose nevirapine Compared with zidovudine for Prevention of Mother-To-Child Transmission of HIV-1 in Kampala, Uganda: 18-month Follow-Up of the HIVNET 012 Randomised Trial, *Lancet*, **362**, No. 9387, 859−868.

Lopert, R. *et al.* (2002), Differential Pricing of Drugs: a Role for Cost-Effectiveness Analysis?, *Lancet*, **359**, No. 9323, 2105−2107.

Marazzi, M.C. *et al.* (2006), Improving Adherence to Highly Active Anti-Retroviral Therapy in Africa: the DREAM Programme in Mozambique, *Health Education Research*, **21**, No. 1, 34−42.

Miller, D. (2001), Distributing Responsibilities Journal of Political, *Philosophy*, **9**, No. 4, 453−471.

Noehrenberg, E. (2004), Objective Patent Study, *Health Affairs*, **23**, No. 5, 280−281; author reply 281.

Nussbaum, M.C. (2006), *Frontiers of Justice. Disability, Nationality, Species Membership*, Cambridge, MA: The Belknap Press of Harvard University Press.

O'Neill, O. (2002), Public Health or Clinical Ethics: Thinking beyond Borders, *Ethics and International Affairs*, **16**, No. 2, 35–45.

Palombi, L. *et al.* (2004), One Year of HAART in Mozambique: Survival, Virological, and Immunological Results of DREAM Project in Adults and Children, 11th Conference on Retroviruses and Opportunistic Infections (CROI); 2004; San Francisco: available at http://www.retroconference.org/2004/cd/Abstract/148.htm.

Pecoul, B. *et al.* (1999), Access to Essential Drugs in Poor Countries: a Lost Battle?, *Journal of the American Medical Association*, **281**, No. 4, 361–367.

Pogge, T. (2005), World Poverty and Human Rights, *Ethics and International Affairs*, **19**, No. 1, 1–7.

Pogge, T.W. (2002), Responsibilities for Poverty-Related Ill Health, *Ethics and International Affairs*, **16**, No. 2, 71–79.

Pogge, T.W., ed. (2001), *Global Justice*, Oxford: Blackwell Publishers.

Quick, J.D. (2003), Essential Medicines twenty-five years on: Closing the Access Gap, *Health Policy and Planning*, **18**, No. 1, 1–3.

Rawls, J. (1971), *A Theory of Justice*, Cambridge, Mass.: Harvard University Press.

Salomon, J.A. *et al.* (2005), Integrating HIV Prevention and Treatment: from Slogans to Impact, *PLoS Medicine*, **2**, 1, e16.

Schmid, G.P. *et al.* (2004), Transmission of HIV-1 Infection in Sub-Saharan Africa and Effect of Elimination of Unsafe Injections, *Lancet*, **363**, No. 9407, 482–488.

Schüklenk, U. *et al.* (2002), Affordable Access to Essential Medication in Developing Countries: Conflicts between Ethical and Economic Imperatives, *Journal of Medicine and Philosophy*, **27**, No. 2, 179–195.

Sterckx, S. (2004), Patents and Access to Drugs in Developing Countries: an Ethical Analysis, *Developing World BioEthics*, **4**, No. 1, 58–75.

Stover, J. *et al.* (2002), Can we Reverse the HIV/AIDS Pandemic with an Expanded Response?, *Lancet*, **360**, No. 9326, 73–77.

Stover, J. *et al.*, (2006), 'The Global Impact of Scaling-Up HIV/AIDS Prevention Programs in Low- and Middle-Income Countries'. *Science*, **31**, No. 5766, 1474–1476.

Wenderlein, D. *et al.* (2004), Aids in Mosambik: Antiretrovirale Therapie erfolgreich, *Deutsches Ärzteblatt*, **101**, 51–52, A3476–A3480.

PART IV

GLOBALISATION, PHILOSOPHY AND CULTURE

Chapter 11

Social Glue under Conditions of Globalisation: Philosophers on Essential Normative Resources

Christoph Luetge

Introduction

The phenomenon of globalisation can be looked at from a number of perspectives. However, the distinctive characteristic of the philosophical perspective is its focus on the normative aspect of a phenomenon. Social philosophy makes no exception: Among social philosophers, it is a widely held assumption that a democracy society depends on specific normative resources of its members and cannot remain stable without these resources. While this is a descriptive claim at first, a consequence drawn regularly is the normative claim that members of democratic societies *should* propagate these normative resources.

This claim, which I would like to call the *social glue assumption*, both in its descriptive as well as in its normative version, is held by the vast majority of authors in the field of social philosophy, in one form or another. I would like to single out three of them here: Jürgen Habermas, David Gauthier and Ken Binmore. In the rest of this chapter, I will try to outline – roughly, at least – which normative resources these three authors regard as indispensable for a stable democracy. I will then discuss the question whether it can be maintained that these resources, which I will call *moral surpluses*, can indeed remain stable, especially under conditions of globalisation.[1]

I will argue that this question must be answered negatively in each of the cases discussed – with the exception of Binmore. Neither of the other two surpluses can remain stable against opposing incentives in PD situations. I will start with Habermas' discourse ethics.

J. Habermas: Democracy Depends on Rational Motivation

Habermas, when arguing for the importance of discourses as grounds for normative theory, makes one fundamental assumption: the participants of a discourse must – at least partially – be motivated by a *rational motivation*.[2] Rational motivation leads

---

1   This question is elaborated on in a much larger study (Luetge, 2007).
2   Cf. Habermas (1981), vol. 1, 50 and 54; Habermas (1983/99), 68 and 119; Habermas 1992, 19.

what Habermas terms *communicative action*. While *strategic action* ('strategisches Handeln') is affected by incentives and sanctions, communicative action ('kommunikatives Handeln') is not, at least not entirely (cf. Habermas, 1983/99, p.68).

It is not easy to find a concise explication for the concept of rational motivation in Habermas' writings. In the 'Theory of Communicative Action' (Habermas, 1981), the existence rational motivation is simply postulated,[3] while Habermas (1981, vol. 1, 50, fn. 42) even admits that this concept has not yet been analysed satisfactorily.

In 'Diskursethik: Notizen zu einem Begründungsprogramm' (Habermas, 1983/99), the justification given relies on the illocutionary effects of a *speech act* (cf. Habermas, 1983/99, p.68): Speech acts are supposed to be able to make actors perform certain actions and refrain from others, in order to escape committing a *performative contradiction*.[4] According to Habermas, a rationally motivated actor is led by the desire to avoid a performative contradiction.

Habermas himself recognises the ensuing problem of justifying the binding force of a speech act. He therefore invents a dialogue with a fictitious sceptic who doubts exactly this binding force. Habermas responds that the sceptic may well hold on to his position, but cannot act from it, as he is invariably bound by the requirements of the 'Lebenswelt': Lebenswelt – according to Habermas – is formed by cultural tradition and socialisation which in turn work through rational motivation. Those trying to escape from it would end in 'schizophrenia and suicide' (Habermas, 1983/99, p.112; my translation).

The problem of the sceptic is taken on again in Habermas (1991). Here, Habermas at first seems to weaken the power of rational motivation by attributing to moral norms only 'the weak motivating power of good reasons' (Habermas, 1991, p.135; my translation). He goes as far as stating that 'the validity of moral norms is subject to the condition that they are observed as the basis of a general practice' (Habermas, 1991, p.136; my translation). This implies that individuals might be allowed to behave 'immorally' when faced with possible exploitation by others, as would be the case in prisoners' dilemma situations.[5] However, it soon becomes clear that Habermas does not consider this a problem of *ethics*, but a problem of *law*: Only within the discourse of law, some norms might be valid but yet not reasonable ('zumutbar') because of their lack of general acceptance.

Habermas therefore develops a conception of philosophy of law, in order to give a systematic account of institutions, which were rather neglected in his earlier work. However, in 'Between Facts and Norms' (Habermas, 1992), it again becomes clear that Habermas does not trust sanctions and incentives to govern modern societies alone. Rather, the citizens must still have certain characteristics: Besides legal rules, they also have to recognise normative claims resulting from idealised discourse assumptions. Habermas still assumes a 'coordination of plans of actions' (Habermas, 1992, p.34) *by language* – thus still assuming the existence of rational motivation

---

3   Habermas (1981), vol. 1, 54; cf. also Habermas (1981), vol. 1, 70.

4   For further explication, cf. Habermas (1983/99, p.100f).

5   Binmore (1994, 1998) and Homann (2002) both assign the PD a central role in their ethical or ethically relevant approaches.

working via speech acts. Thus, Habermas leaves his main claims intact in his later work.

Now the question mentioned in the beginning becomes relevant: Can rational motivation remain stable in view of opposing incentives? One important part of the problem is how to reconstruct the Lebenswelt. In my view, there are alternative, and less harmonious, reconstructions of the Lebenswelt possible in which the binding force of speech acts is much weaker. One major example is the game-theoretic approach that reconstructs all human interactions as being 'riddled' with dilemma situations like the prisoners' dilemma.[6] These situations can be either manifest (as in open market interactions with competition being obvious) or hidden. Hidden PD situations have been overcome by rules and institutions. They are hidden in all the institutions, like police and jurisdiction, that come into effect because of the social contract which enables the actors to escape from the natural state – and the nation state in itself can be reconstructed as a PD situation.

In a phenomenalistic perspective, i.e. one that does not look beyond the surface, it seems as if the individuals complying with these rules are moved by a rational motivation. However, the 'deeper' structures are neglected here: It is not just rational motivation, but rather formal and informal incentives or sanctions that stabilise these rules. This casts doubt on whether Habermas' concept of the Lebenswelt is the only possible reconstruction of everyday practices.

To sum up, discourse ethics regards rational motivation as a necessary moral surplus for modern societies. Institutions play a role, too, but this role is limited and can be neutralised by rational motivation. The question is, however, whether rational motivation can remain stable under conditions of globalisation.

D. Gauthier: Democracy Depends on Dispositions to Cooperate

In his 1986 book 'Morals by Agreement', D. Gauthier develops an account of morals based purely on self-interest. He starts with assumptions fundamentally different from Habermas'.

According to Gauthier, moral problems arise due to PD situations.[7] In a PD situation, the result of the participants' (rational) actions leaves all of them worse off. The solution proposed by Gauthier is that all actors should commit themselves to a certain principle of justice. This principle is the principle of 'minimax relative concession' (MRC),[8] according to which each individual accepts a rule that minimises her highest possible relative concessions to others.[9] Gauthier argues that MRC is to be adopted in a two-step procedure: First, the actors choose MRC *from self-interest*. Afterwards, however, MRC is to *constrain* the actors' self-interest.

Gauthier tries to show that MRC would be chosen by rational, utility-maximising actors for the sake of greater benefits in the long run. However, he recognises that the problem of *compliance* to MRC is not solved easily. Gauthier reminds us of

---

6   Cf., for example, Binmore (1994) and 1998 or Homann and Suchanek 2000.
7   Cf. Gauthier (1986, p.12), p.82, 103f.
8   Gauthier (1986, p. 157).
9   Cf. also Gauthier (1997).

'Hobbes' Foole'. In the *Leviathan*,[10] the Foole is introduced to show that an actor's *acceptance* of a contract is not a sufficient condition to be *motivated* to comply with the contract. The Foole sees the remaining prisoners' dilemma situation. He argues that it would be best for him if all others complied, while he himself could still break the contract.

One way to deal with the Foole would be to rely on sanctions and incentives. However, Gauthier does not want to take this road. Relying on sanctions and incentives would be 'a political, not a moral, solution' (Gauthier, 1986, p.163). This would, according to Gauthier, neglect a crucial difference between morals and interests. Morals is thought to be *more* than 'mere' interest.[11]

Gauthier insists that sanctions and incentives entail costs of supervision and enforcement of norms. These costs would however be greatly reduced if we all kept moral agreements voluntarily. Morals would thus be a more efficient for solving interaction problems. Gauthier thus hopes to substitute political solutions by 'cheaper' means.

In detail, he proposes to *internalise* MRC by adopting a disposition to constrain their actions. Here, Gauthier distinguishes between two ideal types of actors: straightforward maximisers (SMs) and constrained maximisers (CMs). While both types maximise their utility, CMs do so while simultaneously taking into account the utility of other actors. CMs adopt a *disposition* to cooperate, which Gauthier also calls the 'idea of mutual benefit' (Gauthier, 1986, p.157). CMs comply with norms if they expect greater utility in the case of *general* compliance, thereby tolerating at least some degree of free-riding. CMs will thus *not* punish defection by counter-defection. SMs, by contrast, will always try to directly maximise their utility without any internalised constraints.

Gauthier shows that in some evolutionary settings, at least, CMs have a comparative advantage over SMs. If CMs can expect to frequently meet other CMs, they can form a group with stable internal cooperation, resulting in large gains. The comparative advantage of the disposition to cooperate could therefore spread fast within a society. However, if all other actors within a society are SMs, then the remaining CMs must behave like SMs, too. In this situation, morality would have no chance, as Gauthier himself admits.

It is important for Gauthier that CMs are not 'just' very sophisticated SMs who cooperate because they expect greater benefits in the long run. Rather, CMs cooperate even if they do not expect positive retribution.[12] They cooperate because of their disposition. Here, it becomes clear that, contrary to his original intention, Gauthier *disconnects* morals from advantages and benefits.

However, what can help actors out of PD situations, which persist even after people internalise the necessary dispositions? How can dispositions be an *actual* moral constraint if it cannot be ruled out that some individuals pretend to be CMs but do not actually cooperate with others? How many covert SMs can destabilise

---

10 Hobbes (1651/1991), ch. 15.

11 'Were duty no more than interest, morals would be superfluous.' (Gauthier, 1986, p.1.).

12 Cf. Gauthier (1986, p.169f). esp. fn. 19.

a society of CMs? How many CMs are needed to make cooperation among them fruitful (cf. Gauthier, 1986, p.182ff.). While Gauthier cannot be expected to give a figure, he does not even mention the relevant central idea of the PD, whereby *one* (even one *potential*) defector is enough to destabilise a social arrangement or a moral norm. So if Gauthier took PD situations seriously, he would be forced to abandon is theory and thereby his moral surplus.

However, in a rather casual remark at the very end of 'Morals by Agreement', Gauthier seems to introduce an additional concept: education:[13]

... an essentially just society must be strengthened through the development of the affections and interests of the young (Gauthier, 1986, p.351)

This seems to be the moral, not political, solution that Gauthier has in mind. But is this really an alternative to sanctions and incentives? Does education go without sanctions? I think not. And even if Gauthier relied on some concept of anti-authoritarian education, PD situations would continue to be a central problem. The question would then be how norms or dispositions could be enforced if there is no sanctioning mechanism for SMs. Thus, Gauthier, while at some point recognising the problem of implementation, ultimately underestimates it. The introduction of dispositions as a moral surplus cannot be a systematic solution to the problems of modern societies.[14]

K. Binmore: Democracy Depends on the Ability of Empathise

Ken Binmore (1994, 1998) has developed a contractarian approach which he calls 'naturalistic', as it employs, besides game-theoretic concepts, sociobiological concepts, too. A key idea of this naturalistic approach is to abandon all authorities legitimated by metaphysics. Binmore claims that most contemporary political philosophers, like Rawls, Harsanyi, Gauthier and Nozick, still hold on to metaphysical justifications for rules and institutions. The common ground of these authors is the concept of 'commitment'.

Binmore defines a commitment as an 'action in the present that binds the person who makes it irrevocably in the future' (Binmore, 1994, p.161). A commitment is thus a 'binding unilateral promise' (*ibid.*), i.e., a promise that ultimately cannot be revoked. My interpretation is that such a promise does not have to be enforced by sanctions, but can be secured in some alternative way. It is thus not equivalent to a rule which an actor observes because she wants to avoid sanctions or because she expects greater benefits (at least in the long run).

Promises are easily made, but difficult to enforce: It is both difficult to commit oneself as well as to convince others that one has committed oneself (cf. Binmore, 1994, p.162). One possible solution is to provide (financial) 'hostages': for example, a company who wants to commit itself to the protection of the environment can

---

13 Cf. also Gauthier (1997), which stresses, too, the importance of education (esp. 148).
14 According to Binmore (1994, p.26f and 80), Gauthier invents a non-existent enforcement mechanism.

sign an agreement to pay a fixed amount of money if the commitment is broken. While this is a rather simple way, there are other, more subtle, mechanisms of securing commitments via reputation mechanisms. In any of these cases, however, the commitments are *enforced by means of sanctions*. They are not the kind of commitments that political philosophers like Rawls, Harsanyi, Gauthier and Nozick have in mind.

Binmore does not want to continue the line of moral surpluses, but instead proposes a different concept: empathetic preferences.[15] These are to be distinguished from sympathetic preferences in the following way:

An actor A reveals a *sympathetic preference* if it can be deduced from his behaviour that he puts himself into actor B's position *and* adopts B's preferences (cf. Binmore, 1994, p.286). By contrast, actor A reveals an *empathetic preference* if it can be deduced from his behaviour that he puts himself into actor B's position *without* taking on B's preferences. In the latter case, A holds on to his own preferences, while still being able to compare his preferences to B's. So the intuitive idea behind this is that even a *Homo oeconomicus* can adapt his actions better to that of other actors if he can predict their behaviour.

According to Binmore, the ability to empathise[16] may have been an advantage in coordinating human behaviour in hunter-gatherer societies (cf. Binmore, 1994, p.57 and 288ff.). It may have been the evolving *Homo sapiens'* key characteristic.

The influence of empathetic preferences can be distinguishing according to three different time horizons: the short, the medium, and the long run.

In the *short run*, both the personal preferences of an actor as well as her empathetic preferences are fixed. The actor performs the act of empathising in just the way her empathetic preferences tell her. She deliberates 'morally' in the sense of moral norms taken as conventions, as short cuts for long economic calculations of benefits. Here, morals do not influence the decisions of actors deciding about the rules for a social contract, but only the decisions taken *within* this social contract framework. Morals play a 'mere' functional in the short run (cf. Binmore (1998), Chapter 4.6.8).

In the *long run*, all preferences, personal and empathetic, can be expected to change, because the actors adapt to new situations and new rules. Here, the existing social contract is re-negotiated. The personal and empathetic preferences adapt accordingly. Especially, Binmore emphasises that in the long run, all moral content erodes from the preferences. Over *longer* periods time, the actors arrive – via 'moral' empathy – at the same result as if they had been bargaining like *homines oeconomici* all the time. Thus, in the long run, morals serve long-run *interests*. Moral norms

---

15 This goes back to Harsanyi's 'extended sympathy preferences', cf. Harsanyi (1977). By employing the concept of 'empathetic preferences', Binmore wants to highlight the difference between the classic concept of sympathy in D. Hume's works and his modern one, cf. Binmore (1994, p.28), 58ff., Chapter 4.3.1 and Binmore (1998), Chapter 2.5.4.

16 I prefer to use the term '*ability* to empathise', as it is a more general concept than the empathetic preferences. The latter are preferences that a particular actor reveals in a concrete case with regard to one or several other actors. These may change from one actor to another and from case to case.

cannot remain stable if they are systematically opposed to interests, i.e., also to incentives.

In the *medium run*, only the personal preferences remain fixed. The empathetic preferences, by contrast, are brought into an 'empathy equilibrium'[17]. This is defined as a state in which all actors have equal empathetic preferences. This situation has the same result as the long run case: All moral content erodes from the social contract framework. And, while the actors in fact end up with a result that is identical to a *Nash bargaining equilibrium*,[18] they do not perceive it that way: Their semantics leads them to think that they are guided by non-economic 'moral' deliberation.[19]

By distinguishing between the three time horizons, Binmore seeks to define the role of empathetic preferences in society: They are used for coordination, more precisely for reforming existing social contracts and inventing new ones. They are used as a heuristic tool for finding directions in which new social contracts may develop. In this sense, Binmore (1994, p.241) regards empathetic preferences as an important part of morality.

As for their theoretical status, I think empathetic preferences cannot be regarded as a moral surplus in the sense outlined here, for the following reasons:

Empathetic preferences have fewer consequences for their bearers than the other moral surpluses discussed here. In Habermas' works, one gets the impression that he already has in mind a rather precise idea how the citizens should act or at least which rules they should adopt. And he is clearly opposed to treating his ideas in an economic way, lest alone rely on self-interest for their implementation.

This impression does not arise when reading Binmore: Assuming the existence of empathetic preferences does not imply anything for the detailed design of rules and institutions. If A can put herself in B's position, she will in some way try to assess B: on the one hand, if A regards B as rather unreliable or as only interested in short-run gains, she will anticipate B's defection, adapt her own behaviour and tend to 'counter-defect pre-emptively' herself (cf. Homann, 2002, p.98; Homann and Luetge, 2004, p.35). If, on the other hand, A regards B as reliable *and* if there are no contrary incentives for A to defect, A will tend to cooperate. But it cannot easily be said what the outcome of this process will be.

But what is even more important: the ability to emphasise *cannot*, unlike the moral surpluses reconstructed here, *be exploited* by other actors. Consider the following situation: If A constrains her behaviour in a PD situation, e.g., by committing herself to rational motivation, she risks being exploited by B. This can only be avoided if B constrains his behaviour in the same way as A, i.e., by way of sanctions. But if A can just *empathise* with B in a PD situation, i.e., relies on empathetic preferences, she does not necessarily risk exploitation, especially not in a situation where B acts in ways different from A.

---

17 Binmore (1994, p.65); cf. also *ibid.*, ch. 1.2.7, 1.3, and 290ff.
18 Cf. Binmore (1994, p.88). For the Nash equilibrium, see Nash 1950 and 1951.
19 Binmore even regards the ability to empathise as genetically 'hard-wired' (Binmore, 1994, p.133 and 1998, 182), although he does not rely entirely on genetic concepts, but also on Dawkins' (1976) concept of the 'meme', Cf. Binmore (1994, p.65f).

For example, suppose that one of the two prisoners in the classic PD situation (X) is motivated by rational motivation. If the other (Y) knows this but is not motivated in this way himself, he can exploit X without any problem by confessing (i.e., defecting). But if X 'only' has empathetic preferences, this does not necessarily lead to exploitation. It would only mean that X might anticipate the reaction of Y to his own 'moral' behaviour. X could, e. g., use this knowledge to try to turn the tables and exploit Y. In any case, Y cannot gain a unilateral advantage from knowing that X has adopted empathetic preferences, as Y would have to count on the fact that X would anticipate this – by empathising with Y.

The ability to empathise must therefore be distinguished from the moral surpluses discussed above. It does not preclude any particular action, and it cannot be exploited.

Order Ethics: The Ability to Invest

The alternative approach proposed here relies on two ideas: First, norms are seen as functional for social stability. Second the assumptions on the actors' part should be weakened, i.e., the necessary moral surplus should be minimised or even eliminated. This alternative view is a conception of ethics that proceeds systematically from the problem of *implementation* of norms, not from the problem of their justification.[20]

An informed view of economic and social history[21] tells us that, contrary to what some philosophers believe, the questions of norm implementation *and* justification have generally been posed *together*. However, this was not made explicit in former centuries. The implementation of norms that had already been justified was not regarded as particularly difficult, for two reasons: First, there was much less pluralism in terms of values and life styles in pre-modern times, and second, social relations were not yet as anonymous as in modern times. In particular, generally accepted norms could be enforced much more easily through face-to-face sanctions.

Since the beginning of modern times, however, this situation has changed dramatically. As N. Luhmann[22] has proposed, especially, modern societies consist of functionally differentiated subsystems. The actors in modern societies find themselves in social subsystems with completely different governance mechanisms: in the field of ethics, this often leads to laments about loss of values. The question how norms can be enforced becomes therefore much more pressing under modern conditions and must be put at the beginning of a conception of ethics for modern societies. I would like to call such a conception an *order ethics*.

An order ethics is designed to cope with the *problem of social order*.[23] This problem cannot be solved by way of an *individual ethics*. An individual ethics assumes that morally problematic states are caused by actors' immoral motives or preferences. Consequently, this position calls for a change of motives, i.e., for a

---

20 Cf. Homann (2002); Homann and Luetge (2004), Luetge (2005).
21 For such a view on Ancient Greece, see Meier (1998).
22 Cf., e.g., Luhmann (1997).
23 Cf. also Hayek (1973), ch. 2.

change of consciousness. The main mechanism of governance is (moral) appeals, maybe supported by education.

However, in those structures typical of modern societies, i.e., PD situations, an ethics remains fruitless that addresses primarily the individual. An order ethics therefore proceeds from the assumption that morally problematic states are not caused by immoral preferences or motives, but by specific *structures of interaction*. Therefore, moral claims should aim at revising the conditions which apply to all actors, i.e., the rules of the game. The main governance mechanism is the design of *incentive* structures. Moral norms cannot be brought into opposition to the logic of advantages and incentives.

The arguments in the preceding sections make it clear that it is not systematically fruitful to base normativity on anthropological capabilities or characteristics, the moral surpluses. But if these moral surpluses are not sustainable, what are the alternatives? The alternative social governance mechanism that an order ethics would argue for is not based on anthropological findings, characteristics or surpluses, but on *situations*: A modern society that wants to profit from deep specialisation and competition has to switch to a system of governance by rules. With the use of pre-modern governance mechanisms, the benefits of modern societies cannot be appropriated.

Which rules and which governance mechanisms are necessary for an interaction I depends only on the situational conditions of I. For example, there might be situations where informal governance by moral norms still works and where the partners can count on at least approximately equal normative backgrounds. In such situations, governance by moral norms may still be an option. However, these cases are not too frequent in modern societies under conditions of globalisation. The number of interactions between individuals with vastly different cultural, social and normative backgrounds is continually growing fast. These individuals cannot rely on common moral surpluses, they can only rely on common mutually accepted rules – or they might devise new rules adapted to their situation.

The question is whether even for these cases of rule governance some – maybe weak and not anthropological, but rather situational – capability is necessary. Of the concepts discussed here, only the ability to empathise would be a candidate. Notwithstanding this, I want to argue that if we abandon any moral surpluses, there are three minimal – and very general – assumptions that must be given to guarantee functional governance by rules and social stability: *sociality, ability to communicate* and *ability to invest*.[24]

The first two are rather trivial, i.e., there must be some social group and there must be some mode of communication in effect within this group. But the third is more interesting and important. Individuals that always maximise utility in the *short* run cannot form a stable society. This is nothing spectacular and not peculiar to social stability or morals. Every company must be able to invest in the future. In fact, any form of action and cooperation requires thinking and planning, which in turn requires investing, i.e., saving some resources now for greater benefits in the longer run.

---

24 Cf. Luetge (2007), ch. 4.

Together, these three assumptions might be taken as a minimal basis for modern globalised societies which cannot rely on moral surpluses. The actors must only be able to communicate and invest. An order ethics can then go on to only require these actors to a) comply with the rules, and b) engage – from their own interest – in the further development of these rules in mutually benefiting ways. Such further development can only come into effect if the individuals affected agree to it. In view of PD situations, it is systematically not enforceable against the wishes of these individuals.

To sum up, the normative resources that an order ethics regards as most important for modern societies are much different from the moral surpluses that Habermas and Gauthier argue for. While the latter are all conceptualised in opposition to interests, advantages or incentives, this opposition is abandoned within the framework of an order ethics. Here, the ability to invest is considered a minimal condition for preventing societies from destabilising. Like Binmore's ability to empathise, the ability to invest does not require the individuals to act against the logic of advantages and incentives, especially in PD situations. And this applies equally to what I would like to call *heuristics*, i.e., values and ideas from philosophical, religious, scientific, literary, artistic or other traditions. These heuristics can point the actors in new directions where new gains of cooperation may be found. But they are, again, not conceptualised against the logic of advantages and incentives, not as moral surpluses: They do not erode in PD situations.

What I have been arguing for in this chapter is not only a purely theoretical case. It is relevant in particular for the semantics that we choose to employ in public discussion: do we use, in the political sphere, a 'morally driven' semantics which constructs sharp contradictions between values and interests, between rational motivation and incentives? This will lead us into dead ends and into theoretical blockades. Or do we switch to a revised semantics that rather employs concepts like 'investing', 'mutual self-interest', 'mutual gains' or 'win-win-situations'? Then, moral surpluses might be made productive, if they are re-interpreted as part of a heuristics which suggests *investing* in the individuals' own self-interest. But this task of re-interpretation requires much further conceptual work from philosophy and ethics.

References

Binmore, K. (1994), *Game Theory and the Social Contract: Vol. 1 Playing Fair*, Cambridge, Mass.: MIT Press.
—— (1998), *Game Theory and the Social Contract: Vol. 2 Just Playing*, Cambridge, Mass.: MIT Press.
Dawkins, R. (1976), *The Selfish Gene*, Oxford: Oxford University Press.
Gauthier, D. (1986), *Morals by Agreement*, Oxford: Clarendon.
—— (1997), Political Contractarianism, *Journal of Political Philosophy*, 5:2, 132-148.
Habermas, J. (1981), *Theorie des kommunikativen Handelns, 2 Vols*, Frankfurt a. M.: Suhrkamp (Engl *Theory of Communicative Action*, Boston: Beacon Press 1984).

—— (1983/99), Diskursethik: Notizen zu einem Begründungsprogramm, in: *Moralbewußtsein und kommunikatives Handeln*, Frankfurt a. M.: Suhrkamp, 53–125.

—— (1991), *Erläuterungen zur Diskursethik*, Frankfurt a. M.: Suhrkamp.

—— (1992), *Faktizität und Geltung: Beiträge zur Diskurstheorie des Rechts und des demokratischen Rechtsstaats*, Frankfurt a. M.: Suhrkamp (Engl *Between Facts and Norms: Contributions to a Discourse Theory of Law and Democracy*, Cambridge, Mass.: MIT Press 1996).

Harsanyi, J.C. (1977), *Rational Behavior and Bargaining Equilibrium in Games and Social Situations*, Cambridge: Cambridge University Press.

Homann, K. (2002), Vorteile und Anreize: zur Grundlegung einer Ethik der Zukunft, ed C. Luetge, Tübingen: Mohr Siebeck.

Homann, K. and Luetge, C., (2004), *Einführung in die Wirtschaftsethik,* Münster: LIT.

Homann, K. and Suchanek, A. (2000), *Ökonomik: eine Einführung*, Tübingen: Mohr Siebeck.

Luetge, C. (2005), Economics Ethics, Business Ethics, and the Idea of Mutual Advantages, *Business Ethics: a European Review*, **14**, No. 2, 108–118.

—— (2007), *Ordnungsethik im Zeitalter der Globalisierung*, Tübingen: Mohr Siebeck.

Luhmann, N. (1997), *Die Gesellschaft der Gesellschaft*, 2 Vols, Frankfurt a. M.: Suhrkamp.

Meier, C. (1998), *Athens: A Portrait of the City in its Golden Age*, New York: Metropolitan.

Nash, J. (1950), Equilibrium Points in N-Person Games, *Proceedings of the National Academy of Sciences*, **36**, 48–49. [DOI: 10.1073/pnas.36.1.48]

—— (1951), The Bargaining Problem, *Econometrica*, **18**, 155–162. [DOI: 10.2307/1907266]

Chapter 12

Sovereignty of Interpretation: A Dubious Model of Cultural Globalisation

Michael Neuner

Introduction

Against a background of economic globalisation, problems related to culture and cultures are becoming more and more a central topic of ethical consideration (Crane, 2002; Nederveen Pieterse, 2004, p.1). The globalisation-related exchange of goods, lifestyles, and ideas releases creativity. A vital cultural scene requires open spaces, likewise under market economy conditions. What is required is not just the opening, but also the sustaining of creative spaces within the economic field of action. A not yet clearly defined area appears to be forming in accordance with the concept of 'cultural ethics' (Ammicht-Quinn, 2002, p.258, 261), wherein those conflicts can be dealt with which can arise from ethical reflection on the diversity of cultures and subcultures, within the field of tension of economic vested interests. For example, tensions can result from the question to what extent culture and cultural goods should give themselves over to the free forces of the market. Regarding the assessment of the relationship between culture and the market, there are – on a global level – extremely varying and to some extent opposing views (Pauwels and Loisen, 2003).

In this chapter the tense relationship between cultures and the market will be explored using the example of the marketing of the literary character Harry Potter. In doing so, it will be shown that globalisation of the media and of media corporations involves an economically based tendency toward transcultural compatibility of cultural goods. The tendency toward transcultural compatibility can work against a comprehensively understood cultural freedom, a freedom that not only includes media corporations, but also cultural consumers (Hutt, 1936; Rothenberg, 1962). This is particularly relevant if no distinction is made between the economic and the cultural, dual character of cultural goods and services. The freedom of cultural consumers is particularly at risk when global media corporations are systematically pursuing a 'commodification of culture'. This argument is illustrated by distinguishing between the 'idea' and the 'brand' of Potter. It will be demonstrated how globalised media corporations can achieve a sovereignty of interpretation that limits the freedom of cultural consumers, in those instances where the dual character of cultural goods has not been sufficiently taken into account. Here arises the danger that, due to the pressure toward transcultural compatibility, companies will exercise their interpretive power in their own commercial interests and against the interests of cultural consumers. From this is derived the necessity of creating regulatory institutions on a global level. Such institutions should be committed to the concept of cultural diversity, as formulated by UNESCO.

The Cultural Dimension of Globalisation

From the perspective of a local life-world ('Lebenswelt'), globalisation, even today, remains a broadly irrelevant and unknown mirage. However, from the point of view of an external observer with a global comprehension, globality is a variable relevant to the realm of immediate actions; it indicates an extended context of restrictions and options which, via the proliferation of established patterns of expectation, decision-making parameters, rules and procedures for developing rules, has become just as 'real' for other observers within their differing perspective of a local life-world (Willke, 2003, pp.13–14).

For some time now, a whole series of varying developments of the internationalisation of the market place have been discussed under the catchphrase 'globalisation', where the exact meaning of these developments has in many cases remained unclear (Ohmae, 1996; Helleiner, 2001; Beck, 2003; Nederveen Pieterse, 2004; Fuchs, 2005). What is involved is a complex process of partly contradictory forms, ranges, and modes of expression, whereby it is still up in the air whether the result will be a world society, a global nation, a global village, or a global nirvana. The preconditions and conditions evinced by the process are not determined by nature, but rather by culture. The process of globalisation is therefore subject to influence. Scrutiny of the literature on globalisation reminds us that 'globalisation' is not just a neutral term that refers to some observable objective reality 'out there'. What one sees as globalisation is always framed by one's lenses and focus, and the use of globalisation is always associated with claims and arguments about this reality and its implications. Globalisation, then, is a short-hand term aggregating a vast variety of processes and practices, a meta-narrative used both to describe a wide range of observations and to support a similar range of arguments and claims (Fuchs, 2005, p.24). Consequently, empirical dimensions as well as political, social, economic, and ethical implications of globalisation are highly controversial, making it a battleground for different ideas and ideologies. From the perspective of this paper, most importantly, we need to understand how globalisation influences the behavioural options of different actors.

The circumstance which in public discourse causes 'globalisation' to focus primarily on economic considerations (OECD, 1997; Hirst and Thompson, 2005) may stem from its having to do with an economic, industrial process involving the dissolving of borders. Nevertheless, globalisation cannot be reduced to economics. It is not just economic goods, but also increasingly norms and values, knowledge, tastes, symbols, social institutions and practices, i.e., ideas, and therefore cultural goods, that are becoming more and more mobile and transparent, and available without delay regardless of location, due to the networking and global character of the media (Waters, 1995; Cairncross, 1997; Crane, 2002; Pauwels and Loisen, 2003; Fuchs, 2005). Thus, there is little doubt that the process of dissolving borders also encompasses the cultural dimension (Robertson, 2000; Appadurai, 2003).

The culture idea itself is variable, its concepts and definitions being in turn culturally influenced (see, e.g., Kroeber and Kluckhohn, 1952; Carr, 2004). For the points presented below a general definition will suffice: 'Culture' should in general be understood as the production of meaning with regard to the interpretation, construction and deconstruction of social identities that are necessarily orientated toward difference. The culture industry and the media corporations that represent this industry have a central role in this process. These corporations can, theoretically, either support culturally relevant interpretation processes or, through pursuing the aspirations of 'interpretive imperialism' and using the exercise of interpretive sovereignty, they can also massively limit these processes.

Cultural globalisation involves varying degrees of awareness and emotionality in the manner in which cultural consumers see themselves, and with regard to their individuality, life situation, and sense of social belonging. Many of the questions that arise in the context of cultural globalisation can be traced back to their relationship with difference. Simmel has already pointed out modern culture's tendency toward conflict (Simmel, 1918/68). Currently – ideally – a distinction can be made between three scenarios that describe what may be the results of globalisation in principle (Robertson, 2000; Crane, 2002; Nederveen Pieterse, 2004):

- Cultural pessimism as a cultural levelling-out into the 'one-commodity-world': Here cultural globalisation comes across as a global culture industry, and leads to a uniformity of cultural symbols and life patterns in accordance with universally shared image worlds or a pattern of uniform customer goods. Cultural diversity seems acutely threatened: 800 million Barbie dolls worldwide propagate the beauty ideal of the white, US-American middle class.
- As 'glocalisation' (Robertson, 2000): the dissemination of western consumer goods and cultural patterns is accompanied by an increased revisiting of local cultural traditions. Within processes of mutual self-reassurance or reaffirmation, the particulars of local community are remembered and set against global cultural patterns. Glocalisation aims at anchoring the global in the local, the unique and personal, and at the fostering ('Einhegung', *cf.* J. Habermas) of the local within the global.
- Cultural optimism through the formation of 'hybrid cultures': Hybridisation or creolisation is the leitmotiv of this scenario. It means the uniting of varying cultural styles, forms, and traditions, out of which something new arises, a global melange (Nederveen Pieterse, 2004, pp.69–71). Important influences in this stem from the global culture industry, as well as from the cultural communities of civil (and also global) society. In many instances new cultural streams arise, into which endogenous sediments flow, along with the products, styles, and images of global, Euro-American cultural origin.

In order to justify the establishment of the globalisation concept, what needs to be integrated is the development of novel, over-arching structures and functionalities – and disfunctionalities (if the need should arise) – which are more than just internationalisation processes further extended and of greater proportions (Ruggie,

1993; Gamble, 1994; Robertson, 2000; Fuchs, 2005; Hirst and Thompson, 2005). What is novel in a qualitative sense, for one, is that processes observable in the course of globalisation are giving rise to a fundamental dissolution of what until recently have been predominantly territorialised operational relationships (Tomlinson, 1999; Scholte, 2000; Touraine, 2001). Secondly, these processes are suspect of constricting cultural diversity in some sense, and under certain conditions, which can come across as questionable on ethical grounds (UNESCO, 2001, 2005; Bardoel and d'Haenens, 2004). And thirdly it is by no means certain that this constriction of cultural diversity can be overcome via existing institutional arrangements.

If these observations are correct, and if globalisation induces changes in the availability and effectiveness of traditional, political economic instruments at the national level; if on the other hand only relatively weak organisations and institutions for regulating globalisation-related problems exist at a global level so far (Homann and Gerecke, 1999, p.441), and if the widely prevalent detachment from institutions, together with the seemingly considerable accumulation of power in the media field, can present a danger to local cultural communities (Bagdikian, 2000; Crane, 2002; Bardoel and d'Haenens, 2004), then questions arise how to regulate this process, and questions of corresponding concepts and institutions (Touraine, 2001). These questions will be explored below.

Globalisation of the Media and Transcultural Compatibility

Media corporations are particularly significant with regard to the process of cultural globalisation, namely in that these corporations influence the global networking of cultures and subcultures and, to some extent, enable it in the first place. In contemporary societies these media corporations, as powerful interpretive instances, are increasingly determining the construction of reality in accordance with commercial perspectives:

> The company that has the capacity to manufacture its cultural products in large quantities and continuously, that is able to distribute them effectively to many parts of the world, that is in a position to persuade huge numbers of people that what is on offer is something they want to see, buy or listen to, that has the know-how to transform all those single products into a tasty soup of not-to-be-missed experience, that is capable of upgrading its international operations to a privileged position by expanding horizontally and tapping emerging markets worldwide, that is capable of forging vertical alliances at all levels and in all branches of the cultural market, and that can attract the investment money to undertake all those activities – *this cultural conglomerate has power* (Smiers, 2003, p.28).

With the intensification of globalisation pressure, there arises the danger that globalised media corporations may acquire a sovereignty of interpretation which substantially constricts endogenous, culturally relevant processes within society.

The ethical challenges stemming from cultural globalisation are to a large extent tied to the perspectives inherent in the production of dual goods by commercial media corporations. In terms of what they are offering, in their broadest definition, media corporations are not just purveyors of culture, but are also shapers of culture. At the same time as fulfilling their economic task they fulfil a cultural one (Koslowski, 1989, p.13). In that companies in a broad sense simultaneously produce economic and cultural goods, they reveal themselves to have a dual role. On the one hand the goods produced have a private character, and on the other hand they fulfil the societal function of serving the public good.

Problems can arise from this dual role if public interest becomes hurt or if its free unfolding is constricted, due to the pursuit of private – i.e., economic – interests. Counted among public interests is the interest in undiminished conditions allowing for cultural variation, diversity, and plurality, remain. Along these lines, the General UNESCO Conference has concluded that the process of globalisation, facilitated by the rapid development of new information and communication technologies, represents a severe challenge to cultural diversity (UNESCO, 2001).

This concern arises, among other things, from the fact that media corporations are constantly under pressure to increase their productive and allocative efficiency. Via the repeated exploitation of contents, they attempt to expand their traditional brands, to integrate them both horizontally and vertically (AOL-Time Warner 2006; Bagdikian, 2000; Herman and McChesney, 2001; Kunczik, 1997; Smiers, 2003. According to McChesney (1999) corporations without access to this type of synergy are incapable of competing in the global marketplace. A central precondition for the utilisation of synergies is the extensive standardisation of contents: the products have to be 'transculturally compatible' for global marketing. Mergers, strategic alliances, and the convergence of medias, telecommunications, consumer electronics, and computers have introduced into the media arena pronounced integration and concentration processes at a global level (Gershon, 2000; Crane, 2002). From the point of view of media policy these developments are by no means under control. At the same time, the communications and information sector is progressively being deregulated in more and more countries worldwide. Changes in American legislation have been instrumental in initially facilitating the intense vertical integration of media corporations. Notable in this instance is the Telecommunications Act of 1996, implemented under the Clinton administration ('Act to promote competition and reduce regulation in order to secure lower prices and higher quality services for American telecommunications consumers and encourage the rapid deployment of new telecommunications technologies' – United States of America, 1996). This law created the preconditions allowing for international corporations of hitherto unimagined size to arise. Today (2006) the world media market is dominated by less than 10 corporations (Bagdikian, 2000, pp.x–xiii).

A paradigmatic example of this development is the merging of America Online (AOL) and Time Warner Inc. in the year 2000. This merger marked the formation of the largest media corporation yet. In anticipation of over-arching synergy effects, media content and structural networks were bound together on a global scale. In their shared ground, these companies symbolise two trends that will be cultivated by the information economy in the future: economic synergy effects via cross-medial multiple utilisation and convergence of content.

Benjamin Barber notes that 'a free and democratic society depends on competition of ideas' (Barber, 1996, p.123). The developments that, under pressure from globalisation, are coming to fruition raise questions that pertain to the role of media corporations taken as an information and orientation variable within society; questions as to the consequences of cultural globalisation for cultural variation, diversity and plurality; questions regarding the influence the public has on culture, which remains under pressure from the requirement of transcultural compatibility of cultural goods; questions that arise from commercialisation in relation to the possibility of the independent reception of cultural goods.

From Cultural to Interpretive Imperialism

On the side of cultural pessimism, some questions continually return that were already inherent in the 'cultural imperialism debate' of the 1970s (Schiller, 1969; Tomlinson, 1991, *cf.* for models of cultural globalisation: Crane, 2002, pp.2–7). At that time, people were essentially examining the interactive effects of media products, lifestyles and values on other nations and cultures. An attempt was made to demonstrate that the North American culture industry had hegemonic aspirations in its conquest of foreign markets. Today there is renewed argument that globalisation has an impoverishing effect on media services, due to the standardisation of what is being offered. There are a few modern catchphrases now like 'McDonalidization' (George Ritzer), 'Cocacolization' (Zdravko Mlinar) and 'McWorld' (Benjamin Barber), which tend to get used in this discussion.

It is undeniable that in the future the production as well as the assessment of mass media content will be in the hands of just a few profit-orientated corporations, who consider and deal with media contents mainly as merchandise rather than as cultural products. And in some cultural areas, like the youth or popular culture, or in other words in culture detached from reference to traditional aesthetic standards, wherein production is profit-orientated, one can truly speak of a worldwide standardisation. If the situation is one where the contents reflect what appeals to the majority of people, then this development is an expression of consumer freedom. The borders of unification and standardisation are determined in the end by cultural consumers.

Where the cultural imperialism debate went astray, and from where it is to some extent starting out again, is in the assumption that just what is on offer by the mass media alone will lead to a cultural levelling-out effect. The paradigm of cultural imperialism has continued to suffer from its own assumption of structural determinism and has not sufficiently explored the context-specific process of cultural and commodity diffusion, integration, rejection or transformation (Griffin, 2002). An outgrowth of the 'cultural studies' movement in communications research and its concerns for the active role of receivers in interpreting, negotiating, resisting, or even subverting the polysemic meanings of mass media presentations, several landmark studies from the 1980s provided evidence that audiences in both Western and non-Western cultural contexts brought distinctly different patterns of interpretation and media use to bear in their interactions with Western mass media products (Ang, 1985; Liebes and Katz, 1990; Lull, 1991; Morley, 1992; Turner, 2002; Hall, 2003).

The possibility of varying reception and multiple interpretations certainly depends on preconditions that have come increasingly under pressure during the course of globalisation. Particularly significant among these preconditions are the protection of 'openness' and of the 'polysemic potential' of media content (Fiske, 2003). This argument is based on the assumption that every cultural manifestation can be taken to be a structured, interpretive phenomenon, which allows for fundamental and varying acts of interpretation. If polysemy and openness are protected, then central conditions of cultural freedom are being satisfied. In other words, cultural consumers then have the option of individually or collectively imagining something other than the reality construction intended and presented by the culture industry. They may also reject or repudiate the culture industry's ready-made interpretations. As opposed to the case of 'interpretive imperialism', these conditions (of cultural freedom) are formally assumed to be a given in 'cultural imperialism'.

The pressure of transcultural compatibility has the consequence of corporate communication of a phenomenon, for example of a literary character, being increasingly, and in the extreme case in all available medias – trans-medially – conveyed in the *same* pictures, the *same* patterns, the *same* colours, the *same* forms. In this case, the conditions of polysemy and openness are not yet formally compromised; this would first become a reality if a media corporation simultaneously had a total sovereignty of interpretation, in that it discredited or banned all alternative patterns, colours and forms, etc. In this case the freedom of cultural consumers is under pressure. This will be explored below using the example of Harry Potter.

Interpretive Imperialism as Exemplified in the Literary Character Harry Potter

It is difficult to find a success story comparable to the marketing of the literary character Harry Potter. This series of so far six books began in 1997. By the end of 2006 a total of over 300 million books had been sold. The books have been distributed in more than 200 countries and have been translated into an excess of 63 languages, including Ancient Greek and Hindi. The company is the owner of all the utilisation rights for the brand 'Harry Potter'.

Due to the transcultural conformity necessitated by global marketing, the marketing object 'Potter' has to be subjected to a standardisation process. In accordance with defined style criteria, the character 'Harry Potter' undergoes a 'shaping process', the resultant of which is a marketable product. The criteria of conformity are meticulously worked out and listed in a Harry Potter Style Guide. The company guidelines are concerned among other things with forms, colours, accessories like the Potter glasses, as well as with the context in which the brand may be presented. To date worldwide more than 300 companies have acquired merchandising contracts with Time-Warner. Several companies were able to improve their share price just by making it known that they had a license to market Potter. These gains on the stock exchange have amounted to as much as 30 percent more than the previous day.

All guidelines in the Style Guide were constituents of the Harry Potter brand. The license holder had to ensure all guidelines were maintained. Even small deviations were assessed as violations and could as a consequence lead to withdrawal of the marketing license. In the German-speaking world, media company-driven standardisation led, among other things, to a publication ban on alternative illustrations of the Harry Potter character. And on the title page of high circulation newspapers only the company approved version of the Potter character was permitted to be seen.

The media company was faced with considerable opposition to their uncompromising marketing strategy from the public. What was irksome was not the rigid and contractually regulated behaviour toward license owners, but rather the actions levelled against non-commercial websites and Internet forums, at which Potter fans would gather to exchange thoughts. For the affected cultural consumers, the literary character 'Potter' had become a sounding board for their own creativity and fantasies. They had, so-to-speak, reinvented the character according to their own ideas, within a cultural context of shared stories, symbols, and rituals; 'Potter parties' were thrown, 'Potter hymns' were composed, books were continued on further according to readers' imaginings. Everyday life developed its own unusual magic due to the breakdown of stiff habits. In those days it was actually possible to find 9¾ railway tracks, bookstores transformed into displays of literary events, books delivered until all hours of the night, etc.

The company considered itself to be threatened in its marketing pursuits by these free thinking activities of fans, and began to routinely search the Internet for Harry Potter sites. On the authority of its marketing rights, the company also initiated a global campaign of sanction directed toward the operators of non-commercial Potter websites (*Die Zeit*, 2001; *Libération*, 2001; *USA today*, 2001; *Wall Street Journal*, 2000). Subsequently, the company was able to legally ban operation of such sites. This was enabled via arbitration stemming from the World Intellectual Property Organisation (WIPO), a UN special organisation that is responsible for the protection of commercial rights and for the upholding of copyright on the global level (www.wipo.int). The particularly irritating aspect of the action was that it was by no means only commercial operations that were affected by these sanctions. The overwhelming majority were private citizens, mainly children and teenagers. In total over 4,000 addresses were examined, and only 350 were allowed to retain ownership of their domains – after correcting deviations. Any exchange of ideas that took place outside the control of the media corporation was thereby considerably reduced. There were conflicts in other areas as well. For example, the publication of secondary literature for pedagogical purposes using the theme of Harry Potter was massively restricted. These conflicts culminated in a temporary boycott of all Potter products. The globally staged boycott was organised over the Internet by the society called 'Defence Against Black Arts' (www.dprophet.com/dada/guidelines).

Harry Potter as a Cultural Phenomenon

Readers are not passive naive recipients of corporate cultural products. Many readers are drawn to the Potter texts because the books resonate with them or captivate them (Malu, 2003; Turner-Vorbeck, 2003). There are many different ways in which readers supply important textual content by projecting their identity, past experiences, preoccupations, and cultural orientations onto the text. At its most extreme, this suggests that the reader is really the author. This idea is consistent with philosophical postmodernism, which emphasises 'local knowledge' and questions the truth of any collective authoritative interpretation or 'meta narrative' (Heilman, 2003). Thorough reading can be understood as a kind of authoring because readers bring so much of themselves to their interpretations. Some readers actually write their own episodes or rewrite parts of Rowling's stories. They use the 'original' characters, settings, and themes as the basis for the creation of their own stories.

The dubiousness of the media corporation's behaviour first becomes evident if we differentiate between two – equally legitimate – modes of existence with regard to the cultural good 'Potter'. A differentiation can be made between the 'Potter brand' and the 'Potter idea'. An idea is just a notation that is actively or productively interpreted by recipients or consumers of culture. The connection to culture is revealed here, as culture manifests in the interchange of varying meanings and interpretations. The brand world is the world of images and objects. Ideas enable images; one, the idea, evokes the other, the image or brand, without being identical to it. Only ideas allow the observer the freedom to have his or her own imagination. The active aspect of personal interpretation arises from how the perceptual capacity seeks out varying perceptual forms from a background of personal fantasies, out of which is derived a specific constellation inspired by the text. What comes out of reading is not *factum brutum*, is not simply established, but is rather the achievement of a reflexive process. While alternative interpretations discover the uniqueness and wilfulness of the Potter character, the obtrusive interpretive design of the brand lacks originality, magnetism, and complex depth.

Thus, Harry Potter was initially just an idea, polysemic and open to any desired interpretation, but then he became a protected trademark. Having become so predetermined, packaged and priced, the sorcery apprentice has rapidly lost the charm of the improbable. The well-oiled, smug marketing machinery has shut out the observer, reducing him to a passive consumer. Potter has become a product. The conjuring tricks continue, but the magic is gone. On the one hand we have plastic brooms, on the other hand-made magic wands; on the one hand we have the Game Boy Edition, on the other the book interpretations; on the one hand there are the plastic figurines, on the other the mutual interest groups. From the point of view of consumers' cultural freedom, it has been an unfortunate development that it was not possible to have both: the brand usurped the idea not just in an economic, utilisation rights sense, but also in a cultural, life-world ('Lebenswelt') sense.

To describe a strategy whereby the exercise of interpretative power leads effectively to a constriction of polysemy and openness of media content, we suggest at this juncture the term 'interpretive imperialism'. Interpretive imperialism undermines the conditions of aesthetic experience, these conditions being outlook, imagination, and reflection. Alternative, life-world interpretations of ideas often cannot withstand the levelling-out of content induced by the pressure of global media production. As a culturally relevant strategy on the part of global media corporations, interpretive imperialism can be defined from two perspectives. The *organisational* perspective entails the legally binding, prescribed imaging regulations that state how an idea, a literary character, a text, etc., should be received, in accordance with the conceptions of the media corporation. The *functional* perspective should be understood as all promotional and defensive strategies whereby a media corporation presents and distributes its own commercialised image of the idea in the form of a marketable object, and whereby it constricts and suppresses alternative, non-commercial expressions of the idea.

Cultural Diversity as a Guiding Principle

Globalisation is still not a synonym for the homogenisation of cultures; nevertheless, structural conditions are arising whose result is to facilitate standardisation. The globalisation process currently under way encourages the growth of private goods in the media field, yet under certain circumstances threatens to undermine the protection afforded to global public goods like the preservation of culture. The global media actors are profit-motivated corporations, who mainly understand media content as merchandise rather than as genuine cultural products. With the accumulation of power in media markets, there is a growing need for global regulation. At the same time, national politics is waning in influence, particularly in the area of establishing norms and regulations (Castells, 2001).

Culture and economics are becoming increasingly bound up with each other in a globalised world. Cultural life and cultural industry benefit from each other in their respective fields of activity. This leads to the question as to the mutual relationship between economic and cultural value assessments. This has less to do with the debate regarding the merchandise character of culture, and more to do with the undecided but increasing conflict, taking place in the context of globalisation, between copyrights, artistic freedom rights, and the freedom of cultural consumers on the one, and trademark and patent rights on the other hand. The conflict is heightened by the fact that at the global level there are varying dominant points of view with regard to the relationship between culture and the market. For the advocate of free trade the economy remains the means of organising human needs. In this view, culture is just one way of conducting business among many. The USA has traditionally been convinced that the significance of cultural goods chiefly depends on the assessment of their content on the market (Boddy, 1994; Pauwels and Loisen, 2003; Sauvé, 2004). Cultural products are equated with regular economic products. The opposing position, most fiercely advocated by France and Canada, considers the concept 'culture as merchandise' to be harmful to society, in that the value of culture far outstrips that of the market. They argue that cultural products are also carriers of values, identities, and world views.

At the level of global institutions there is recognition that cultural products and services evince an economic and cultural double character, which is a connecting conceptual link between UNESCO and the WTO. Since the 1990s, culture and media have been dominated by a liberalisation debate, which largely stems from the General Agreement on Trade and Services (GATS). The international trade in audiovisual productions is an economic factor of the first order. For the USA, the culture industry is their largest export after the aviation industry. There is hardly a more contentious issue in the liberalisation debate than the question of whether the process of opening up markets can be approached in a way that is 'culturally acceptable'. In the context of the debate regarding liberalisation of the audiovisual sector, some members, such as UNESCO, the European Union, and also some single countries, have interjected the concept of 'cultural diversity' into the debate. Although the various actors with their differing accents and issues are clashing, this concept builds a bridge between the opposing views of culture and media markets. The concept of cultural diversity recognises the unique societal position of cultural goods and services, which cannot be dealt with using a purely commercial approach. The concept also supersedes the definition of the special status of cultural goods, in that the uniqueness of each individual and his specific identity is recognised (Smiers, 2003). It also accepts the non-cultural aspects of cultural production.

As a guiding formula, the idea of cultural diversity remained non-binding for a long time. This changed on November, 2 2001. On this date the general assembly of UNESCO passed the 'Declaration on Cultural Diversity' (UNESCO, 2001). The objective was to emphasise the significance of cultural diversity on a national as well as on an international level, and simultaneously to raise awareness as to its fragility in the age of globalisation. In Chapter 4, UNESCO proclaims that the defence of cultural diversity is an ethical imperative. All persons shall have the right to participate in the cultural life of their choice and conduct their own cultural practices (Chapter 5). In Chapter 11 of the declaration, there was explicit mention of the concern that 'market factors alone cannot guarantee the preservation and promotion of cultural diversity'. The concept of cultural diversity was given further clout in that at the 32nd general conference (General Conference of the United Nations Educational, Scientific and Cultural Organization) on 17 October 2003, UNESCO proclaimed the intention to develop a 'Convention on the protection and promotion of the diversity of cultural expressions'. The objective of the initiative is to maintain cultural diversity within the parameters of globalisation and liberalisation in the context of GATS. In establishing the declaration of 20 October 2005, a solid foundation was laid for recognising the special status of cultural goods and services which, as carriers of identities, moral convictions, and meanings, cannot be viewed as mere merchandise and consumer goods (UNESCO, 2005, p.2). Apart from Israel, the USA was the only other country not to sign the convention.

From a strategic perspective, the concept of cultural diversity creates opportunities to reconcile the various positions. Until recently there was a very open approach, leaving room for a whole range of definitions. Cultural diversity is now simultaneously both: a rigorous theoretical concept and an important political objective. It remains to be seen how the concept will prove itself in actual performance.

References

Ammicht-Quinn, R. (2002), Kulturethik, in ed Düwell *et al.*, pp.258–263.
Ang, I. (1985), *Watching Dallas: Soap Opera and the Melodramatic Imagination*, London: Routledge.
AOL-Time-Warner (2006), *AOL Time Warner Factbook 2004*. Online available: http://ir.timewrner.com/downloads/factbook_2004.pdf (last visit: 2 March 2006).

Appadurai, A. (2003), *Modernity at Large: Cultural Dimensions of Globalization*, Minneapolis, Minn.: University of Minnesota Press.

Bagdikian, B.H. (2000), *The Media Monopoly*, Boston: Beacon Press.

Barber, B. (1996), *Jihad vs. McWorld*, New York: Ballantine Books.

Bardoel, J. and d'Haenens, L. (2004), Media Meet the Citizens. Beyond Market Mechanisms and Government Regulations', *European Journal of Communication*, **19**, No. 2, 165−194.

Beck, U., ed. (2003), *Global America? The Cultural Consequences of Globalization*, Liverpool: Liverpool University Press.

Boddy, W. (1994), U.S. Television Abroad: Market Power and National Introspection, *Quarterly Review of Film and Video*, **15**, 45−55.

Cairncross, F. (1997), *The Death of Distance. How the Communications Revolution Will Change Our Lives*, London: Orion Business.

Carr, S.C. (2004), *Globalization and Culture at Work. Exploring Their Combined Glocality*, Boston: Kluwer Academic Publishers.

Castells, M. (2001), *The Rise of the Network Society*, Malden, Mass.: Blackwell.

Crane, B. (2002), Culture and Globalization. Theoretical Models and Emerging Trends', in ed Crane *et al.*, 1−25.

Crane, B. *et al.*, eds. (2002), *Global Culture: Media, Arts, Policy, and Globalization*, New York: Routledge.

Die Zeit, (2001); Wem gehört Harry? By Wolfgang Gehrmann, *Die Zeit*, as of 15 March 2001, Hamburg.

Düwell, M. *et al.*, eds. (2002), *Handbuch Ethik*, Stuttgart: Metzler.

Fiske, J. (2003), *Television Culture. Popular Pleasures and Politics*, London: Routledge.

Fuchs, D. (2005), *Understanding Business Power in Global Governance*, Baden-Baden: Nomos.

Gamble, C. (1994), *Timewalkers: The Prehistory of Global Colonization*, Cambridge: Harvard University Press.

Gershon, R.A. (2000), The Transnational Media Corporation: Environmental Scanning and Strategy Formulation, *Journal of Media Economics*, **13**, No. 2, 81-101.

Griffin, M. (2002), From Cultural Imperialism to Transnational Commercialization: Shifting Paradigms in International Media Studies, *Global Media Journal*, **181**, 2−28.

Hall, S. (2003), *Critical Dialogues in Cultural Studies*, London: Routledge.

Heilman, E.E. (2003), Fostering Critical Insight Through Multidisciplinary Perspectives, in ed Heilman, 1−10.

Heilman, E.E., ed. (2003), *Harry Potter's World*, New York: RoutledgeFalmer.

Helleiner, G. (2001), Markets, Politics, and Globalization. Can the Global Economy Be Civilized?, *Global Governance*, **7**, No. 3, 243−263.

Herman, E.S. and McChesney, R.W. (2001), *The Global Media. The New Missionaries of Corporate Capitalism*, London: Continuum.

Hirst, P. and Thompson, G. (2005), *Globalization in Question. The International Economy and the Possibilities of Governance*, Cambridge: Polity Press.

Homann, K. and Gerecke, U. (1999), Ethik der Globalisierung. Zur Rolle der multinationalen Unternehmen bei der Etablierung moralischer Standards, in ed Kutschker, 429-58.

Hutt, W.H. (1936), *Economics and the Public*, New York: McGraw-Hill.

OECD (1997), *Globalisation and the Changing Nature of the Firm, OECD Paper DSTI/EAS/IND/SWP (97)16*, Paris: OECD.

Koslowski, P. (1989), *Wirtschaft als Kultur. Wirtschaftskultur und Wirtschaftsethik in der Postmoderne*, Vienna: Passagen.

Kroeber, A.L. and Kluckhohn, C. (1952), *Culture. A Critical Review of Concepts and Definitions*, Cambridge, MA: Kraus Reprint Company.

Kunczik, M. (1997), *Media Giants, Ownership Concentration and Globalization*, Bonn Friedrich Ebert-Foundation.

Kutschker, M., ed. (1999), *Perspektiven der internationalen Wirtschaft*, Wiesbaden: Gabler.

Libération (2001), La Warner confisque Harry Potter. Après avoir acheté les droits des livres, la firme s'en prend aux sites créés par des fans', par M.− J, Gros, *Libération*, le 30 avril 2001 (Paris).

Liebes, T. and Katz, E. (1990), *The Export of Meaning. Cross-cultural Readings of Dallas*, Oxford: Oxford University Publishing.

Lull, J. (1991), *China Turned on: Television, Reform, and Resistance*, London: Routledge.

Malu, K.F. (2003), Ways of Reading Harry Potter: Multiple Stories for Multiple Reader Identities, in ed Heilman, 75−95.

McChesney, R. (1999), *Rich Media, Poor Democracy*, Urbana: University of Illinois Press.

Morley, D. (1992), *Television, Audiences, and Cultural Studies*, London: Routledge.

Nederveen Pieterse, J. (2004), *Globalization and Culture. Global Mélange*, Lanham: Rowman & Littlefield.

Ohmae, K. (1996), *The End of the Nation State. The Rise of Regional Economies*, New York: The Free Press.

Pauwels, C. and Loisen, J. (2003), The WTO and the Audiovisual Sector , Economic Free Trade vs Cultural Horse Trading?, *European Journal of Communication*, **18**, No. 3, 291−313.

Robertson, R. (2000), *Globalization: Social Theory and Global Culture*, London: Sage.

Rothenberg, J. (1962), Consumers' Sovereignty Revisted and the Hospitability of Freedom of Choice, *American Economic Review, Papers and Proceedings* **52**: 269-83.

Ruggie, J. (1993), Territoriality and Beyond: Problematizing Modernity in International Relations, *International Organization*, **47**, No. 1, 139−174.

Sauvé, P. (2004), *Trade Rules Behind Borders. Essays on Services, Investments and the New Trade Agenda*, London: Cameron May.

Schiller, H.I. (1969), *Mass Communications and American Empire*, New York: Kelley.

Scholte, J.A. (2000), *Globalization. A Critical Introduction*, Houndmills: Palgrave.

Simmel, G. (1918/68), *The Conflict in Modern Culture*, New York: Teachers College Publishing.

Smiers, J. (2003), *Arts Under Pressure. Promoting Cultural Diversity in the Age of Globalization*, London: Zed Books.

Tomlinson, J. (1991), *Cultural Imperialism: A Critical Introduction*, Baltimore: Hopkins University Publishing.

Tomlinson, J. (1999), *Globalization and Culture*, Cambridge: Polity Press.

Touraine, A. (2001), *Beyond Neoliberalism*, Cambridge: Cambridge University Publishing.

Turner, G. (2002), *British Cultural Studies*, London: Routledge.

Turner-Vorbeck, T. (2003), Pottermania: Good, Clean Fun or Cultural Hegemony?, in ed Heilman, pp.13–24.

UNESCO (2001), *UNESCO Universal Declaration on Cultural Diversity*. Adopted by the 31st session of the General Conference of UNESCO, 2 November 2001, Paris: UNESCO.

UNESCO (2005), *Convention on the Protection and Promotion of the Diversity of Cultural Expressions*, 20 October 2005, Paris: UNESCO.

United States of America (1996), *Act to Promote Competition and Reduce Regulation in Order to Secure Lower Prices and Higher Quality Services for American Telecommunications Consumers and Encourage the Rapid Deployment of New Telecommunications Technologies*, Washington, DC: USA. Online available: www.fcc.gov/telecom.html (last visit: March 2, 2006).

USA Today (2001), 'Potter' Web Fans Organize Boycott, by Elizabeth Weise, *USA Today*, 22 February 2001, Virginia: McLean.

Wall Street Journal, (2000); Harry Potter Fan Web Sites Can't Shake off Warner BrosBy Stephanie Gruner and John Lippman, *The Wall Street Journal*, 21 December 2000, New York City: *The Wall Street Journal*.

Waters, M. (1995), *Globalization*, London: Routledge.

Willke, H. (2003), *Heterotopia: Studien zur Krisis der Ordnung moderner Gesellschaften*, Frankfurt a.M.: Suhrkamp.

Chapter 13

Business Ethics in Globalised Financial Markets

Peter Koslowski

Space, says Leibniz, is the order of all things that are simultaneous, time is the order of all things that are non-simultaneous. Space and time order the things. The things that are simultaneous are arranged through the space, the things that are non-simultaneous through the time. All things are in space and in time and therefore spatially and temporally ordered.

The Extension of the Simultaneity in Space and the Decrease of the Non-simultaneity in Time of Humankind through the Process of Globalisation

With the Internet and the new technologies of communication, the basic order relations of the human being, space and time, have been changed, and thereby the simultaneity and the non-simultaneity of the things for the human being have changed as well. Leibniz's definition describes the absolute space and the absolute time, not the space and the time of the human being. The definition is, however, also valid for the space and the time of the human being: It holds true that the space of the human being is the order of the things that are simultaneous for the human, and that the time is the order of the things that are non-simultaneous for the human being. The space of the human being is made up by the things which are simultaneously accessible for the human. The time of the human being is determined by what is non-simultaneous for the human. The time is the things in their succession, the space is the things in their simultaneity.

With the Internet the relations of simultaneity and temporal succession as well as the relation of the centre and the periphery change. Through the Internet, also far away places which were formerly not simultaneous for us become simultaneous. Transactions and information over large distances, that were formerly non-simultaneous and outside of the individual's space or range of decision-making, become simultaneous and move into the individual's range of decision-making. Transactions that were formerly to be carried out only with great delay and therefore did not belong to the human's space, to the human's space of simultaneity, become simultaneous and move into the individual's space or range of decision-making. The individual's space of decision-making and action increases because the control of large spaces in simultaneity becomes possible.

Financial investments contain always the element of entrepreneurial decision-making and control. To the degree in which effective control becomes possible over great distances, the spatial range and the simultaneous control possibilities for investments increase. With the aid of online-brokerage, a portfolio of shares can be controlled from every place of the world without high transaction costs.

The process of globalisation resulted in the years 1990s in the extension of finance investments to areas which before were not the aim of such investments, particularly the countries of the former East bloc as well as China and India. At the same time, the instrument was created by the Internet, by online-banking, and online-brokerage that facilitated the information circulation and transmission about the new investment space. Globalisation brought these countries into the relationship of simultaneity and virtual proximity with the finance centres of the Western metropolitan cities, moved them into the decision-space of these centres.

The Globalisation of the Capital Markets as a Central Feature of the Process of Globalisation

Three large extensions of world-wide financial investments were caused by the process of globalisation which, in the field of financial investments and markets, is not only a process of spatial extension but also of intensification. The first factor, the spatial extension in geographical respect to new countries, was closely connected with the second factor, the extension and intensification of financial information, and the third factor, the social extension of financial investments to new groups of investors in the population. With the extension of financial investments to wider circles of the population that up to now did not participate in the capital market, a third element of extension appears in the historical dynamics of globalised capital markets besides the spatial and informational extension and expansion.

The following processes must be regarded as the central definitional features of globalisation according to Klaus Müller:

- Liberalisation of the financial markets
- Internationalisation of cross-border ecological dangers
- Trans-national mergers of corporations
- Circulation by mass media of Western images and patterns of consumption
- Increasing streams of trans-national and transcontinental migration
- Decreasing effectiveness of the policy making of the nation state.[1]

Müller names the liberalisation of the financial markets at first place, and, in fact, one will have to refer to the liberalisation, internationalisation, and extension of the financial markets as the strongest influential factor in the process of globalisation. The increasingly location- and space-independent, ubiquitous access to knowledge and information is common to all the mentioned features of globalisation. The decision-maker's space and range of decision-making have become global, the time for effectuating the decisions instantaneous, since knowledge about the entire world is faster available and can be documented better on storage media than in former

---

1   Müller (2002).

times.[2] The decision-space becomes larger, the decision-time, the time to gather and process information about far removed places becomes almost negligible. The space made up by the things that are simultaneous for the human increases. In reverse, we can only perceive globalisation since our information systems provide us with instantaneous knowledge about the global reality or at least about parts of it. With the Internet and the globalisation of information processing, another effect is happening. The former difference, or even hiatus, between the centre and the periphery of the knowledge is increasingly levelled or even abolished. The catalogues of the largest libraries of the world are now accessible from the most remote village of the world via the Internet as far as this village has a telephone line to the outside world.

What is meant by the social extension of financial investments and financial institutions? The main driver towards this extension are the pension funds. Peter Drucker published his book the Unseen Revolution: How Pension Fund Socialism Came to America in the year 1976.[3] The retirement or pension funds led already in the 1970s to a socialisation of investment. They further enforced the tendency recognised already by Marx in the joint-stock company, the dissolution of the class of capitalists into a larger group of capital owners or into a kind of socialised capital ownership. The question whether pension fund capitalism is already real socialism must be left unanswered here. The pension and investment funds as well as the widening of ownership of shares through online-brokerage contain an element of the socialisation of the property in the means of production and are a drive towards the expansion of the capital market.

A further factor driving towards the expansion of the capital market is the attempt of many employees observed in the USA since the 1980s to improve their income through speculation in shares and thereby to provide a second income for themselves.

All the four tendencies mentioned have caused an expansion of the capital market with the effect that a volume of the investment amounts and a volume of trade in shares have occurred that had been unknown before in economic history. The expansion and the worldwide internationalisation of financial investments and of the capital market are probably the most important feature of the present globalisation. As in the other fields of globalisation, globalisation is also in finance more than mere internationalisation. It implies not only that a corporation becomes internationally active and is present in many other countries. Globalisation requires, rather, an integration of the national capital markets into a global capital market, that the corporations act globally also with respect to corporate finance in an integrated space of financial investment and refinancing since global investment has become technically possible through the new global means of communication and the Internet.

---

2   Shiller (2001) points to the fact that installing the first transatlantic telephone cable has had a similar effect as the Internet on economic growth and on a stock market boom. It is, however, important to note the difference that the Internet, unlike the telephone, facilitates also the instantaneous documentation of the long-distance communication.

3   Drucker (1976).

On the Ethics of the Capital Market

How can one analyse ethically the institutions of and the individual actions in the capital market? From the approach of ethical economy developed by the author,[4] the ethical presuppositions of the functioning conditions and of the rationality of the capital market and the actions therein are at the centre of an economic and ethical analysis of the capital market. A decisive test for the functioning conditions of a set of institutions or of a market is the question whether being active in these institutions or in this market causes unintended side-effects which contradict the institutional objective or purpose and disturb its workings. If the side-effects become considerable, institutional changes must be carried out. If, for instance, the trade runs smoothly but extreme 'churning' of investors occurs, institutional precautions against this churning must be taken. Churning of investors describes a situation in which high commissions and fees are paid due to a high volume of share trading but in which these fees and commissions paid by the investors are higher than the investors' returns on investment. The situation is particularly problematic if the investors are not made aware of this by an appropriate disclosure of the fees and commissions by the brokerage firm or bank.

Before one asks whether the ethical quality of an action within an institutional setting, of an acting person's intention and values, the question must be asked as to the norms, the rules and duties of this institutional setting. To be able to determine the rules and duties, it is to be asked what the right law would be in the institutional setting under consideration. The question about the ideal right or the right law and right order of rules is to be answered according to Radbruch by applying three principles: first, the question about the purpose of the institutional field or institutional setting that is supposed to be ruled by norms, secondly, the idea of justice as formal justice and equal right of all acting or being concerned by the institutional field under consideration, and thirdly, the principle of legal security that requires that those who act in the institutional field are able to form constant expectations with respect to the perpetuity of the law and the continuity of the jurisdiction. Without constancy of expectations with respect to the legal norms, no effective legal order and no adequate ethics are possible.[5]

If one applies these principles to the institutional setting of the capital market, at first the purpose of the capital market is to be clarified. A set of institutions as complex as the market for capital and corporate control serves, in general, several purposes that can even stand in a relationship of tension towards each other. The purposes or functions of the capital market can be distinguished into four partial purposes: 1) the saving function: the capital market absorbs savings; 2) the wealth function: the capital market is used for the storage of purchasing power over longer periods of time; 3) the liquidity function: the capital market offers investors the possibility to convert their financial assets into cash again to have liquid financial means at any time; 4) the economic policy function of the capital and money market: Through capital market policy and monetary policy, the economic policy maker can

---

4   Koslowski (2001) (Orig. 1988).
5   *Cf.* Radbruch (1973).

influence the economic situation and trade cycle and can control macroeconomic demand.[6]

Through a rise or decrease of the money supply the government induces an increase or reduction of the demand for shares and in this way influences the share prices. A rising or lowering of the share prices increases, in turn, reduces the consumption expenditures of the economic agents since the individuals' consumption expenditures are influenced by the value of their wealth assets. If the share prices, and therefore their perceived wealth, are higher, the investors have a higher net wealth and will increase their consumption expenditures. If the government reduces the money supply and induces a rise of the interest rate, it causes a decrease of the share prices. Decreasing share prices cause the share owners, the consumers, to consume less because they have the perception that they are less prosperous.

By means of the money supply and the interest rate, the government can influence the value of the wealth invested in shares and, thereby, the rate of consumption that is partly determined by the capital value of the shares the consumers hold. In this way, economic policy is able to influence the trade cycle, accelerate it or slow it down. The American Government stabilised, for instance, the share prices in the years 2002–03 through a politics of easy money to maintain a pattern of high consumption rates by keeping the value of the private wealth in shares stable since both, share prices and consumption expenditures, threatened to decrease even further in the recession. As consumption is also a function of the consumer's net wealth, private consumption had been pushed by a policy of easy money and by the increased share prices induced by the low credit rates credit enabled by the easy money policy.

In the capital market, the objective of the efficient allocation of capital stands at the centre. The question where capital is supposed to be invested is of the greatest importance for every economy. The objective of optimal capital allocation implies the solution to the question, in which projects, technologies, industries, regions, etc. the economy invests and which future projects get a chance and receive investment. Since the investors decide *ex ante* which developments they hold to be the right and desirable ones, their decisions are always burdened with high uncertainty. The consumer in the market decides, on the other hand, *ex post*, after the investment being done, what he likes in the supply of firms that have made their decision in the past. The market decides after the investment being made which investment decisions of the firms have been right.

Fundamentally, three social decision mechanisms are available to an economy for capital allocation: the economy can leave the allocation decision with banks or with the government as in a centrally administered economy or with a specialised market of its own in which savers/investors as suppliers of capital and enterprises as demand for capital coordinate their plans and their expectations by the price mechanism. A capital market corresponds better to a democratic society as a coordination mechanism for the allocation of capital than the coordination through large banks or through centrally administered economic direction by the government.[7] The capital market is, like other markets, a means to diversify and to control economic power

---

6 For the functions of the capital and money market, *Cf.* Rose (2000, p.6ff).
7 This position was also taken by von Nell-Breuning (1928a, p.9 and 1928b, 52).

since it creates competition between the supply and demand of capital. This market as venture capital market is furthermore open to new ideas and offers a chance to the new and the unknown yet and even to the outsider.

If the capital market is supposed to take over this function, however, a high degree of speculation is needed. Speculation is inevitable and even desirable for two reasons in the capital market. On the one hand, future possible returns on investment can only be speculated about to a certain degree, since the future demand for products and goods can not be known today yet. It is a phenomenon known also from philosophical and theological speculation that the speculative starts where complete information and complete empirical knowledge are impossible, where, however, there is at least some empirical insight. The greater overall scheme is inferred from fragmentary experience and incomplete empirical knowledge.

Stock market speculation is not only a game and gambling, but an anticipation of future developments based on incomplete information and empirical data that include also the anticipations of the anticipations of the other speculating players and contains also an element of gambling. The theories of the justification of the speculation in the nineteenth century took as a basis mostly the question whether the stock market speculation is gambling or betting. Gambling was held not to be ethically justifiable whereas betting was taken to be ethically permissible. The result of the considerations in nineteenth century on speculation was that speculation is a bet and not gambling and that, as a bet, it is ethically permissible because in the case of betting more strict institutional conditions and a stronger intellectual element of correct anticipation of reality are given than in the case of pure gambling where the correct anticipation of the future outcome results just from good luck.

The inevitability of speculation results from the problem of uncertainty about the future. In the capital market, two central uncertainties play a role, the uncertainty about the future profits of enterprises and the uncertainty about the future development of the value of enterprises or their shares, about their future capital value. Correspondingly, speculation aims at both, at the correct anticipation of the firm's profits or – in the case of the joint stock company – of its dividends paid and at the correct anticipation of the development of the stock, of the share price.

On the other hand, speculation is also necessary to create those volumes of trade for shares that are necessary to fulfil the liquidity function of the capital market. The strength of the share market is that the shareholders' long-term investments in enterprises can be liquidated and reconverted into cash at any time – even if not always with a profit. This liquidation of long-term investments and their transformation into cash is, however, only possible if there is professional speculation and professional share trading because investors would run otherwise the risk of meeting no effective demand for their wish to sell and liquidate and would be locked into their investment.[8]

For both reasons, for the inevitable uncertainty about future corporate profits and for the necessity to create liquidity in the market for shares in corporations, speculation is inevitable in the capital market, and no efficient capital market

---

8   *Cf.* also Koslowski (1997).

conceivable without speculation. The resentment against stock market speculation finds, therefore, no rational justification.

Since speculation is useful and satisfies the purpose of the capital market, it should not be hindered. Popular slogans that one should stop speculation do not find justification since they contradict the functional conditions and objectives of optimal capital allocation in the capital market. Also the possibility of low-priced 'people's shares' that the German Government proclaimed and offered to the public in the shares of the privatised state firms for telecommunication and the mail service, Deutsche Telekom as well as Deutsche Post (German Mail), must be criticised from the understanding of the inevitability of the speculative character even of these shares. Since the share market is necessarily speculative, there can not be a low-priced share which would be certain to rise and not be subjected to speculation and uncertainty about its future price. Every stock, also the stock of former state monopoly firms as the telephone or mail service, is subject to the share price risk and the fluctuations of the stock market. It is one of the weaknesses of small investors that they usually underestimate the risks in the development of the share price. The realistic assessment of risk is also a postulate of the ethics of business. The sense of reality is a morally relevant quality.

Instead of propagating and offering assumedly low-priced shares, it would have been more reasonable to follow the objective of developing a people's capitalism instead of issuing 'people's shares'. In a democratic society, it is desirable that as many people as possible participate in the decisions about investments and enterprises, and in this way about future economic strategies, and that the entire economic knowledge of a nation and the individuals' appraisal of future share value enter the valuations of the capital market. In this sense, the objective of a 'people's capitalism' which serve the efficiency of the capital market is quite desirable. To achieve the objective of an efficient capital allocation, the concentration on of a few 'people's shares' is, however, not a viable strategy. Rather, an investment activity scattered as widely as possible amongst social groups and an investment as widely diversified into the stocks of innovative and small enterprises should be aimed at.

If one summarises the purposes or functions of the capital market, it becomes visible that the efficient allocation of capital into purposes of investment under conditions of information efficiency and capital liquidity or the transformability of the investment into liquid means are at the core of the objectives and the conditions of functioning of the capital market.[9]

In this way, it becomes possible to answer the question which ethical and economic values must be taken into account in the globalised capital market. To fulfil information efficiency and the liquidity function, as many parties in supply and demand in the market for capital should be active to make the volumes of the supply and demand for capital so large that real markets for corporate control and corporate strategies arise. The globalisation supports, therefore, the information efficiency and the liquidity of the capital market through the enlargement and greater liquidity of this market. An efficient capital market requires sufficient liquidity so that investors

---

9   *Cf.* also Picot (2000).

are not locked into their investments.[10] On the other hand, the wealth preservation function and the savings function of the capital market require that the fluctuations in the value of shares do not reach too large amplitudes in the capital market. As a result, two criteria must be realised in the capital market at the same time: on the one hand, the investment and disinvestment decisions in the capital market must allocate capital to its best use quickly and smoothly. On the other hand, the high degree of allocation and reallocation as well as the level of trading volume must not cause exaggerated and unnecessary fluctuations in the share prices that make savers and investors feel insecure and drive them out of the capital market.

The conditions of the high mobility and efficient allocation of capital, on the one hand, and the conditions of the stability of the share prices in the capital market, on the other hand, stand in a relationship of a certain tension towards each other that also influences speculation. On the one hand, the speculation in shares must trace every even very insignificant change in the chances for profits from investments and make visible in the market. On the other hand, speculation must also avoid causing artificial value fluctuations that do not have any basis in the substantial value of stock.

From this Janus-headedness of speculation follows that speculation is supposed to be, on the one hand, highly speculative and to find out the smallest changes and differentials of value, but should, on the other hand, not produce any artificial volatility. In the formation of the value orientation that should direct the actions of capital market participants, a tension arises here in speculation that speculates because of the volatile value changes of shares between the speculation that destabilises shares prices and the speculation that stabilises the volatility of share prices.

It must not be overlooked, however, that the stock market speculation rewards such speculative anticipations which have anticipated improbable value increases correctly. By this measure, the capital market rewards at the same time highly speculative speculation that curbs the price fluctuations and takes price volatility out of the market.

Speculation can be regarded in general as the phenomenon of price arbitrage between different points of time. In the same way as spatial arbitrage produces a

---

10 John Boatright (1999, p.116) shows how the missing possibility to liquidate high volumes of shares at the same time can be a problem for large pension funds because they are frequently not in the position to formulate their protest against low performance management teams by selling large packages of the shares they hold in these firms without undergoing a high share price risk. They must, therefore, influence the management directly through influence on the management decisions and stay invested in the enterprise. A pensions fund as CalPERS (California Public Employees' Retirement System) that manages assets worth 80 billion dollars would find it difficult to sell shares of General Motors worth 1 billion dollars at once without causing a loss of their value in the stock exchange. – The change of the form of capitalism from the private property and owner capitalism to the "pension fund capitalism" is indicated by the following figures: "In 1970, individuals held more than 72 percent of shares, while institutional investors (pensions, mutual funds, insurance companies, and private trusts and endowments) accounted for about 16 percent. By 1990, the holdings of institutions had risen to more than 53 percent, with private and public pension funds owning approx. 28 percent of the equities of US firms." (Boatright, op. cit., p. 114).

profit from mediating between price differences between different places in space, temporal arbitrage or speculation makes profit from mediating between differences in prices between different points in time. When a merchant, due to his knowledge about differences in the prices of goods in two cities, transfers the goods from the city with a low price and high supply to the other city with high price and low supply[11] he contributes to levelling the prices at the two places and earns a profit from the economically useful action of spatial arbitrage.

Speculation engages in arbitrage between the value variations of different points or epochs in the course of time. The speculating person who speculates *à la hausse*, goes long, assumes that the corporate shares that he buys today will have a higher value in the future. As long as the speculators follow the general opinion in their speculation, they will not make any especially high speculative profit. If, on the other hand, they speculate against the prevalent opinion, their speculative gains will be considerable, provided they have been right. At the same time, these speculators will play a price-stabilising role when the price of the share has risen, since they will provide a higher supply of the share in question that will curb the share price at the point in time. A normativity of the processes effective in reality becomes visible here in as far as the speculators' interest in realising a profit through the correct but improbable speculation goes hand in hand with the common interest of the market to stabilise share prices through a higher supply of those shares that are in high demand and that the speculators supply. If speculation made profit only by strategies increasing volatility, it would attack and destroy the legitimacy conditions of its own existence.[12]

On the Ethics of Financial Consulting

The question as to the ethical duties of financial consultants addresses the individual ethics of the correct action within the framework of the institutional setting of the capital market. Consultants are obliged, due to their fiduciary position towards their customers, to act in the customer's best interest, not in their own best interest. They are subject to fiduciary duties and duties of due diligence, duties that have been further differentiated in American law and its business ethics than in Continental European civil law and business ethics. These duties include the duty to prudence and due diligence or adequate care in working for the customer. Every performance of financial consultants that does not protect the customer's interest is not diligent or prudent. It is a breach of their duty and of the fiduciary relationship with the customer.

In the capital market, the financial consultant is tempted to engage in 'churning', 'twisting' or 'flipping' the customer. The temptation to breach the fiduciary duty is always around. Churning is the excessive trading of stocks that creates only

---

11 Thomas of Aquin: *Summa Theologiae* II-II, qu. 77, art. 3(4), discusses this question and grants expressly an important, morally justified, economical function to arbitrage and the arbitrageur.

12 Cf. for the business ethics of speculation and insider trading Koslowski (1997), 61-90.

commissions and fees for the bank or the broker but does not produce any benefit for the customer. Recommendations of shares and of trading actions which lead to churning represent a breach of the broker's obligation as the customer's trustee to recommend only suitable investments and to reveal the risks linked to them. The financial consultant stands here under diverse role expectations which often lead to conflicts of interest which are ethically relevant. As an employee of a bank the consultant must realise, for instance, the customer's interest in a profitable investment and, at the same time, the interest of the bank in commission payments, etc.

Non-professional day traders that are churned not so much by their consultants, but by themselves are a special case. According to investigations of the German Federal Agency for the Supervision of Financial Services (*Bundesanstalt für Finanzdienstleistungsaufsicht*, BaFin), many day traders lose their invested capital through incessant buying and selling of the same shares because they pay ever increasing amounts of commission for their trades to their online banks or brokers. The commissions eat up frequently the profits from share sales which the day trader has only in view.[13]

Twisting is the replacement of an insurance contract through a new one that does, however, no represent a real improvement for the insured, but creates only commission for the insurance broker and produces cost for the insured. Flipping is the replacement of a given credit contract by one or several new ones that also pretends to create an improvement for the credit applicant in his debtor situation without realising it since only the credit broker earns in these transactions by earning commissions.

All three phenomena of churning, twisting, and flipping are a breach of the fiduciary relationship. They are not only a breach of the value of good consulting but a positive breach of the consultant's fiduciary duty. In serious cases, this breach of duty can not be combated only through an ethical value orientation of the financial service provider, but must be sanctioned by the law, i.e. by the sentencing of compensation payments and, where appropriate, of criminal punishment. However, this legal sanction is appropriate only, where a fiduciary relation has actually come into existence. Where customers renounce that a fiduciary relationship has been established and explicitly want to act according to the maxim *caveat emptor*, the buyer be aware, they cannot claim an increased fiduciary duty of the financial service provider afterwards.

---

13 The Director of the Dept. III, German Federal Agency for the Supervision of Financial Services (Bundesanstalt für Finanzdienstleistungsaufsicht, BaFin), Günter Birnbaum, presented his agency's findings on day trading in his lecture 'Einflussfaktoren am Kapitalmarkt: Autoritäten, Paragrafen, Leitbilder' (Performance Influencing Factors in the Capital Market: Authorities, Paragraphs, Guiding Ideas) at the conference 'Ethik des Kapitalmarkts' (The Ethics of the Capital Market) organised by the Deutsches Netzwerk Wirtschaftsethik (German Network for Business Ethics) and others at the Siemens Forum Munich, Germany; on 12 October 2001.

Mergers and Acquisitions: the Capital Market as the Market for Corporate Control and the Importance of a Globalised Competition between Management Teams

In the newest development of the global capital market, it becomes increasingly visible that a central function of the capital market is not only the allocation of capital, but also the allocation of management capability and knowledge so that they find in each case their best use. The capital market is not only the market for capital, but also for corporate control, for corporate governance. Corporate control that is secured by the acquisition of the majority of the shares of a corporation becomes more and more important in the present day capital market. Its trading is part of the function of the capital market to secure the optimal allocation of capital. The ownership of the majority of the stocks of an enterprise provides the control over this enterprise. The acquisition of 51 per cent of the shares represents a radical advance in control as compared to the acquisition of 49 per cent. This advance is also expressed in the increased relative price of a majority share ownership.

Corporate control or corporate governance is carried out increasingly either by purchasing the majority of the corporation's shares, even against the will of the of the target company's management, or by mergers.

The question must be asked why there has been such an increase in mergers and acquisitions (M&A). The globalisation of the world economy is an engine for M&A. Through the purchase of other companies, the company taking over gains advantages for its corporate network. The network advantages through the integration of whole new companies that continue to exist frequently as independent divisions of the firm after the merger gain in importance as compared to the classical vertical integration or to the efficiency increase through economies of scale of a mere increase in size.

The purchase of stages of product development and of production processes through the purchase of the companies which own the know-how of these stages leads to a shortening of the time for research and development. A company taking over can buy knowledge and know-how through the takeover. The takeover results in shortening the development of new products and processes.

A completely new form of using the time zones becomes possible: in research and development, 24 hours a day, work can be done globally on the same projects provided a company acquires different companies with research and development activities in the same product that are active in all time zones.[14] Through the acquisition or sale of an enterprise or of parts of it, a corporation can carry out adaptations of the corporate structure, size, and borderline to other corporations which would require more time if the firm built up new parts of the corporation within the old organisation. In this way, the borderline of the corporation becomes more fluid and varying. Also, the complexity and increased obsolescence of products requires increasingly the acquisition or merger instead of research and development within the firm, not at last, in order to save time for R&D.

On the other hand, it is objected to the increasing number of hostile and of friendly takeovers that only a small number of corporate takeovers succeeds. Studies

---

14 *Cf.* Jansen (2000, p.5f).

made by the consulting firms Price Waterhouse and A. E. Kearney show that 40.000 mergers occurred worldwide in the period 1996–2001 that had a total value of 5 trillion US-dollars. Eighty per cent of the merged firms did not earn the capital costs of the merger transaction. Thirty per cent of these mergers were either reversed or the firms bought were sold again. A. E. Kearney estimates that the rate of failure of mergers is about 60–75%.[15]

These numbers are, however, not necessarily an argument against hostile takeovers since they do not consider the effect of the takeover threat on the management of companies which were not taken over. The effect of the takeover threat on the management of all firms in the market is that all management teams are forced by this threat to increase or at least to maintain their performance level. The effect of a takeover threat and of a lively market for corporate control is a kind of general prevention against the shirking of management, against a too comfortable life of management teams.

The effect of the general prevention measure against management shirking that the takeover threat exerts is not reflected in the number of successes of the takeovers that actually occurred. The possibility and the threat of being taken over represents a general prevention of the market for corporate control against shirking or becoming lazy of management teams. In judging the effect of the takeover threat, it is not the number of mergers and takeovers that actually occurred and were successful or unsuccessful that is decisive but the general threat and prevention of management shirking through the general takeover threat.

How are so-called hostile takeovers to be judged ethically which occur against the explained will of the management of the company taken over? For the economic and ethical value of mergers and acquisitions, the question about the economic legitimacy in the sense of economic functionality of the hostile takeover is central. Is the hostile takeover to be refuted as a hostile process or does it serve the purpose of the capital market to secure and improve the optimal capital allocation and the control of corporate control? The central legitimation for hostile takeovers lies in the right of the owners of a corporation to sell their part in the property of a firm to those that offer them the highest price for these parts or shares of the firm. If the owner of the firm is the owner of the majority of the shares, the central legitimation for hostile takeovers is derived from his right to exchange the management if he reaches the justified conclusion that the management damages the enterprise or does not realise the maximum value creation of the enterprise.

From the logic of the owners' property right and of the owner or shareholder principle results that the management of the target enterprise must not refuse, if a takeover threat occurs, any offer that gives the shareholders the possibility of selling their shares at a price that is usually above the given share price. Measures of defence that hinder or stop this possibility of selling the shares must be judged, therefore, as value destruction because they deprive the owners or shareholders of the possibility to sell their property, their shares, at higher value. The functional use of hostile takeovers is unquestionable in case of an inadequate performance of the

---

15 Quoted in Schweikart (2001).

management of the target corporation or in case of the substantiated expectation that the management team taking over will create a higher corporate value.

In Germany, the objection is frequently raised against the owner- or shareholder value-principle[16] that it violates the consensus principle, the principle that the firm should be managed with the consensus of everyone active in the enterprise, with the consensus of all stakeholders. It is also referred in the German context to the co-determination legislation applicable to German large-scale enterprises which safeguards the employee representation a share in the decision-making in the firm's management on the supervisory board level and, therefore, limits the shareholders' right to determine the management without consulting the employee representation.

The Anglo-American model, on the other hand, emphasises the external control of the management and the enterprise through the shareholders' right of control, which is a control coming from outside of the firm in contrast to the internal control by stakeholders in the German model. At the foundations of the Anglo-American model, one finds fairly realistic assumptions about the dangers that the enterprise faces by its internal stakeholders. Situations are conceivable and likely in which the management and the employees prefer management decisions that make life easier for them at the shareholders' expense by using up he firm's value and the shareholders' capital, e.g. by paying the owners or shareholders none or too small dividends or returns on investment and by concealing this value destruction to the shareholders and to the stakeholders themselves. If one assumes that all members of an organisation are tempted to have an easy life for them personally in the organisation and that this tendency is counteracted by the owners or shareholders from the outside, it is recognisable that the control of the enterprise by the shareholders is necessary. The shareholders are the countervailing power against the collusion of the firm's members.

Amongst the explanations given for hostile takeovers, it is especially the 'free cash flow-hypothesis' introduced by Jensen that points to the danger of the management's shirking in mature corporations and industries.[17] In mature industries, high positions of free cash flow arise, high returns from turnover and depreciation which should be paid out as dividends to the shareholder and be reinvested by them in other projects or firms in order to secure the efficient allocation of capital. It is, however, in the interest of the managers of these firms to leave the free cash flows in the enterprise since they increase thereby the degree of their freedom and their potential for shirking in the firm by lowering the control of the capital market on their performance by diverting dividends into internal revenue of the firm.

The threat of hostile takeovers to be taken over by international management teams and investors in globalised markets reduces the management's inclination to keep returns on capital or profits in the firm. It also prevents the tendency to expand the firm's turnover without appropriate profits at the expense of the shareholder value. If the management's income is made to be dependent on its performance and this performance is measured in turnover the management will again expand turnover at the expense of dividend.

---

16 *Cf.* on the debate Koslowski (1999).
17 Jensen (1986).

The causality that the free cash flow hypothesis analyses can also be described as the more general phenomenon that people feel entitled to lean back and work in a less hard way if they have founded and built up something, be it an enterprise or any other achievement. This is, of course, not in the interest of the institutions for which they set up something. On the other hand, the necessity arises here in the case of a hostile takeover to appreciate the building up achievement and to compensate by compensation payments that share that the management caused in the added value of the enterprise that had not been paid for by the management's contractual income. The criticism of high compensation payments or 'golden parachutes' paid to managers that are fired because of hostile takeovers as it is frequently expressed after hostile takeovers must be put into perspective.

A further argument for the necessity to allow, if not to encourage, hostile takeovers is the argument that the shareholders, in general, are not able to be present all the time in the firm and can not defend their interests continuously within the firm, particularly not in the large joint stock firm with a large number of small 'anonymous' shareholders. In this situation, the investors or shareholders are able to prevent their 'exploitation' or their being taken advantage of by the management only through the right to hire and fire the management or at least to threat to be able to fire and displace it in a hostile takeover.

The Consensus of those Concerned as Internal Self-Control *versus* Competition as External Control through the Takeover by the Competitor: Two Models of (Corporate) Governance

In the German model of corporate governance, it is assumed that the consensus of the groups concerned makes already sure by its very quality of being a consensus that the best decision is taken for the enterprise and that consensus will secure that the decision best for the company is realised. Disagreement or decision-making without consensus between the groups working in the enterprise and concerned by its fate is regarded in this model as a sign of crisis and of inadequate management, whereas consensus is regarded, in full agreement with Jürgen Habermas's consensus theory of truth, as the guarantee of the correctness or 'truth' of the decision taken.

It is easily recognisable that fundamental philosophical differences in the conception of governance, constitutional arrangements, governing, and control come into play at the debate about corporate governance and the constitution of the firm, at the question of consensus principle *versus* shareholder value principle. The questions about corporate governance reach as far as to the debate about the political constitution.

In the German or, more broadly, in the Continental European understanding of the republican constitution and government, the idea of self-government through consensus, the general will model, is very influential although representative government prevails in fact. In the Anglo-American understanding of the republic, the idea of representative government through the representation of voter groups and the competition and alternating rule of competing political teams in politics and competition between management teams in the economy are the guiding idea. In both realms, in politics and in the economy, not the idea of consensus but of competition for voters or shareholders coming from outside of the decision-making groups is central in the American tradition, whereas internal consensus or agreement between the insiders in politics and in the economy is characteristic for the Continental European tradition since Rousseau's idea of the general will, the *volonté générale*.

The process of globalisation of capital markets supports the competition principle, not the consensus principle. It requires and introduces the globalisation of a market for corporate control and, therefore, the principle of competition between management teams, not the idea of a consensus of insiders in the economy. A foreign investor who is not an insider in the industry of another country cannot rely on insider consensus as a means of controlling the performance of a management team of a foreign firm he wants to invest in.

Consensus does not guarantee the truth of the decisions made in consensus. A consensus of stakeholder groups is conceivable that decides at the expense of other stakeholders who have been contingently or systematically absent when the 'consensus' had been formed. It is also well possible that all stakeholders of a firm decide and act under illusions – and might even have a systematic interest to confirm each other in these illusions – about the actual state and performance of the republic or of the firm. These illusions of insiders about their performance might be so pervasive that it can be destroyed only through the possibility that an outsider breaks through the delusion of the insiders' consensus from the outside by using the competition for corporate control and external alternative management teams for opening up the 'consensualised' firms.

In the debate in the European Union about corporate governance, the constitution of the firm, and the role of capital markets, basic principles of corporate governance are at stake. The EU Commission urged Germany in 2001, to make the take-over directive of the Commission actual law in German legislation and jurisdiction. This directive requires the strengthening of corporate control through facilitating hostile takeovers and abolishing laws hindering market competition. Regulations are to be removed that allow the state or state owned firms to have privileges of restricting competition. Prominent cases are the Volkswagen-Law that grants special voting rights to the State of Lower Saxony as the main share holder of Volkswagen Corporation or the law that gives state owned banks the privilege that their liquidity is guaranteed by the state as in the case of the state banks (Landesbanken).

It is of philosophical interest that the former Commissioner for Industry, Mario Monti, has expressed the view that the European Union cannot make any difference between firms that are owned privately and firms that are owned by the state. State ownership in firms can not justify, according to Mario Monti, an institutionalised competitive advantage since this advantage disturbs the competition between private and governmental or semi-governmental firms.[18]

One can look at this postulate from two perspectives. One could object that the EU Commission questions by its policy the distinction of state and society or

---

18 So Mario Monti, *Then Commissioner of the EU, at the Annual Meeting 2001 of the Verein für Socialpolitik*, German Economic Association in Magdeburg on 27 September 2001.

economy which has been emphasised particularly in Germany.[19] The commission seems to deny the special standing of the state among the other social institutions since it refuses to grant any special position to firms in which the state holds shares compared to those firms that are completely privately owned. On the other hand, one has to raise the objection against this position that giving a privilege to the enterprise in which the state holds shares cancels the very distinction of state and society by creating a third hybrid form of political-economic control that is neither economic nor political.

The hybrid of the state-owned business firm follows neither the market principles of competition, consumer sovereignty, and profit or loss nor the political principles of voter sovereignty and orientation on the common good. The semi-governmental firm is neither fully subjected to economic competition and completely for profit, nor is it completely not-for-profit and orientated at the common good. It can make profit, but the use of this profit is then decided frequently on political grounds that can neither be checked by the market nor by the voter. The semi-governmental firm belongs neither completely to the sphere of government and the state nor completely to the societal and economic sphere. It distorts, in fact, competition in the sphere of the economy and society since it can make use of privileges against its privately owned competitors.

The dynamics of the EU single market move here into the same direction as the dynamics of the global world market. Within the single market of the EU, it is difficult to give good reasons why Volkswagen should have competitive advantages due to the fact that the State of Lower Saxony holds a major part of its shares as compared to its French competitors like Peugeot or Renault that are, however, also partially state owned. It is hard to see why the politicians elected for running the State of Lower Saxony or France should have a higher competence to run Volkswagen or Peugeot or Renault respectively than managers coming from industry. The criterion that state and society, government and economy, should be functionally separated requires, for the sake of the protection of the essential state functions, that the hybrid forms of joint stock companies that are half state- and half privately owned should be given up in favour of companies that are fully privatised joint stock companies and a small number of companies that are fully state-owned and act completely in the public interest where this can be justified.[20]

If one asks the question which basic value orientations and which identifications with basic principles stand behind the dispute about the permissibility or non-permissibility of hostile corporate takeovers, one is led to the opposites of consensus and competition, self-control and control from the outside. The German model of corporate governance is based on the consensus principle and the self-

19 *Cf.* Koslowski (1982).

20 A well-founded judgement about the special position in Germany of the State Banks (Landesbanken) of the German States and of the savings banks is not easy to make. The support of these banks by the liquidity guarantee of the government makes credit for small- and medium-sized enterprises less expensive and can, therefore, be useful. On the other hand, this guarantee is paid by the tax payers who might not be interested in seeing their money to be used for this purpose.

control of insiders and stakeholders. It allots a subordinate role to the control of management from outside of the firm by the capital market. The essential control of the corporation is supposed to be carried out as the self-control of the stakeholders within the firm. The Anglo-American model of corporate control, on the other hand, assumes that consensus does not necessarily imply efficiency and does not secure high performance since the emphasis on the value of consensus furthers the self-indulgence of those participating in the consensual discourse and eases their rash satisfaction with solutions and decisions pleasing them.

Traditions are influenced by and specific to culture and religion. Cultural tradition and even religious denominations play a role in the positions on political and corporate governance. In the Puritan, Calvinist-Protestant tradition, there seems to be a stronger distrust in the individuals' self-control and self-appraisal than in the Lutheran-Protestant and the Catholic tradition. The denominational and, therefore, cultural differences have shaped the different models and ideas of republicanism which have developed from the American and from the French revolution.

According to the Anglo-American Puritan model, the persons concerned and also the leaders of government and business are unable to judge their own performance properly due to the distortion of human judgement by self-interest – or theologically speaking due to the distortion of human intention and self-interest by original sin. When we are supposed to judge our own performance we are always in a conflict of interest, in the conflict between our interest in objectivity and our self-interest to appear to be good to ourselves and to others.

On the other hand, the consensus model of republicanism, of political government and corporate governance, based on the assumption of the identity of the governing and the governed assumes that the consensus or Rousseau's *volonté générale* is the truth-generating element of political and other governing processes that removes the distortedness of self-interested decision-makers into decision-makers that are orientated at the common good or the *volonté générale*. It is the conviction of this tradition that consensus nullifies the conflict of interest between self-interest and objectivity.

The identity-philosophical interpretation of democracy as the unity of the governing and the governed dominates the German and Continental-European political philosophy. Its understanding of government from Rousseau and Hegel to Habermas is not as theoretically superior as this tradition suggests to itself. It is based on the questionable basic assumption that there is an absolute identity of subject and object, an idea that originates from Hegel's and Schelling's philosophy. In the same way as Hegel's absolute subject becomes conscious at the absolute object and in identity with this object, the nation as an object becomes conscious of itself in the subject of the state. Government and people are an absolute subject-object in which the nation or people becomes self-conscious. Consensus is the highest form of this subject-object in which there is identity between subject and object, state and society, governing and governed.[21]

---

21 Through the transition to popular sovereignty, the national state enables society to influence 'itself' politically according to Habermas (1998, p.100). According to

From this supposed identity of the subject and object of political power, the identity-philosophical thinking deduces that a nation's becoming subjective-objective or conscious takes place in the republican state in the consensus of the governing and the governed. Consensual governance leads to the identity of the state and the nation/people, the legislator and the legislated, the author and the addressee of the law. Through this identity of consensus, political rule is sublated or abolished and transformed into self-government. Discourse-theoretical approaches to corporate governance transfer the consensus and identity-theoretical model of political government to the firm and its governance. They postulate that stakeholder discourse and consensus in the firm ought to be the principles of corporate governance and control.[22]

From the viewpoint of a general anthropological theory of human self-interestedness and of the human beings' missing objectivity towards themselves, the discourse theory of human decision-making remains below the complexity of the task of controlling power. The tendency observable in the corporatist state to collusions and coalitions of influential interest-groups or lobbyists forces one to emphasise the need for the control of political and economic power through competition, through individuals and institutions that come from the outside to check organisations. Hostile takeovers are one of the possible control mechanisms against mistaken forms of consensus and of coalitions between the management and the stakeholder or pressure groups within the firm. Hostile takeovers, therefore, should be rather encouraged than hindered by the legislation on corporate governance. A greater control of the management of large-scale enterprises through competing management teams and their takeover threat will result in an increased performance of these firms.

The need for a limitation of the consensus principle does not exclude to retain elements of the co-determination legislation as it is mandatory for German large-scale enterprises. The option for some worker participation does not imply, however, equal voting rights of the employees at the supervisory board level. Rather, it requires an end to the accumulation of power by the trade-unions in the supervisory board of large-scale enterprises as it developed in Germany where many CEOs claim that they cannot decide against the worker representation in the board dominated by the unions that usually organise and represent the employees. Co-determination in the form of employee representation on the supervisory board does not violate the owner- or shareholder value-principle if and only if the clear majority of votes and therefore the right of the last decision remain with the owners or shareholders. At present, this is not the case in Germany. An enormous insider position has been built up by the unions since their representatives sit in practically all supervisory boards of large-scale enterprises as the representatives of the employee representation.

The participation or do-determination principle can increase corporate performance when it understood as a principle of representation and not as a consensus principle and when it is instituted together with the control principle of

---

Schachtschneider (1994, p.4), the republic is founded on being in the 'state and constitution of freedom from rule'.

22 This position is taken in publication of a discourse theoretical approach to business ethics in the group around Horst Steinmann, *Cf.* Scherer (2003).

hostile takeovers. The co-determination as representation of the employees on the board increases the learning capacity of the organisation and also fulfils a pacification function in conflict situations within the enterprise as long as the majority vote of the shareholders or owners is safeguarded.

The synthesis between the Anglo-American principle of the capital market as the market for corporate control and the German principle of co-determination as employee representation in corporate governance on the board level is possible also under conditions of globalisation. This synthesis can improve the firm's ability to discover chances and weaknesses within the organisation and to use this knowledge for increased performance. The synthesis of the capital market control model with the co-determination model of corporate governance is likely to be superior to the 'pure' models of either the capital market control or the co-determination governance model. Globalisation will move corporate governance in the European Union in the direction of such a synthesis. It is likely that this model will radiate from the EU to the global financial markets.

References

Boatright, J.R. (1999), *Ethics in Finance*, Malden, Mass.: Blackwell.
Drucker, P. (1976), *The Unseen Revolution: How Pension Fund Socialism Came to America*, New York: Harper & Row.
Habermas, J. (1998), Die postnationale Konstellation und die Zukunft der Demokratie (The Postnational Constellation and the Future of Democracy), *In Habermas, J Die postnationale Konstellation (The Postnational Constellation)*, Frankfurt am Main: Suhrkamp.
Jansen, S.A. (2000), Mergers and Acquisitions. Unternehmensakquisitionen und - kooperationen Eine strategische, organisatorische und kapitalmarkttheoretische Einführung (Mergers and Acquisitions. Corporate Acquisitions and Corporate Cooperations. A Strategic, Organisational, and Capital Market Theoretical Introduction). (Wiesbaden: Gabler), 3rd ed.
Jensen, M.C. (1986), Agencies Cost of Free Cash Flow, Corporate Finance, and Takeover, *American Economic Review*, **76**, 323–329.
Koslowski, P. (1982), Gesellschaft und Staat, *Ein unvermeidlicher Dualismus (Society and State. An Inevitable Dualism)*, Stuttgart: Klett-Cotta.
—— (1997), Ethik der Banken und der Börse, *Finanzinstitutionen, Finanzmärkte, Insider-Handel (The Ethics of Banking and of the Stock Exchange. Financial Institutions, Financial Markets, Insider Trading)*, Tübingen: Mohr Siebeck.
—— (1999), Shareholder Value und der Zweck des Unternehmens' (Shareholder Value and the Purpose of the Enterprise) in *Shareholder Value und die Kriterien des Unternehmenserfolgs (Shareholder Value and the Criteria of Corporate Success)* ed Koslowski, P., Heidelberg: Physica, pp.1–32.
—— (2001), *Principles of Ethical Economy*, Dordrecht: Kluwer. German Original: *Prinzipien der Ethischen Ökonomie*. (Tübingen: Mohr Siebeck 1988).
Müller, K. (2002), *Globalisierung (Globalisation)*, Frankfurt, New York: Campus.

Nell-Breuning, O., von (1928a), Grundzüge der Börsenmoral (Fundamentals of Stock Market Morals). (Freiburg i. Br.: Herder).

—— (1928b), Volkswirtschaftlicher Wert und Unwert der Börsenspekulation (The Economic Utility and Disutility of Stock Market Speculation) Stimmen der Zeit (Voices of the Time) 114, 46-56.

Picot, G. (2000), M&A aus Sicht der Kapitalmärkte (M&A from the Point of View of the Capital Markets), in *Handbuch Mergers and Acquisitions (Handbook of Mergers and Acquisitions)* ed Picot, G., Stuttgart: Schäffer-Poeschel, pp.33–52.

Radbruch, G. (1973), *Rechtsphilosophie (Philosophy of Right)*, 8th edn, Stuttgart: Koehler.

Rose, P.S. (2000), *Money and Capital Markets. Financial Institutions and Instruments in a Global Marketplace*, 7th edn, Boston: McGraw-Hill.

Schachtschneider, K.A. (1994), Res publica res populi, Grundlegung einer allgemeinen Republiklehre. Ein Beitrag zur Freiheits-, Rechts- und Staatslehre (Res publica res populi. Groundwork for a General Theory of the Republic. A Contribution to the Theory of Freedom, Law, and State), (Berlin: Duncker & Humblot).

Scherer, A.G. (2003), *Die Rolle der Multinationalen Unternehmung im Prozeß der Globalisierung (The Role of the Multinational Corporation in the Process of Globalisation).* (Heidelberg: Physica; Ethische Ökonomie. Beiträge zur Wirtschaftsethik und Wirtschaftskultur – Ethical Economy. Studies in Economic Ethics and Economic Culture, Vol. 7).

Schweikart, N. (2001), Der getriebene Chef. Shareholder value überall – das US-Modell setzt sich durch' (The Haunted Boss. Shareholder Value Above All – the US Model Gains Dominance), DIE ZEIT, no. 20, 10 May 2001, 26.

Shiller, R.J. (2001), *Irrational Exuberance,* 6th edn, Oxford: Princeton University Press.

Name Index

Subject Index

For Product Safety Concerns and Information please contact our EU
representative GPSR@taylorandfrancis.com
Taylor & Francis Verlag GmbH, Kaufingerstraße 24, 80331 München, Germany

www.ingramcontent.com/pod-product-compliance
Ingram Content Group UK Ltd.
Pitfield, Milton Keynes, MK11 3LW, UK
UKHW021005180425
457613UK00019B/814

* 9 7 8 0 3 6 7 6 0 3 7 2 4 *